T0363815

The Return Trip

Maya Golden

RISING ACTION

Cover Illustration © Nat Mack
Distributed by Simon & Schuster
Copy Edited by Marthese Fenech

ISBN: 978-1-990253-66-9
Ebook: 978-1-990253-67-6

BIO026000   BIOGRAPHY & AUTOBIOGRAPHY / Personal Memoirs
SOC060000   SOCIAL SCIENCE / Sexual Abuse & Harassment
BIO002010   BIOGRAPHY & AUTOBIOGRAPHY / Cultural, Ethnic & Regional
/ African American & Black

#TheReturnTrip

Follow Rising Action on our socials!
Twitter: @RAPubCollective
Instagram: @risingactionpublishingco
Tiktok: @risingactionpublishingco

Foreword

Written by Tennie McCarty, LCDC, ADC III, CEDC-CEO/Founder, Shades of Hope Center of Healing

It's an honor to write this foreword for The Return Trip. I first met Maya Golden in May of 2015, when she walked through the doors of Shades of Hope Center of Healing. I was immediately struck by her presence—a combination of strength, poise, and an unmistakable sadness in her eyes. Maya came for an Intensive program, not fully knowing what she was stepping into, yet willing to trust the process. Throughout the week, she demonstrated compassion and support for others while deeply engaging in her own work around the trauma of sexual abuse.

In The Return Trip, Maya outlines her experience with the weeklong intensive therapy program at Shades, describing the rigorous mental, emotional, and physical healing she underwent. While her account offers a glimpse into the program's transformative nature, it's difficult to fully capture the depth of healing that takes place there. Shades of Hope is one of the few centers in the United States offering this type of Intensive, providing a unique short-program with long-term healing that helps individuals, families, couples, and adolescents alike to address and process their traumas. Through these intensives, Shades not only treats the individual but also fosters healing within family systems, helping loved ones to better understand and support one another on the path to recovery.

In my 40 years of working with thousands of clients, I have rarely seen anyone embrace the healing journey as Maya has. She not only faced the truths of her past—both the abuse and her abuser—but also bravely confronted how these experiences impacted her throughout her life, from childhood and teenage years into college and beyond. Maya is one of the few survivors I've known who has openly addressed the impact of her trauma, including her struggles with sex addiction in adulthood.

The Return Trip isn't just a book—it's a courageous exploration of the dark realities of sexual abuse and the way it can lead to destructive coping mechanisms later in life. Maya's story exemplifies the profound effect that trauma can have on one's identity and behavior, especially when left unspoken. As I've often said, "We are as sick as our secrets." When trauma remains hidden, it breaks a person down from the inside, making true healing a journey from the inside out.

What sets Maya apart is her honesty, especially around her adult challenges and the choices she made as a result of her trauma. She shares openly about her experiences with sexual acting out and other addictions. For many survivors, there is a split—the "day child" lives a seemingly normal life, while the "night child" is burdened with the hidden darkness of abuse. In Maya's case, this split intensified when she went to college, and her struggle with isolation grew. When we turn inward and isolate, we can end up reliving the pain repeatedly, and the abuse becomes part of our very being, affecting our bodies, our actions, and our relationships.

Maya's courage in writing The Return Trip moved me deeply. Her story resonates with my own experiences as a survivor of childhood sexual abuse. She shares vulnerable memories, from her early years through high school and into college, bringing the reader into her trust. For instance, as a successful sports reporter, Maya faced being labeled as a "little black girl" at events, which echoed my own painful experiences growing up. My father referred to me as "the black baby," and his blatant preference for white features left me feeling inadequate. Only later did I realize the abuse and racism embedded in those labels. Maya's honesty about her own identity and the impacts of racism is a gift to the reader, and I believe that her story will resonate profoundly.

Whether you're a survivor of sexual abuse, someone dealing with addiction, or simply a reader with an open heart, The Return Trip offers a journey of awareness, compassion, and healing. Maya not only highlights the pain of abuse and addiction but also shares a pathway toward recovery. In these pages, she presents both the problem and a path forward—reminding us that true healing is possible.

By the last page, I'm certain you'll be as grateful as I am for the powerful journey Maya Golden has created. Prepare to be moved, inspired, and deeply changed.

For Buster and My Sweetie Peetie

This memoir is the author's story. The memories and experiences are from her recollection and may not reflect the experiences of those featured in the book.

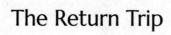

The Return Trip

Part 1

Chapter One

Homecoming

2014

Today is the day I am going to die. Few people wake up with this knowledge; death row inmates, war criminals awaiting execution, terminally ill cancer patients, maybe. What's that Bible verse? "No man knoweth the day or the hour," or something to that effect? During my southern Baptist upbringing, I wasn't attentive enough to have it committed to heart.

But today, I know. I just know.

I'm okay with it—the dying. Detached and numb, I've watched my life experiences pass by, as if I were a mannequin in a storefront window.

Dying is a formality.

Four days ago, I was on Cloud Nine. But that joy soon became another thing snatched away from me. Happiness isn't meant for me. So today is the day.

The air purifier, set on high, blasts at a pitch meant to drown out the cars beeping and lawnmowers whirring outside. I throw back the too-heavy-for-the-summertime comforter, the pits of my T-shirt now damp with sweat. I'd been cocooned in that comforter for at least ten hours, seven of those in a dreamless, black sleep thanks to two Xanax pills.

From the other side of the closed bedroom door, muted by the white noise, a children's show is playing on the television, and my two-year-old son, Charlie, giggles as he babbles with my husband, Everett.

I stretch, then adjust my sticky underwear back into place before padding barefoot, phone in hand, to the bathroom. My steps follow the choreography of a

3

beleaguered mother's daily morning routine: shoulders hunched, eyes half shut, feet barely lifting with each step over the carpet.

But there is one deviation—I have an assignment this morning—my Mission: Possible.

Toiletries, medications, and beauty products clutter the cabinet suspended to the wall. I reach over eye drops and nail polish bottles that haven't been opened in years, colored with seductive red and flirtatious pink lacquers, until my hand locates translucent orange bottles. The contents rattle like a morbid maraca, the soundtrack to my determination. Muscle relaxers (a common gift from my mother), antidepressants, various painkillers, and my sweet, savory friend: Xanax.

Quite a few pills—but maybe not enough?

Not enough to be *sure*.

When I was twenty, my then-psychologist told me that most suicide attempts from pills and alcohol fail and result in severe brain damage. I can't dwell on this. The perfectionist, hyper Type-A in me isn't going to let me half-ass this job. This will be another checkmark, another gold star on my list of successes. The Final Act done well.

An automated message greets me unceremoniously after dialing the number to my pharmacy. It sounds as lifeless as I feel. The tip of my finger taps the screen as I enter each prescription number. Two brand new, filled-to-the-childproof-lid bottles to add to my exit collection would soon be waiting for me to pick up.

The phone and I return to bed. The sheets and thick comforter touch my chin. A tiny voice outside the door sounds closer than before.

"Mama?" Charlie calls.

Wincing, I wait. *Please go away.*

"We're letting Mama rest," Everett replies. "Come on, buddy."

"No!" Charlie wails in resistance.

The doorknob jostles.

"Nope!" Everett's voice is at the threshold and the twisting knob stills.

My eyes remain on the door, waiting for it to be thrust open. My two-year-old enters my room most mornings like a SWAT officer. The fact that I haven't died from a heart attack from one of these abrupt daily awakenings might be the miracle that is lost on me. I have been bargaining with God for so long—for something. Hell, maybe that I hadn't been startled to death yet by an anxious toddler was it.

But the tiny voice retreats. My entire body exhales.

I check social media, look at the "news" on Twitter, and stare at the clock. The pharmacy opens at 9:00 a.m., and it's around 7:30. Prescriptions won't be ready as soon as the store opens, yet I will emerge from the bedroom with enough time to make the fifteen-minute drive into town and be there when it opens. I need my final destination cargo quickly because later this morning, we will leave East Texas for my hometown of Garland, two hours west.

I am left alone in the bedroom. And in my aloneness, I think. I mull over about what will happen later that afternoon. I am tired, so incredibly tired.

Should I write a note? Tell them all why? No. They know *why*.

Then I think of my son. What will they tell Charlie? All he will know is that his mother was here, and then one day, she wasn't. As he grows older, transforming from my beautiful, curly-haired toddler into a lanky, gangly teenager, will he still remember me? Will he remember my face from something other than old pictures on an iPad or in a frame? Will there even be pictures of me in frames? Or will every reminder of me be wiped away like dust off a coffee table?

Will he know that I loved him? Will he remember what it felt like to snuggle in my arms and drift into a protected sleep? God, I would fight a hurricane for that kid.

My soul holds a microphone up to my brain, as I have done during a thousand interviews, and interrogates, *But, Maya? Are you sure?*

"Yes," I whisper to myself. I frown as my lips part. Then another deep exhale. "No."

Do I want my son to grow up with a legacy that he wasn't worth his mother sticking around for? That she couldn't tough it out for his sake? Will he be full of the same rage, the same self-doubt, the same never-good-enough attitude that vexed his mama from age five?

I can't do that to him—but this is not about him. It's about me, and I can't anymore.

Maybe I should write a note.

A month earlier, my thirty-fourth birthday had passed without hullabaloo. This was customary; I never wanted to celebrate my birthday or for anyone to celebrate me, for that matter.

When I was a teenager, I'd gotten it in my head that twenty-three was a good age to die. I'd watched all of the adults in my life moving through the banal realities of grocery shopping, exhaustive desk jobs, and forced family outings, and rebuked the notion that would ever be me. All the early twenty-somethings I'd known were flashy and fashionable, free to date and explore sex, unburdened by the shackles of responsibility. Life after twenty-three seemed to turn stale like a forgotten loaf of bread in the pantry.

But when I reached twenty-three, I was having so much fun living my new life I had no desire to end it. I'd made it another eleven years before the thought struck me once more.

I scramble out of bed again, heading back to the bathroom to wash my face and scrub the morning breath away. Tossing on a pair of jeans and a T-shirt, I slide polished toes, part of my façade from four days before, into a pair of flip-flops and smooth my relaxed hair into a ponytail. I open the bedroom door.

Everett and Charlie are in the dining room, huddled over a yellow train that lists numbers and the alphabet. From the volume of the sounds it exudes, it has fresh batteries. It chirps and sings while it flashes.

No one speaks to me. I am treated as a passerby, which—quite frequently—I am. I either emerge from the bedroom to fetch something to eat before climbing back into bed, or I am there to inspect whatever state the house is in after a morning of play.

I'm a wanderer, passing through on my way somewhere else.

"Hey," I say to Everett, then clear my throat. My raspy voice is lower than usual from the lack of use.

Everett barely raises his head, and I notice the slight lift in one of his brows. At least I know he's heard me. The sweet morning greetings and kisses to start the day stopped not long after Charlie entered the world.

"I need to go to the pharmacy to get my medicine before we go." I clear my throat again.

"Alright," Everett says, sounding disinterested. His gaze shifts back to our son. The hairs on Everett's head and in his goatee are grayer than the week before. He wears a pair of gray and black basketball shorts, and he sits on his heels. His skin is redder than a tan from summertime yard work. The sunburn reduces the stark contrast in our skin tones, giving him at least some color that doesn't look so pale next to my brown skin.

I try hard not to look too closely at Charlie. He doesn't have Everett's green irises, but he has his smile and his chin. His owl eyes, long lashes, and arched brows he got from me. He's so busy fiddling with his toy he doesn't even look my way or say hi.

"Do you want me to pack his stuff?" Everett calls after me as I turn the knob to the door leading to the garage.

"No," I reply curtly. *You'll probably fuck it up.* I don't say it, though. I know the exact contents that need to go with us. It's best I do it myself. "I'll pack for him when I get back." I close the door behind me.

As I back my SUV down the steep incline of our driveway and roll out onto our street, I am struck again by the lackluster feel of this day.

The Texas sky is cloudless, with ribbons of orange and gold sunlight stretching out over the rooftops and storefronts as morning creeps over them. It is July, and that same Texas sun will send heat waves rising off the highways in another two hours.

Melodies play through the car speakers as I drive, but I don't hear them. Usually, as soon as I am in the car on a drive by myself, I crank up the 90's station and imagine Janet Jackson, Paula Abdul, and Mariah Carey concerts. Sometimes I nod along to gangster rap, pretending to relate to the lyrics about slinging dope and getting money. Who the hell am I kidding? I grew up beside a country club.

These days, though, I usually have my precious passenger in the backseat, so the divas and Snoop Dogg are often replaced by the nasally, cherubic voice of Elmo. Always. Fucking. Elmo.

To my surprise, three cars are already ahead of me at the pharmacy drive-through.

I grab my phone and do a quick Google search. *What do the scriptures say about suicide?*

My life is already shit, but finite shit. An end will come, if not today, then someday. But hell, fire, and suffering for an infinite number of years isn't exactly the starring role that I'm lining up to audition for.

I read a few top results. A Bible-analysis website says Judeo-Christianity condemns suicide, but the Bible does not explicitly. Alright, not too bad. A Christian forum says the real question is can we lose our salvation? From the comments posted by so-called preachers and ministry leaders, none of this is looking good for me. I'm so desperate to find something to validate my position and fragile state of mind that I venture into the abyss known as the second page of the Google search.

Surely God isn't that vengeful? God knows my story; certainly, there is some sympathy waiting for me at the judgment gates? Didn't He let the molestations happen to me in the first place?

Therapy hasn't fixed me, marriage didn't fix me, having a kid didn't fix me, and a job in TV didn't fix me. Nothing I've ever done has been enough. The empty void of "enoughness" is impossible to fill. Every award, every compliment, every success I've shoveled into it has only been sucked into the same black hole, never to be seen again. I've been in a never-ending battle to feel good enough to be able to stand myself.

The line moves. Two cars, then one, then I'm at the window. I pay for my Xanax and Celexa.

"Thank you, ma'am." The young man at the window smiles at me. "Have a great day!"

"You—" I have to clear my throat again. My voice is still scratchy. "You too." The edges of my lips jerk upwards as I flash my teeth—my TV smile.

I pull away from the drive-through window and head back towards the house. The drive to the pharmacy had been my defibrillator, keeping my heart thumping. The organ in my chest feels close to flatlining with the prospect of returning home.

I enter the house, shopping bag in hand, and Charlie smiles at me as he pushes his train in a circle from the dining room to the kitchen over and over.

"Hell-o," he says, emphasizing each syllable as he continues to improve his speech. The train flashes and chimes and plays "The Wheels on the Bus."

"Hey, little man." I give him a wry smile and head to the bedroom. Everett's tattered duffle bag is on the bed with a pile of neatly folded clothes. He does not greet me, and I don't acknowledge his presence with so much as a "Hey." We pack in silence.

I pick out one of five weekend bags on my closet shelf and drop the shopping bag with my new prescription haul inside. While Everett packs in the bedroom, I shut the door to the bathroom. The medicine cabinet door pops open with a loud click, and I grit my teeth, looking back at the door, wondering if the noise has been heard. The bathroom door remains closed. After a few breaths, I grab three more orange bottles and lower them gently into the weekend bag.

I return to the bedroom, my weekend bag cradled against my breasts. As I walk into the room, Everett walks out.

I throw a change of clothes, some pajamas, and clean underwear into the bag. I'm not really sure why. This is a one-way trip, but for the sake of appearances, I pack. That is something I'm good at—illusions.

In Hindu philosophy, my name, "Maya," means illusion. In Buddhism, it means delusion. It feels like I was destined to live behind a veil—an illusion filled with delusions.

Everett and Charlie are in the dining room, entertaining themselves with another buzzing, flashing toy. I stealthily pry open the refrigerator door and retrieve a bottle of Jose Cuervo Gold.

While the other house occupants remain busy, I head out to the garage and tuck the cold glass bottle of shimmering liquid underneath the driver's seat. My father unknowingly taught me this trick.

In a few hours, my buddy, Jose, and the cantina of pills in my bag will guide me into the permanent sleep I'm craving.

My husband and I are quiet in the car.

I chose to drive. It's my trip; I'm in charge. I'll get us there.

It's mid-morning, just before noon, and I feel like I'm driving an oven down I-20. The Texas sky is a river of blue without a single cloud to shadow the journey. It's already in the '90s, and I have a two-hour trip with hot pavement below rubber wheels ahead of me. Sweat stains are re-forming at the pits of my shirt. A sip of the cold stuff under the driver's seat would help, but the thought of drinking and driving offends me. I don't want to cause physical harm to anyone but myself.

Charlie sits in his car seat as Baby Einstein soundtracks and Elmo serenades us. Always, always Elmo.

"Again!" He requests specific tracks on the CD repeatedly. Like a droid, I press the back button to replay the songs.

Everett's thumb slides upward, over and over again, on the phone in his lap. I remind him constantly about radiation from cellphones and the dangers of sitting it so close to his nuts, but today, I don't bother.

My eyes are on the road ahead—my shoulders inch closer towards my ears with each mile. I grip and release the steering wheel a few times, rolling and flexing my wrists. I am always tense on the highways. As strange as it sounds, it's one of the reasons I often volunteer to drive. I feel in control of the vehicle, and better equipped to handle or maneuver a sudden swerve or slamming of the brakes by other drivers. I don't like being a victim.

East Texas's piney woods and hills give way to flat cement lots filled with shopping centers and Tex-Mex restaurants. The towering evergreens that line the side of the interstate dissipate as we cross the Dallas County line; pines and cedars are replaced by street lights, gun outlets, fried chicken fast-food chains, and supercenters where you can buy a gun with your groceries.

I press the back button, and Elmo sings about the parts of the face again.

We turn off the highway and pull onto the main road that leads to the area I grew up in. However, in Garland, Texas, Broadway Street isn't a glamorous thoroughfare like its famed counterpart in NYC. It's peppered with squares of patched asphalt and potholes that cause the car to bounce and scrape the road so violently that I cuss under my breath.

But down the street, there's a popular barbeque joint that has stood at the intersection across from my high school since the '80s.

Fragrant smoke, mingled with the alluring scent of ribs roasting to fall right off the bone, always billows from the side of the building. Stacks of wood for the pit are piled high behind a fence. The red, white, and black façade of Soulman's Barbeque is a staple of our town.

I take in the view of my hometown as if making a new memory, but little about it has changed. The same gas station on the left, the same Karate center wedged in the corner of the strip mall, the same shaved ice stand that also illegally sold cigarettes to students at South Garland High School in the '90s. And the same Soulman's Barbeque.

Elmo's saccharine peppiness has shifted into a ballad.

My grip on the steering wheel tightens. The strain radiates up my bicep and into my neck that's as straight as a flag pole. Elmo's voice floats into my ears, now inexplicably no longer immune to his sound.

If someone believes in you and thinks you are enough ... You'll start to see what everybody else sees in you.

Oh my God.

My arms tremble despite my grip on the steering wheel.

That's not a lump in my throat—maybe it's my heart? Maybe it has leapt upward to remind me it's there, to feel it beating? No. Something else has lodged itself in my windpipe: a rising sadness.

My heart beats faster, rocking my chest back and forth, shouting, "You are alive!" Suddenly, the tailspin of grief and hope blur my vision, and all around me are shadows.

My eyes flick to the rearview mirror, and I glance at my son.

My son. He believes in me. He believes I will take care of him, and love him.

He believes I'm enough.

Contentment floods his innocent face as he listens to Elmo's words. Always, always Elmo. The lyrics bring heavy tears to the brim of my eyes. I fight them back. I don't do tears, but God, I can't stop them. And I can't swallow away the thing wedged in my throat, making it harder to breathe.

The tears run down my cheeks, leaving wet circles on the neck of my shirt. I feel each tear swell as I suppress the sobs that threaten to break free from my belly.

I glance over at Everett. He's still scrolling. He doesn't see the tears, doesn't pick up on my broken breaths. I'm in a car with two other people, and I feel alone.

Then, I look up.

I look up as we glide past the Soulman's Barbeque sign.

I read it, and the last of my resolve shatters.

"God sees you."

Chapter Two

The Carol Burnett Show

1985

The summer I prepared to enter kindergarten, I was already like a pony—all legs. I was five and didn't have many friends yet, so I was looking forward to school and being around other kids. *Sesame Street* had made school seem like the happening place to be, and in a couple of months, it would be time for me to enter the Texas educational system.

Our house was at the corner curve in the road of Flannigan Street, one of at least forty other family homes in our subdivision. Flannigan was a racially diverse street and indicative of the kind of hopeful change my parents felt as Black Americans in the 1980s. There was a white family that lived across the street. Next to them was an interracial couple—an Indigenous woman from Oklahoma who was married to a Black man. They had a son together, Dustin, and he and I would later become playmates, despite the four-year age gap between us. Our neighbors to the right were Indian immigrants who frequently visited, bringing us meals of traditional Indian foods and gifting us a porcelain white elephant with brass tusks for our mantle, a gift for protection and prosperity.

My parents worked hard to maintain the taupe and brown brick with brown wood trim on the exterior of our home. Ours was a brand new three-bedroom, two-bathroom house, and we were the first family to reside there. I assisted my mother and father over the next few years in helping them to lay squares of St. Augustine grass and to plant hedges around the front of the structure. The new house became a home.

Inside, my mother had decorated it like a mansion. Dark cherry and mahogany woods were part of the dining room table and sofa and chair legs of the Queen Anne furniture. She chose the colors: sky blue, peach, and white for the decor. To me, the furnishings resembled a sunset. Her love affair with swag curtains started in that first house, and I remember her slumping over a sewing machine, pulling and tugging at peach linen fabric until she had created curtain panels for the bay window at the front of the house. I fearfully watched her tenaciously ascend a ladder, her 4'11" petite frame (though she swears she is 5'1") balanced on tiptoes as she hung curtains at every window in the house. As I watched her shift from one perilous position to the next, I expected her to topple off that ladder at any moment, but she never did.

One of my earliest and most vivid memories is of a four-year-old me, sitting cross-legged on the floor of my bedroom in our home. My bony little elbows were pressed against the windowsill as I sat on the nearby carpet and stared at nothing in particular through the open, floor-length window. This was a comfortable position for my tiny frame to lean in and dream. When the Texas temperatures allowed for an open window during the spring months, gentle afternoon breezes slipped past the window screen to caress my cheek, lulling me into a trance.

My eyes felt void of sight, but my remaining senses were attuned to what I felt and heard: the wind on my skin, the sound of cars on the nearby road, the chirp of birds, the trilling of insects or the hiss of cicadas. If you had called my name then, I might not have heard you. I would slip into a dream-like state so deeply that I no longer felt present. I could go anywhere in my head with details of cinematic quality, vivid faces, places, and landscapes so elaborate they felt like reality. There, wherever *there* was, in my head, I felt the emotions of the stories I made up so profoundly that I often shed real tears as dramas and tragedies played out in my young mind. I was more than Maya, stuck in her conventional, American bedroom. I could be more than myself. Dreaming of being taken away and out of the moment became an even bigger part of my life as I grew older.

We weren't rich, even though the way my mother dressed us and the way she decorated our home would have led you to believe so. We were a Black-American, middle-class family. To me, that first house was elegant but cozy, and my parents taught my brother and me to appreciate homeownership. Unlike the apartments I had first grown up in, this felt like *our* space. It was where we belonged together.

By then, Mom had accepted a job at a jewelry company as a collection supervisor. Until I was three, she had stayed at home to keep me from going to daycare. She worked the evening shift to be with me until she had to leave for work by late afternoon. A year earlier, my father had left his position at a cosmetics warehouse to take a job with a budding tech company—Apple. A babysitter would care for me for a couple of hours in the evenings before Dad usually pulled our navy Monte Carlo, nicknamed "Blue," into the garage around dinnertime, sitting down at the table with me to dig into whatever Mom had made for us to eat. Typically, the babysitters would be a cousin or one of my older brothers. My parents always felt that family members were the safest and most trustworthy.

My mother's son from her previous relationship was called JJ by everyone because of his initials. She'd gotten married to her high school sweetheart, his father, straight out of school. Over the years, snippets of why they had divorced were revealed to me when Mom felt I was old enough to understand. She mentioned a few beatings, his affair, and the final straw: when four-year-old JJ had jumped between them during an argument. Although JJ was seven years older than me, we were raised together. I had never considered the *half* part of our relationship as I grew up. To me, he was my whole, cool, older brother.

I had one other brother who I know by name only, my father's son from his first marriage, nicknamed Captain. During my father's second marriage, he became an uncle to a nephew that he had raised like a son—Nathan, who was nine years older than me. Nathan came to visit regularly, and some summers, he stayed with us, but he lived with his mother for most of the year in another part of Dallas. Dad took Nathan under his wing like his own, always welcoming him to stay.

I didn't know much about Nathan's mother or why she and my uncle divorced. I was told that it was "grown folks' business." All I knew was that I had met her on a few occasions, and her last name, Lovely, seemed to belie her true nature. Kids and dogs, they say, are good judges of character, and whenever I was near her, I felt uneasy. She was "lovely" in the way a laxative is after days of constipation.

Though Nathan and I were nine years apart, we shared a birthday. This was an instant source of resentment on his part. My birth ushered in not only a cousin for him but a nuisance.

As Dad tells it, once I was brought home from the hospital and placed in my crib, Nathan hovered over the bedding, inspecting me. He then declared, "That girl is cross-eyed," and walked away. I am not cross-eyed, and most of my family found this story humorous years later. Though I felt as though there was something else there that no one else could see or feel—a sinister contempt for me from the first moment we met.

During the school year, JJ was usually at football or basketball practice and was not at the dinner table with us in the evenings. As it became apparent he was an exceptional athlete, Mom worked it out with the coaches that if he was to attend evening practices, his kid sister had to be there too. Given that he was already a talented player, they agreed to babysit me. I'd sit in the bleachers and watch as JJ ran routes on the field or hustled back and forth on the court, dribbling and tossing up a jumper with grace and ease. I heard the clash of helmets and pads, a whistle blowing as the smell of the freshly cut football field grass wafted under my nose, my chin resting in my hand as I watched the action or daydreamed. I heard the squeak of sneakers on the polished hardwood courts, and smelled the pre-teen boy sweat and musk filling the un-air-conditioned gym as they shouted at each other for the ball. I listened to the coaches' instructions and watched the players huddle up. Other times, I was uninterested and sat in the coaches' office playing memory card games or doodling on the coaches' notepads.

With school out, JJ often spent the entire summer at his father's house, and I had free reign to hijack his favorite toy, the Sega video game system in his room, or to lift and lower the trellis on his daybed over and over again while he was gone.

When my female cousins couldn't watch me for those brief two or three hours between Mom's departure for work and Dad's return home, my parents hired a friend of JJ's to babysit. She didn't talk much, so it's not like we sat around having oodles of fun and braiding each other's hair. She simply came by to make sure I didn't burn the house down or let a stranger inside to murder me.

When Nathan came to visit, there was no need for a sitter. He was fourteen, a teenager, and my parents trusted him to be responsible enough to look after his cousin.

The sitter wasn't with me one afternoon during the summer of 1985 when JJ was at his father's. But Nathan was. I couldn't tell you what month it was June, July, August, the day of the week, or the hour. Those details are blocked from my memory, sequestered details that seem inconsequential in the grander picture. I also couldn't tell you what exactly I was wearing—although I know I was wearing shorts.

I can remember what my bedroom was like because it was in my bedroom that a line in the sand altering the purity of my childhood was drawn. My bedroom was a white and purple haven with a canopy bed, the top enclosed by ruffles that swayed whenever the fan was on. The matching comforter was dotted with little lavender flowers and more ruffles. My dresser was cream and embellished with gold spray paint.

On top of that dresser sat a brown and black television with a long, metal antenna that shot out like alien tentacles. It had clear buttons that were square and hard to push, and the edges would sometimes poke into your skin or indent your index finger or thumb if you didn't press it just right to change the channel.

The details of "the when" are fuzzy for a reason. Part of me doesn't want to remember. My memory fails me there, an obstacle to what followed, and is fragmented with only the worst parts left. What I *can* tell you, what I do remember: what happened and how I felt.

I was in my bedroom watching that television when I heard Nathan call my name from the bathroom. There was urgency in his voice when he shouted, "Maya! Come here!" I hopped off my bed and scrambled up the hall towards the closed bathroom door, where I paused. I could see the light from inside through the crack under the bottom of the door. Before I could respond, he shouted my name again, this time an exclamation of excitement to entice my young interest.

"You gotta come here!" he shouted again, not realizing I was already on the other side of the door. "There's a worm in here!"

I typically recoiled from anything that slithered or had more than four legs and wasn't a puppy, but the urgency in his voice titillated my little brain.

I don't remember if he opened the door or if I turned the doorknob and pushed it open. All I can tell you is that somehow the door opened, and there stood my cousin, pants off, with a fully erect penis.

I screamed. It was the shriek of a little girl who, shielded and protected as she had been, knew something was wrong. The cry of a frightened child who sensed impending danger and harm. The screech of something innate telling me this was all wrong.

I turned to run, to retreat to the refuge of my room, but his teenage body, long arms, knocked-knees, and much bigger than mine, took quick strides and seized my arms from behind. My forty-pound frame didn't stand a fighting chance against his fourteen-year-old, pubescent physique. Still, I struggled like a gnat in a spider's web to wiggle free.

"Don't run," he said softly as he held my arms. I resisted for a moment more, but there was a calm in his voice. Fear pulsated with every beat of my heart, but the gentleness of how he addressed me, how he commanded me not to run, stilled every limb in my body.

The hallway was dark, save for the light coming from the opened bathroom door, as he guided me towards my bedroom, where the only illumination came from the glow of the television screen.

He had me lay down on my stomach on top of the covers of the bed. I remember the feel of my shorts being dragged down my legs along with my underwear and the coolness of the air conditioning striking my small, exposed parts.

The mattress dipped with the weight of his body and mine as he climbed on and behind me in some fashion, either straddling me or between my legs. I never looked back. Not once. I focused instead on the television screen, the blue-greenish glow of light cast across my face and making silhouettes of our bodies on the wall beside the bed.

A rerun of *The Carol Burnett Show* played that afternoon, and as my cousin rubbed his erection between my legs, I watched Carol sing and dance, drawing hoots and howls from the audience with her and the cast's vaudeville variety of comedy.

As Carol's mouth opened wide and she belted out a song, I felt the warm, smooth hardness and pressure against me over and over again.

"Does it hurt?"

His voice drew me from Carol's world for only a second so that I could lie.

"Yes," I said, my five-year-old voice even smaller than usual in my ears.

"No, it doesn't!" he contradicted with clear irritation. I took that as my cue to keep quiet as he continued.

I'm not sure when he stopped or why. I don't recall if he orgasmed. What I recall most is the antics of a red-haired comedian because I never looked back. Not once.

When he was done, he told me to sit up, and he helped to pull my shorts and underwear back into place. I didn't quite understand what had happened, but I knew it was wrong. I knew that my cousin was not supposed to touch me that way. No one was supposed to touch me that way.

If a love scene came on during a movie we were watching as a family, my parents would tell me to turn my head or cover my eyes until it was over. I knew something was going on that I wasn't supposed to see, but I was only mildly curious to peek. Plus, my parents had been careful with whom they had entrusted my care.

My ability to daydream was transformed that day. I didn't simply create castles and epic tales in my head for my own young entertainment. I could put myself in a trance-like state. Now I could take myself out of my head, out of my body, out of the sensations against me. I found calm and peace in the midst of chaos and fear. I could control my thoughts even when I was not in control of what was happening. I could generate the eye in the hurricane. Now my mind could find its way to a place where I was secure.

"Don't tell anyone," he said as I avoided eye contact. He spoke to me as if I was his accomplice, as if we had robbed a bank together, and this was our escape plan.

I was now an unwilling partner in his crime. "You tell, and *you'll* get in trouble," he emphasized.

My ears perked up at the "you," and my eyes darted to his face in a panicked glance. His brows lifted ominously for emphasis, and I looked away again. He was my older teenage cousin, treated like a brother in our home, and I believed him. He was old enough to understand rights and wrongs and how to navigate discipline from parents.

All I could do was nod my head in silent agreement.

Chapter Three

Silence is Golden

I sat as still as a grandfather clock in the middle of the velvety backseat of Blue as Dad sped towards the Hamilton Park neighborhood of North Dallas. The long Monte Carlo rode like a space shuttle in orbit, gliding up the highway, the suspension rising and lowering effortlessly over every dip. My legs were inert, my knees locked together. But when we reached a long curve in the road, my shoulders and chest swayed like a pendulum.

A half-hour before, Dad had come home and announced it was time for Nathan to go. I wanted him gone. I didn't want to see his face for one more second. I didn't want to smell the wet, sulfurous reek of his breath or his musty, aroused, teenage scent. I didn't want to be within five feet of him.

But there wasn't a feeling of "Oh! Dad's home! Now I'm safe." My father was not my savior that day. Instead, he was a harbinger of my fear. I was steeped in dread and terror, stewing in despair at possible punishment.

You'll get in trouble.

Four words. Such a short sentence would burden me for the rest of my life.

The childish dismay spun inside my head like stirred-up hornets, swarming down my throat and stinging the insides of my belly. I was poisoned, filled with venom, and I believed in my soul. If Dad had taken more than a glance at me as his work-weary feet stomped across the threshold of the garage door, he would have known.

I felt like I looked different. I certainly felt different. I *was* different.

My anxiety post-molestation had about an hour to birth itself as a Gollum-like ghoul while Nathan headed across the hall to JJ's room to kick back and play video games.

Having known very little about sex at the start of that day, I had to process what had been done to my body by my cousin. I grappled with shame and guilt through the worldview and intellect of a five-year-old.

You'll get in trouble.

My father was so beaten up from his work shift that he never gave me more than a glance. When I heard the garage door open, I emerged meekly from my room and stood in the living room. As memory serves me, I usually came bounding to the doorway to greet him, excited that Dad was home. This time, I didn't.

I don't recall him saying *hello*. He stood in the doorway, jiggled his keys, and said loud enough for Nathan to hear him over the sounds of the video game, "Time to go."

Nathan rode up front in the passenger seat, making chit-chat with Dad as we drew closer to the Dallas city skyline at sunset. He failed to mention how he had violated the innocence of the little girl—a girl who was like a sister to him—a couple of hours before.

I watched the back of their heads sway, father and nephew, almost in unison, as I sat mutely, my thighs and knees clamped like a hydraulic press. What was between those thighs was no longer safe, and the burden to protect it was up to me.

Saying I felt dirty would liken that first time to getting grass stains on the knees of my jeans. This was a different kind of dirty. The hornets in my brain were rotting, and the carcasses they left made my entire body feel putrid. Especially "down there."

"Down there" wasn't just for going to the bathroom anymore. "Down there" didn't just differentiate me as a female. "Down there" seemed, at least from that moment forward, to exist for the pleasure of someone other than me.

We pulled onto the street of Ms. Lovely's house. Teenage boys were outside dribbling basketballs and taking shots toward a goal that faced the street in front of one of the houses. I slumped down in the backseat as the car came to a stop. As Nathan opened the car door to step out, Dad cranked down the window, winding the knob until it was low enough for him to exchange polite greetings with his ex-sister-in-law.

Nathan said, "Goodbye," before flicking his eyes towards me. I looked away, and he hopped out, slamming the door behind him. I didn't hear Dad's reply.

Dad and Ms. Lovely continued their conversation as I listened through muffled ears. It felt like cotton balls were wedged in my ear canals. The world around me was animated, picturesque, and moving. I watched the boys dribble but did not hear the pounding of the ball on the cement. I watched as they laughed and shit-talked one another but only heard it as a whisper. My father's words to his ex-sister-in-law were equally as muffled in my ears. I did not turn to watch Nathan's spindly figure climb the elevated steps towards the front door where his mother stood.

Dad waved goodbye and spun the wheel sharply into a U-turn, and I exhaled. It seemed for the first time in almost two hours that my tiny lungs released all of the pent-up air that had escaped in only short bursts before Nathan departed fully from my presence.

As we headed back towards our home, my hearing became clearer. The smooth R&B voices on Soul 73 AM radio serenaded us, but I didn't pay attention to the lyrics. I leaned forward, my arms folded and resting on the back of the headrest of the front seat, my head in line with Dad's as he kept his gaze on the road.

We exchanged no words. The radio and the hum of the tires on the road provided the only sounds inside the car. There were other vehicles on the road at that hour of the day in the city, but I didn't see them pass. As we traveled, it felt like everything in the entire world was encased in that Monte Carlo. The most important thing in my world was silenced inside our car like a tomb.

From the side of my eye, I stared at my father's profile. I flicked my eyes at his skin, the color of earth, and his short afro, and longed for some unspeakable force to prompt him to realize that I was not okay.

I can remember, at that moment, wanting so very badly to tell him what had happened. There was a persistent urging in the back of my mind. *Tell him! Tell him exactly what Nathan did to you! Tell him right now!*

And then, I sat back in the seat.

But you'll get in trouble, a second little voice hissed like a snake from another part of my brain.

I watched Dallas pass by through the windshield. I remained silent. I made a choice to say nothing. I would keep everything that happened that day to myself.

We are all born with intuition, a feeling in our gut about right and wrong or things meant to cause us harm. A feeling that courses through us when something is off-kilter. It was that intuition that made me run when my cousin emerged from the bathroom with his pants down.

Looking back now, I realize my intuition told me then that I would never be the same. I remember very clearly thinking my life was forever changed. Not solely from the abuse but from my decision to remain silent. I was not sure how I knew. I just knew.

My intuition was right.

Chapter Four

Post-It Notes

2014

In the waiting room chair, my body drops so low in the deep plushness the armrests are at my shoulders in a suspended hug—almost wrapping me up but stopping short of holding me. My gaze doesn't leave the floor-length, oil-painted canvas of Christ. It's so large it's difficult to look at anything else.

I examine the painting intently. Jesus is cradling the broken body of a limp white man, propping him up like a divine crutch. The anguished man's legs hang like tentacles from his torso, as useless as jelly. His eyes are shut as life seems to ghost from that marred form. His mouth is open, either with death's final exhale or gasps for more lifesaving breaths. Jesus' cheek presses to the man's hair tenderly, his face full of love and compassion. A halo of gold surrounds his divine head.

Below the man's jelly legs, a stream of bright red blood flows into a crack in the dark earth. Brown skin or white skin, female or male, I am just as broken as he is. Four days before, I'd also been just as close to death.

The door to the office opens, and my head drops, and I avert my eyes. I don't have my phone out. Otherwise, I'd pretend to scroll as people do when they want to avoid social interactions or being seen. I always hate the moment when one patient is leaving and has to walk through the waiting room. I keep my eyes cast down towards my purse, hoping they don't see my face or, even worse, recognize me.

My counselor says a friendly goodbye to the patient; I don't look at them. My head remains down until I hear the whine of the front door's hinges.

"Hello, young lady," Counselor greets. "Come see me."

I don't move or uncross my legs until the creaky hinges stop, and I hear a metallic snap. I know then that we are alone. I slip my purse strap over my shoulder when I finally stand, feeling the weight and pulling against the tendons near my neck. Inside are plastic baggies of Teddy Grahams and packages of fruit snacks, along with a couple of diapers and a thin pack of wet wipes. My coin purse and overstuffed make-up bag used to make my purse heavy enough, but now I walk around with a dumbbell harnessed to my side loaded with emergency supplies for Charlie.

My body leans, a little crooked from the purse as I stand. A cocker spaniel emerges from the office door and walks to the toes of my shoes. She tilts her head up at me, black snout rapidly moving as she sniffs. Two ears that look like tan shag rugs sit on either side of two black marble eyes that lift to my face.

I bend down, careful to keep the heavy purse from swinging forward as I pet her head.

"Hello, Ms. Sadie," I say in a gentle voice.

I take a step towards Counselor in her office doorway, and Sadie turns, trailing at my heels. The dog stays close. In fact, when I'm seated on Counselor's leather sofa, Sadie sticks with me. I put my purse on the side table, and the dog hops onto my cushion, curling into a fuzzy stress ball next to my thigh.

Mindlessly, I lay a hand on her fur and stroke. There have been days when she's welcomed me, sniffing as she assessed me, and determined I was fine enough for her to return to her dog bed in the corner.

Not today.

"Tell me how you've been," Counselor says, taking a seat in her leather rocking recliner across from me. She grabs a clipboard and, in her custom, tucks one leg underneath her. Her smile reminds me of Sally Fields. There's a motherly warmth in it that says you can trust her. Her first name could be that of a man's. Maybe that's why I liked her so quickly the first time I entered her office four years ago. I've always felt more at ease around men than other women.

Except for today, when I am reticent. I feel like the herald of some awful news to be disclosed to a family member—cancer, or a fatal car accident, perhaps. In my mind, I'm sitting like the grim reaper, shrouded in my dreary cloak, a scythe propped up against the sofa as I hold it, ready to swipe at Counselor's pleasant smile. My news *is* of death and sorrow. But I also carry words laced with something I fear even more from those I respect: disappointment.

"Well." I emit a skittish giggle that sounds like a sitcom laugh track in my own ears. My eyes lower away from her face to the tiny hairs on my arm. I begin to twist and pull at a few of them; the sting reminds me I'm alive.

"I need to tell you something, and I'm worried," I add.

I don't see it, but I imagine her tilting her head as she watches me.

Her voice lifts with her question. "What has you worried?"

"That you'll be disappointed in me." Then, for the second time today, I begin to cry. The first wave of tears came in the car on the ride to her office as I imagined telling her what I'd almost done.

My worry shakes hands with my shame. They slap each other on the back, old friends reuniting again, and take seats on either side of Sadie and me, boxing us in. Feeling the sting of arm hair almost tweezed away by my fingers, I return my hand to Sadie's fur and pet faster this time.

"Maya," Counselor says in a tone like a fifteen-pound weighted blanket wrapping around me. "You could never disappoint me if you're being honest about what you feel."

I gulp and stop petting Sadie. I begin to speak, but the words don't seem to come from my own lips. "A couple of days ago, I had intended to go home," I explain. I blurt out the next few words as if saying them faster would quickly get rid of the situation. "I was going to kill myself when I got there."

Released. Like the Leviathan in that essential oil-infused office, I'd acknowledged it out loud. Before that moment, it felt like another one of my many secrets. The inhales and exhales through my nostrils vibrate the tiny nose hairs with the force of each breath, so much so that I can feel them moving. I can hear my breathing with the hi-hat tapping of my heart against my sternum. It beats like a jazz melody, a chaotic timing that somehow finds a pace. I grab a clump of hair on my arm and pull. If I could turn to mist and sink into the creases of that sofa, I would.

I find the courage to look at Counselor, more out of curiosity than actual bravery. The corners of her eyes and lips dip, and I watch her chest and back sink into the recliner. It's not the disappointment in her body language that I'd feared she would show: it's sympathy. I hadn't caused chaos. I had raised concern from at least one person on this planet.

"First, thank you for telling me," she says with a sincerity that slows the beating of my heart to a legato tune. "Now, tell me how you got to that point."

There is a pause. It's probably only seconds, but it feels like half an hour. With the back of my hand, I wipe at my cheeks as I throw light upon the events of the last few days.

⋘⋙ ❁ ⋘⋙

The downtown Dallas Omni Hotel was resplendent. It was recently opened, and everything inside had the crisp newness that had not been rubbed away yet by many travelers flowing in and out of its doors. The marble floor shined like a pool of reflective water. Over my head, modern spherical chandeliers glittered in the afternoon light which poured through the windows. My high-heeled strappy sandals tapped in rhythmic cadence with the sway in my hips as I pulled my suitcase behind me. I was glad I'd dressed nicely for the trip. My dark jeans, considered dressy by Texas standards, fit the curve of my legs and bottom, sticking out from a flowing navy and white blouse.

I'd checked my hair and blotted my oily nose and forehead before exiting my car in the parking garage adjacent to the hotel. Driving in the Texas summer heat had drawn droplets of sweat and oil to bead up over my makeup, and I'd slathered on enough deodorant for two people to stay as fresh as possible.

Fleeing. That's what I had done. I peeled out of the driveway of my home back in East Texas. It felt like the days when I was in college: single, and my only concern was whether I had enough gas money.

I scanned the hotel lobby for familiar faces. I recognized a few older men from television forming a line at the check-in desk. A piece of paper taped to the granite counter read "Media." Suitcase in tow, I fell in line behind the men.

A blonde in a dark blazer and starched white shirt smiled when I stood in front of her.

"Good afternoon, ma'am; checking in?"

"Yes," I said, utilizing my broadcast voice. It drops a bit lower and is projected unnecessarily. I hadn't used it in a while, but I felt important and wanted to sound it, too.

She took my identification and a credit card, manicured fingers typing in numbers on her keyboard before she slid two bright red door keys towards me in a small envelope. I put my ID back in my purse before inspecting my room number and the card keys. They gleamed with the athletic conference logo on the front. *Fancy.* For us, for this occasion.

My chin lifted as I held my room keys in hand and rolled my suitcase towards the elevator. I pressed the button for the eighteenth floor and waited with a few other guests.

I couldn't actually afford the stay at the hotel. What I will make for the piece of work ahead won't even cover the room service I will order twice, let alone the room.

I'd finagled a freelancing gig through a friend who was a sports director at one of the network affiliates in East Texas to cover a football conference's media days. It's an annual gathering each July of the who's who of the college football world—coaches, athletes, and media personalities.

Those days spent in the bleachers and coaches' offices, watching JJ and his teammates, created a deep love of sports within me. I felt a sense of ease, comfort, and familiarity on a football or baseball field or on a basketball court as I did in my bedroom.

I'm back in my element, shining, but like a charming piece of costume jewelry, the shining veneer will soon tarnish.

I'd been out of the TV industry for three years. My career in local TV news had started out like therapy. It was the polish to my perfectionism, the bragging rights that gave me a sense of worth. I had Emmy award nominations, several Associated Press awards, and a distinguished Excellence in My Market award from the National Academy of Television Arts and Sciences. Yet, in constructing that lustrous career, my dream became corrupted and ultimately another nightmare. I'd wake up tired and found that even the cordial greeting of the station's receptionist as she welcomed me would grate on my nerves like an electric drill. I sat at my desk with my jaw clenched so tightly that after a few weeks, my chin and lips started to develop numbness. When I did sleep, it was for twelve hours. When I didn't sleep, I watched the ceiling fan swirling over the bed, trying to think of another angle for a good story the following day.

I was also the first female sportscaster in the market's history. Real and perceived, a lot was riding on that job for me. I had to prove that my brain and little vagina could handle discussing football formations and routes and breaking down highlights. I had to hold my own walking into field houses, which were, by their very nature, boys' clubs.

The anxiety, the manic will to be the best, left my brain feeling like it was inside a batter mixer, constantly churning, swirling, never resting. Before my eyes were barely opened each morning, I'd grab my phone and check my emails, message boards, and other news sites for any breaking sports information. I was the first female sports director in the fifty-year history of our market. Good wasn't enough.

When Everett and I moved in together, I was twenty-six, and he was thirty. We'd been dating for a year. When you work sixteen-hour days with someone, you either hate them or fall in love. Everett and I fell in love. He worked behind the scenes in the production booth while I was on-air in the studio, but he was often planted on the sofa in the sports office, flirting, and I couldn't resist him.

Everett would roll over in the mornings, sleep still crusting his eyes, and watch my hyperactive state each day as I fever-scrolled. He begged me to take some time to relax or watch TV. So, I did. I watched the sports networks to see what other headlines I might have missed.

Near the end of my TV contract, I had been looking around for other work. The burnout seeped like slow poison into other parts of my life. I was moody and exhausted, and I became fixated on my on-air appearance. I began taking colon-cleansing pills and drinking only organic juices to lose weight. It worked fine until one night when Everett heard me screaming from the bathroom. I was curled up on the floor, holding my stomach that was violently cramping after a bout of diarrhea. Everett contemplated calling 911, but I begged him not to.

"Promise me you will stop taking those damn pills," he said as he helped me back to our bed. I agreed like a scolded child. The pills stopped—for a little while.

By twenty-nine, we were engaged and a couple of months away from our wedding ceremony. All I could think was that I couldn't enter this big phase of my life feeling so inadequate every single day. After a ten-year TV career, I'd extinguished my flame to a charred wick.   One of the biggest lies I ever told was when I walked away from that career one month before our wedding. It stunk as if manure had fallen from my lips, "When I'm done with something, I'm done. I'm done with TV."

I took a new gig as a communications director for a local education firm. The desk job was appealing on paper. I'd still be connected to the news industry through press releases and video sharing. I also acted as the spokesperson, so I still had the occasional joy of being in front of the camera to wet my whistle.

But the job was mundane. I wasn't cut out for nine-to-five work. I'd sat down at my desk and held in tears two weeks into the gig. I had left a high-stake, high-energy, high-stress environment for ... I wasn't exactly sure. It was a new position, and I got to make up the work as I went along. The problem was that there wasn't much work initially, and I wasn't built for a sedentary existence. Still, I put up the front that I was happy with my new job and stayed.

Since leaving TV and marrying Everett four years ago, I'd done some blogging and written some freelance articles for a locally published magazine. Still, I hadn't covered anything like media days. It was exhilarating to be moving back into that space, but things had been tense at home before I left.

I was preparing what I needed from the trip, and my internal gas tank was almost on E. Charlie was on the floor in the dining room, scooting around and playing with his toys. Everett stood in the doorway of our media room as I put my audio recording equipment and notepads in a pile along with the print-outs provided by the conference.

"Do I need to go to the store before you leave?" he asked, hands on the door frame as he tilted his head and chest forward in a standing pushup.

"What?" The question jarred me from the mental checklist of items to pack I was going through.

"Do I need to go to the store before you leave?" He repeated slower, as if I was sluggish to understand. His hint of a Texas twang was more pronounced as he dragged out the words.

I stood up straight over the collection I was gathering and looked at him. "Why?" I asked, incredulous. I felt the hyphens forming on my forehead as I frowned and squinted at him.

"We need a few things for Charlie, and we are almost out of milk and eggs," he explained and lifted his brows.

My exhale was deliberately loud, and I rolled my head around on my neck. "I'll take care of it," I said—one more thing to do before my dash to freedom from my mundane life.

"Only if you have time," Everett backpedaled. He let go of the door frame and lifted his hands defensively.

"That sure didn't sound like an 'if you have the time' kind of a remark," I grumbled.

"What's that mean?" Everett snapped back.

"You know what I mean!" I shot venom like a viper straight at him. "I've got enough shit on my plate right now. If we need stuff at the store, then yeah, maybe you go get what we need!"

"Alright, that's cool." He shrugged. "I'm fine with it."

"Then why the hell did you ask me all passive-aggressive?" I shrieked, balling my hands into fists at my sides.

"I'm not being passive-aggressive." Everett's voice lowered and sounded more commanding, brooding.

"Bullshit."

"It's fine, Maya. I'll go to the store then. Fine." His face screwed up with irritation as he turned to walk away.

It wasn't the question about grocery shopping that set me off. It wasn't even the underhanded way my husband suggested it would inconvenience him to do the shopping instead of me. It was the added work—another thing for Maya to be responsible for. Postpartum had only exacerbated the depression I'd been trying to hold back, like trying to dam the Nile River with my hands.

Charlie was a fussy infant that didn't even attempt to sleep through the night until he was about nine months old. He was thirteen months now and sleeping *mostly* through the night. I was getting up every morning, feeding him, getting him dressed, dressing myself, attempting to do something with my hair, and taking him to daycare; rinse and repeat five days a week. Everett helped when he could, but since he'd left his job in television to become a teacher the same summer of Charlie's birth, he had to be at the school early most mornings for hall duty. Work, now far busier than when I had started, had become more frantic as I was trying to fix one crisis after another. When we did have the luxury of our parents wanting to keep Charlie overnight, Everett and I slept. We were too exhausted for sex, a phrase I would never have attached to our marriage before the birth of our son.

Charlie's birth had been the catalyst for my Post-Traumatic Stress Disorder diagnosis. There was nothing traumatic about my pregnancy or the delivery itself. It was what followed.

My own broken childhood became the impetus for my style of mothering. I was the Martha Stewart on steroids of new moms. I was going to *mom*. My child would not want for anything, emotionally or physically.

I thought the euphoric bliss that connected to every cell in my body when I held my son for the first time would last for days. I felt ashamed that it didn't.

After months of depression and sleep deprivation, Everett's indirect suggestion that I needed to go grocery shopping while packing for an important trip was the added tension on the already taut violin string that was my body.

"If going to the store is fine, then why did you ask me about it?" I shot the words at Everett as he turned to walk away.

"It's not a big deal," he grumbled. "Damn."

The cuss was a match that had been struck in a room filled with propane.

I bent over and picked up the tripod for my recorder, and I side-armed it like a knuckleball pitch. I shot it toward Everett's legs with such force it grazed his shin as he barely had enough time to move out of the way. It connected with so much velocity against the trim around the bathroom door that chunks of white wood splintered and flew through the air. The shards of wood and the tripod fell to the carpet near Everett's feet, and his head whipped up from inspecting his legs and the wall to my face.

"Are you crazy?" he shouted, eyes bewildered. His mouth hung open as if he was looking at a charging rhinoceros coming straight at him, and running would be useless.

I stood still for what felt like an hour.

"I'm tired!" I finally exclaimed. "Do you hear me? I'm tired!" My voice cracked, and I began to whimper. "I'm exhausted!" My hands covered my face, shielding me from Everett's gaze and hiding the tears I didn't want him to see. My shoulders wobbled as I bent over, and then the agonizing groan rose through my throat, guttural and pained.

"Maya," Everett said, his voice soft as I sobbed.

"Don't." I held my hand out and waved him off. I stood up straight and walked out of the room, brushing past him and stepping over the chunks of wood on the floor. I didn't look toward Charlie in the dining room. I headed straight for our bedroom, and I slammed the door so hard that a picture frame on a little mounted shelf next to the door toppled over to the floor. The short glass vase with fake daisies wobbled but didn't join it.

We hadn't said too much to each other before I left for Dallas. I don't recall apologizing. Instead, I looked ahead. I awaited the upcoming trip to media days like the anticipated moments after finishing an intense workout—gasping in breaths for relief, body and dry throat soothed by a cold, refreshing drink, and thanking God that it was all over.

Even the smell of the air at the Omni Hotel and the vibrations of conversations felt like peace. At lunchtime on Day 1, I'd silently gone through the buffet line using tongs to grab dry chicken and a ladle to scoop an Elmer's paste-like mass of mashed potatoes on my plate, silently wondering where I would settle myself.

I entered the smaller ballroom and looked around like the girl from out of town who had enrolled at a school where no one knew her. I'd been out of the sports news business long enough that I felt more like a spirit drifting through my haunt than a sportscaster that belonged there.

The sports team from the Dallas station where I'd started my career had assembled at a table, and as soon as their weekend sports guy looked up and met my searching eyes, he waved me over like the coast guard spotting a drowning woman in a churning sea.

I sat down for this professional family reunion. All around me, it smelled like aftershave, the musk of hazelwood cologne, and hotel banquet food.

A guy I'd known when working in East Texas was roaming the room and stopped at the table. He'd gone bald long before he was thirty-two, both out of shaving and out of the natural deterioration of his hair follicles. He was a frat brother, the "bro," the used car salesman that always had a sly comeback or a way to make sure his hand found a spot on the small of my back.

As he sat at the crowded circular table, he noticed the marquis-cut diamond surrounded by other diamonds on my ring finger.

"Let me see that thing," he said with a nod toward my hand.

For a moment, I'd forgotten it was even on, so I frowned before the realization of what he meant made me "Oh!" with understanding. I held my hand out, fingers outstretched, and yet he still felt the need to grab my hand.

"Wow, he did good!" he said, brows lifting in admiration at the prisms the diamonds cast under the ballroom lights.

"He did do good." I gave an uncomfortable laugh and pulled my hand away.

"You know," he said to the table. "This one was supposed to be my wife." Thumbing at me like he was pointing out a show cow at the state fair.

I gave a bashful giggle and then felt disdain for myself. None of what he said was true; we never even dated. I let grown men I had no interest in openly flirt and objectify me, and my response was to let out a coquettish flutter of laughs like a mindless twat.

As the hotel staff cleared our plates, Austin guy looked at me, balling his fist and putting it on his hip with a cheeky grin as he leaned against the table.

"A group of us is heading out tonight, going uptown. Food, drinks. Some dudes from Oklahoma. I can text you if you want to join us?"

The invitation could have come from a Xenomorph, and I would have accepted.

"Yeah, yeah." I nodded eagerly. *Get me drunk.*

We were to meet up in the lobby after we had filed our stories after the six o'clock news.

I'd already been wearing full makeup from making the press rounds earlier in the day, but I touched up my look in the hotel room mirror, adding a signature shade of red lipstick as I puckered and tested my pout. I'd packed a sheer Bohemian blouse to wear over a lacy tank top with matching shorts that were also covered in lace. As I turned and inspected my body in the full-length mirror, I looked over my shoulder, arching my back and inspecting the same body that had brought a child into the world. There were faint, light-colored stripes on the sides of my thighs, but my ass was still lifted and firm. I'd stopped breastfeeding almost seven months ago, so when I turned and cupped my breasts and let them go, their descent back into place didn't seem too jiggly and low. *A good three inches above the belly button,* I said to myself with a nod. I dabbed perfume behind my ears and brushed my hair one last time.

I wasn't looking to hook up with anyone. The thought of engaging in extramarital sex was repulsive. I would flirt, sure, hop online and enter a sex chat room on any given day, absolutely. But actually bedding someone other than my husband? I wasn't angling for any reason to fast-track my course to hell.

I wanted the possibility to be there, lurking under every interaction and conversation. *Take me to your room.* I wanted to feel sexy. I wanted to feel hot the way I did before I was married and a mom. I wanted to feel the way I did when I was twenty-three and not contemplating my mortality. I may not fuck anyone that night, but I sure as hell wanted them to want me. I slid on a pair of high-heeled strappy sandals, binding them around the ankles. I wondered if my shorts may be a little too short.

"Look-at-you," Austin guy sang, mouth gaping as I sauntered towards the glass doors of the lobby.

The shorts were too short.

Our destination was McKinney Avenue, a place lined with restaurants and bars for young professionals and the Dallas elite looking to blow off steam after work. One of the Oklahoma sports guys offered to drive us all in his truck. I slid into the backseat of the cab wedged between Austin and a silver-haired man. We were packed like pickles in a jar on that backseat, pressed tightly, our bodies suctioned together. Austin didn't seem to mind it as we bounced and swayed in unison over every Dallas pothole and curve in the road. I told myself a normal person would feel uncomfortable wedged between strange men that tightly. I hadn't felt normal in a long time.

As we cruised through Dallas evening traffic in that truck that felt like a NASA prototype for an expedition on Mars, the flesh of my outer thigh, exposed in those too-little shorts, rubbed against the thigh of the silver-haired man. We hit a dip in the road, and I couldn't control it when my body lurched to the side and my breast firmly pushed up against his bicep. I sat back and corrected my positioning as quickly as I could.

"I'm sorry," I blurted because it felt like what I should say. I wasn't sure I even meant it.

"Oh." He gave a low sigh and a chuckle. "It's fine." He spoke it slowly, words oozing like molasses. A sweetness to them dripped with something more, a hint of something more tantalizing if I'd been given a taste.

I sat back, very aware of the bodies on either side of me and how neither seemed to mind when my thighs rubbed theirs. A pinky finger seemed to have strayed at some point to brush against my skin.

When we reached the parking lot, we poured out from the truck like a clown car, one, two ... then seven, and I stretched my arms over my head and deeply inhaled the smoggy air of a Dallas summer night. The atmosphere hung heavy with humidity all around us, thick with car exhaust and the smell of grills and fryers at work up and down the avenue.

Our party sat at an antique, rectangular dining table on the patio under streams of suspended lights and speakers blasting music from a stereo somewhere inside. Sitting down on that wooden bench, elbows resting on the table, I felt like I'd woken from a coma into a pleasant new reality.

Someone ordered a round of drinks. I'm certain I ordered food, but I don't remember eating. I only remember the first few drinks until I began to forget how many I had consumed. With alcohol in my system, I felt the most like my authentic self. The burn of the spirits ignited the reclusive inclinations in my soul. Afterall, I'd consumed my first glass of wine at the age of two. It was an early introduction to a comatose lullaby. I was relaxed and looking at the world through one of those polished filters you can select on Instagram—vibrant and more vivid even under my heavy lids.

Without TV, I felt I had lost part of my self-worth. That night, I had it back.

Austin said something about me being the "coolest chick" he knew.

"If I was a dude, I'd be a better fuck than any of you," I slurred. I pointed to my crotch. "It would be bigger than all of yours." I motioned around the table dismissively. The men erupted in laughter. I sipped my drink, a mischievous grin on my lips as I peered over the top of my glass. This garnered a chorus of dissenting remarks and a discussion about sexual techniques.

I waved them all off and motioned with my fingers together in centimeters to each guy seated around me. *Small.* I spent the night flirting and telling bawdy jokes filled with innuendo and feeling like a goddess. Alcohol wasn't my crutch; she was my pedestal. Together we were a dynamic duo, stars of a burlesque show. Alcohol and I made for one hell of a show and a good night.

I climbed back into the truck with the fellas and one other lady. We were a giggly bunch by then and much more talkative than we had been on the way to the restaurant—seven folks reeking like seven individual distilleries.

"How big of pimps do you guys look like walking in as a group with just two ladies?" I asked one of the Oklahomans as the bright lights of the lobby hit my eyes, forcing me to squint.

"How big of a pimp do *you* look like, walking in with five dudes?" he retorted and sent me cackling.

Austin invited me to the hotel bar. I was drunk but not drunk enough to forget my marriage. I declined.

When I got home the next evening, I tried to show Everett the pictures from the trip.

"Why are there so many pictures of that coach?" he asked and kept moving. I was all but chasing him with my phone, tapping to show one picture after another as he dodged and switched directions. He gave only partial attention as he kept moving ahead of me with no certain destination.

"Because," I whined like a teenage girl, disappointed that he didn't share my level of enthusiasm. "What's the matter? Hey!" I finally raised my voice. "I'm trying to talk to you. What's the matter?"

"I'm just tired, Maya," Everett said and cocked his head to the side.

"Was Charlie fussy?" I asked and glanced at my son, who had been running in the same circle around the kitchen table since I'd gotten home.

"Of course, he was fussy," Everett retorted.

"Oh," I said, and the last few days flipped through my mind like a kaleidoscope. Heavy guilt latched on to me, a boulder tied to a rope tied to my waist as the cliff I was standing on crumbled.

"Hope you had fun," Everett muttered, barely loud enough for me to hear.

Shame is a funny thing. It can so quickly turn to rage. Everett's snide comment was like a dart into my happy, bright balloon. I watched him enter the darkness of our bedroom and followed him like my feet were in flames, long, hurried strides right behind him.

He walked into the bathroom with me so close the tips of my toes almost tripped up his steps.

"Hey!" I shouted again. He turned and looked at me, brow furrowed with anger. "You said you were okay with me going. Don't get all pissy on me now. I'm sorry if Charlie was fussy, but that's nothing new! Hell, that's why *I* needed a break!"

"And what about my break? What about my time? You come home every day and close yourself up in the bedroom. You barely spend an hour with Charlie and me in the evenings. You get in bed on your phone, take your bath, and come out long enough to eat or say goodnight, and then you go right back to bed. I need time to myself too, Maya!" Everett's face contorted as he shot the words back at me.

The call-out only made me feel worse, and the shame at the truth of what he spoke boiled like magma in my veins.

"I told you I'm tired!" I waved my arms as I stood in the bathroom doorway. "What do you think that means?"

"You said that like I'm not tired too! I'm doing everything you're not. You act like we don't do anything but cause you more stress, so I don't say anything. But don't stand there and complain about being tired like I'm not coming home every day and immediately stepping into dad mode. When you disappear, who do you think is taking care of him?"

"I'm not disappearing," I lied.

"If you don't want to be here with us, fine, then go somewhere else. I'm tired of you making excuses. You act like you don't want to be here, so don't be here!"

My head jerked back, and my eyes narrowed. "What are you saying?"

"You heard me."

I didn't want to be there. I really didn't want to be anywhere.

I had no idea where Charlie was in the house, but I was certain he heard our raised voices.

"I finally, finally got to take a few days to do something for myself, to do something I enjoy, and you can't even support that?" My resentment towards Everett was reaching a crescendo.

"I support you every day!" Everett yelled. "You act like you're the only parent in the house, but I'm the one actually in there raising our son!"

I turned and grabbed the short glass vase with the fake daisies from the shelf by the door. I hurled it at Everett's crotch this time, not even allowing him the chance to dodge it like the tripod a few days before. It bounced off his body with a muted thud and fell to the bathroom tile with a high-pitched crackling. A large shard broke off and lay beside the vase.

Everett trembled with anger as his face reddened. My chest heaved, and I felt like clawing at him with my fingernails. But the minute I looked into his eyes, I felt regret. I felt like a crazy person. I wanted to apologize. I did—but I was also tired of saying 'I'm sorry' every day of my life to the entire world.

"That is the second time you've assaulted me!" Everett shouted. He didn't retaliate. He didn't strike back or strangle me because that wasn't the type of man he was. I found the formality of his word selection at that moment odd. *Assaulted*. I was not only guilty of assault; I'd been acting criminally for days, weeks, months. Years.

I turned away from him and covered my face as I began to sob. Everything inside me felt like oil in a cup of vinegar—the crazy and the sadness, the anger, and the hopelessness had all accumulated on the surface. The vinegar below it was full of bitterness. It was how my soul felt: sour.

That was the day I decided I would kill myself.

In a couple of days, I knew we would be going to Garland. Around the time I became a mother myself, my parents' house had started to feel like a mausoleum. I would rather stick the end of a cactus up my ass than sit in my mother's immaculate living room with white cushioned sofas and chairs, ivory swag curtains, and taupe Berber carpet. It constantly smells like Lysol or the faint remnants of bleach or chemical scrubs like Comet. With its pristine decor, I still feel like a child, worried I would mar the furniture or smudge the carpet and face a tongue-lashing. Hard to relax when you are terrified of messing something up. The safety of that house had been violated, despite the white oasis she had created through decorations and furnishings. She couldn't whitewash or bleach away my history or my pain.

There was something poetic to me about returning to that very house to die. They wouldn't be able to move through the halls or breathe in the dank air of that old house without thinking of me.

When I look up at Counselor, I gulp and shake my head. I swallow down nausea and sadness, bile in my stomach that roils like snakes in a barrel. "I don't think I'm meant to ever be happy. And because I think that—I didn't want to live anymore." To avoid her reaction, I turn to the side table, snatch up a few Kleenex, and blow my nose as quietly as I can. The sound is still wet and sloppy.

I finally look up at her and reluctantly admit, "After everything, the abuse ..." I can't continue; I don't want to acknowledge it anymore. "I'm still not sure that I want to live."

There are no words spoken in return. She grabs a stack of Post-It notes off the table beside her and writes something on it. She peels the top note away and stretches her arm out, handing it to me.

The sticky attachment sucks at the tip of her finger as I pull the note away and read it. "Shades of Hope."

Chapter Five

The Angels in Heaven Done Signed My Name

1991

I t was hot in the church, and I was restless, an eleven-year-old crammed on a pew with at least a dozen other people, most of them bathed in too much perfume that itched my nose and made it hard to breathe. The remnants of the stained, burgundy, crushed velvet cushion under my backside had lost any plushness years ago, and the hard, wooden back of the pew wasn't adding to my comfort.

Yet another Sunday afternoon, two hours into a far-too-long sermon. Like most Black girls in Texas my age, I obediently sat through the grueling marathon at our Baptist church. Even if the air conditioner had been on, it would have been sweltering because of all the bodies tightly packed into pews. There wasn't a single clock in the sanctuary, and I wondered if this was on purpose so the congregation's only squirming would be from the sting of the pastor's words to us sinners and not from restlessness. The only time we could count on the benediction, the dismissal from church, taking place as close to one o'clock for the 11 a.m. service was when the Dallas Cowboys had a noon kickoff. No preacher in the area wanted to risk holding everyone hostage through the start of the second half of the game.

I neither loved going to church nor did I hate it. It was simply a part of life that was expected and accepted as a Black child.

Then, I heard it.

Our pastor's booming voice read Matthew 18:10 with conviction: "Take heed that ye despise not one of these little ones; for I say unto you, that in heaven, their angels do always behold the face of my Father, which is in heaven."

My head shot up. My pastor looked out into the crowd of attentive faces and said, "Every child is protected by an angel."

My shoulders hunched towards my ears, and I felt my body grow hot. It was not the type of warmth you feel with a fever. It was a burning from my core that rose like lava to the crown of my head. Rage. *Where in the hell was my angel?*

I couldn't tell you a single word that came next in the sermon. I knew as I sat on that rickety church pew that I had spent the last six years of my life molested by my cousin. As I sat beside church ladies waving fans with images of Martin Luther King, Jr., and John the Baptist holding his hands over a white Jesus in the river, I remembered how I had been preyed upon, touched, and rubbed by a multitude of other boys as well.

I tuned out what the preacher was saying and focused on a question as I seethed with anger and confusion. *Where was God, and why wasn't He helping me?*

I don't know how long I sat there mentally interrogating the Holy Trinity and every single heavenly host. Someone had some damn explaining to do. *Every child?* Wasn't I a child? Did my guardian angel day drink? Whose watch was I on, and why were they failing so epically at protecting me? I called bullshit on the pastor, the church, and everything it stood for right then and there.

Maybe I wasn't Christian enough? Maybe it was as my mom's friend Barbara said. She seemed to think she was a better Christian than the rest of us and was always spewing Bible verses because she'd taken a few classes at a theological school. Whenever my mother dealt with anything uncomfortable, her friend's guidance was the same: *pray about it.*

Had I not been praying for protection? For salvation? I was persistent in getting on my hands and knees at the edge of my bed every night, eyes shut so tight my eyelids wrinkled and my nose scrunched, my palms glued together, and I recited the prayer I had learned as a preschooler:

Lord now lay me down to sleep

I pray to the Lord, my soul to keep
And if I should die, before I wake
I pray to the Lord, my soul to take

Should I be adding more to it? Should I pray for five minutes and recite individual names like Mrs. Donaldson, the church secretary, did? With her perfectly curled, silver hair under a straw hat, she read with a sense of duty and confidence in having a status position in the church. Through the wire-framed glasses balanced over her nostrils, Mrs. Donaldson read the church announcements and then the sick and shut-in list. We prayed for those in need, bowing our heads so long the tendons in my neck strained. Should I have been following her lead?

I wanted the touching to stop. Though, according to the guy standing in the pulpit, shouting into the microphone and pointing his fingers and stomping his feet for emphasis, I shouldn't have had to pray for it. I was a child. Protection allegedly came with the territory.

Like hell it did.

At some point in the day, my eleven-year-old brain moved on from my bone to pick with God and shoved the anger to a corner of my brain. I pushed it down, crushing it, throwing my weight over the thoughts and emotions like an overstuffed suitcase, flipping down brass locks until I could be sure it was securely latched and not to be reopened.

I entered second grade in 1987, and the abuse continued whenever Nathan came around. But he wasn't the only predator in my life. There was a slew of violators during my early childhood, and I ended up as prey in the incubus-like claws of deviant little boys again and again. I didn't want to process what kept happening. More dirty laundry was stuffed into a suitcase, one for each transgression—one suitcase, two suitcases, three suitcases, until I had a warehouse full of baggage.

As a result, I became familiar with sex, the unholy knowledge of the carnality of the flesh, far too young. I was never the one to initiate it, but somehow, I was a perpetual target.

I felt unclean with this knowledge. I imagined it must have been how Eve felt when she bit into the forbidden fruit. Once exposed, she didn't want to know anymore. She wanted to go back to a simpler time, to an innocent time—a time without danger or harm.

So, I convinced myself that the only way I could get clean, the only way that God would come through on this promise of protection from the angels, was to get baptized.

After a Sunday sermon, the choir began to sing, and the pastor stretched out his hand as the deacons placed chairs before the altar. The burgundy chairs, with their elaborate gold arms and legs, sat as a trio in front of the congregation, a sea of hats, fans, and flamboyantly-collared suits and bright broaches.

The Sunday prior, I'd made the mistake of mentioning to my mom during the car ride home from our grandparents' Sunday supper that I wanted to join the church. She nodded but didn't make a big fuss about it. Or so I thought. When we arrived at church the following week, the Reverend called me into his office. I was more afraid of going in there than I ever would have been of going into the principal's office, even though I hadn't been sent, not once.

He asked me to sit down as he sat in his chair behind the desk. His light grey suit was still smooth, the only wrinkles at the bends of his elbows. Usually, after a sermon, the suit jacket was gone, and his white dress shirt was crumpled and pit-stained from the theatrics on the pulpit. Given he wiped at his bald head with a handkerchief as he shook hands with parishioners for a half-hour after service, I had expected that handkerchief to be in his hand and his head shining with sweat when I entered his office, but he looked quite fresh.

He said something like, "Maya, your mom said you have made the decision to join the church."

Eyes wide, I nodded. Jesus, I told her that, yes. I didn't expect her to rush off to the pastor and proclaim my words like an addition to the New Testament.

"Yes, sir," I said.

He began asking a series of questions that I guess was the pre-test before you can be dunked into the holy water. We were Baptists, so there was no sprinkling on the forehead. There was a full submersion, which I found frightening.

He asked if I was accepting Christ as my Lord and Savior, and I said a weak "Yes." He asked if I believed that Christ had died for my sins. I think there was a pause, but I said yes. He asked if I believed that my soul would be born again by being baptized. At this, my voice was louder and stronger. "Yes," I said with courage.

He smiled, congratulated me as if I won the lottery, and told me at the end of his sermon, during the altar call invitation to discipleship, that I would need to come and sit at one of the front chairs. I agreed and left that office as fast as I could. I went into the sanctuary and sat down beside my mother and grandmother. Mom patted my leg.

There was no turning back now. I did believe those things. I learned about Jesus and his teachings, reciting speeches during the Easter and Christmas programs for years. But the eleven-year-old me wasn't doing it out of a calling from above or a desire to abide by the holy spirit. I wanted to be clean. I wanted to be free of the abuse and the dirtiness of my body "down there."

That Sunday afternoon, before that congregation of about a hundred, I some-how found the strength to rise from a pew and take one step right after the other, not making eye contact with any of the people in the church. I walked to the front, past silver-haired Mrs. Donaldson and the candy lady, Sister Banks. I sat my butt into one of those gilded chairs, folded my hands in my lap, and stared down at them as the church shouted "amen," "hallelujah," and "praise God." The Reverend came down from the pulpit, mic in hand, and told everyone about our conversation in his office.

"This child is dedicating her life to Christ!" he exclaimed, and the mic screeched its feedback. This prompted another chorus of amens and enthusiastic applause. I remember him saying that the angels were doing backflips and flying at supersonic speed because of my decision. I looked up into my mother's smiling face a few rows down, thinking whoever my angel was, I sure as hell hoped they were finally happy with me.

A few weeks later, on the first Sunday of the month, came the big dip. I'd dressed for church in the binding layers my mother usually helped me into on Sundays—satin and velvet dresses with sashes and balloon sleeves, thick opaque tights that made my legs itchy, a petticoat, and patent leather Mary-Janes. During the summer months, I was a walking Easy-Bake oven in all those clothes.

I wore my swimsuit underneath—another layer—a neon green and black striped one-piece I'd had since I was six. It fit me at eleven, my flat chest and angular hips not yet developed enough to stretch the Lycra to its limits. I slipped a white gown provided by the church over it and a shower cap around my head to protect my relaxed hair.

The baptismal tub was in a space as narrow as a storage closet behind the choir stand. A mural of Jesus's baptism could be lifted and lowered like a theater backdrop to separate that cold cement space from the pews filled with wine-red robes of hand-clappers belting out gospel tunes. A white ceramic tub with a rusted ring around the drain was filled with tepid water.

I looked at the smooth, gray cement walls and the old, discolored tub with optimism; this was where my spiritual transformation would take place.

On the steps that lowered towards the tub, my line of sight was above the open window. My forehead and shower cap were all you could see as my eyes scanned the congregation and those that would bear witness to my metamorphosis.

The Reverend entered the tub from the other entrance, walking down the stairs in rubber coveralls to protect his suit pants. One of the deaconesses came up behind me, placing a guiding hand on my back. I looked back at her, and she was dressed like an eighteenth-century nurse. The rigid white hat on her head of dyed, honey-blonde hair looked like a hybrid of a sailor's cap and the nurse's Flossie. Her white skirt suit, thick-soled shoes, stockings, and white gloves made this moment feel medical. My heart thumped, and my mouth became dry as I wondered if I might surge with electricity or even flat-line once I hit the water. I hoped what awaited me was salvation, but then fear whispered into my ear, "What if it's damnation instead?"

I shuddered.

Was I worthy enough to do this? I looked at the deaconess with reservation, but she took my hand and squeezed it, a comforting, motherly squeeze. I looked back at the Reverend, and he outstretched his hand, a gesture meaning I needed to lower into the water.

I stepped down, my feet on the wet steps that led into the tub. Then I was half submerged, and the water formed goosebumps on my arms, the water rising around my cool, bare legs until I stood waist-deep beside the Reverend. The hem of my gown gathered and floated on top of the water.

A deacon appeared at the top of the other stairs and put one hand on the wall to balance himself as he stretched the microphone towards the Reverend's mouth, holding it to broadcast his words to the congregation. I was too little for them to see me. Some of the choir members turned around to peer down at me, and I looked up, feeling a voyeuristic intrusion at my moment to get in good with God. I cast my eyes down to the floating white fabric over my brown twig legs.

The Reverend began to recite the scriptures he had memorized. I heard none of them. My mind was on the water that was about to envelop me like a less-fun day at the water park.

I flinched at his first touch before he cradled me behind my back. He raised his other large hand up into the air before lowering it over my entire face like a fleshy veil. He pushed me back into the water, dipping me under before lifting me back up as I sputtered and felt the burn of water shooting up my nose.

The Reverend put a hand on either of my hips and lifted my small body with ease, handing me to a deacon and one of the other deaconesses who wrapped a towel around me.

Organ music played an upbeat song as the Reverend congratulated me, and the church clapped and sang in praise, "I've been born again."

As I walked towards the bathroom, dripping wet and shivering, I felt no different than when I took a bath the night before. *Maybe it took time.* But whatever transformation was supposed to happen, I didn't feel it inside. I wasn't glowing like a magical unicorn appearing from a sacred forest. I didn't emerge from that wet cocoon with a set of shimmering new wings to carry me away. I examined my arms, my legs, and my face in the bathroom mirror for signs of a glint, sparkles of gold, even a halo.

No. Still just Maya.

I took my first communion that same day.

Maybe I needed the food to change, like a second step in the process.

"This is my body which is given for you; this do in remembrance of me," The Reverend piously recited. "This cup is the New Testament in my blood, which is shed for you."

I drank unsweetened grape juice from a tiny glass that looked like one of my father's shot glasses and ate a piece of a bland cracker that was so stale it stuck to my back teeth. I chomped it down like a nibble of chalk.

As the deacons went around to each pew and collected the emptied glasses, I surveyed my arms and hands: muted brown skin, no sparkle.

I did not feel an ethereal surge aligning itself with my blood cells, transforming the red in my veins into a golden, renewed vessel moving within me. I was not levitating. I did not feel the change within me that I hoped would transcend my experiences, granting me immunity from the demons of the world.

Still Maya.

When my family gathered at my grandparents' house that afternoon, I, feeling no different, made a plate for supper in the kitchen while my grandmother commented on the ceremony to the rest of the family.

"Maya looked like a black cricket coming up out of that water."

Chapter Six

Serenity

2012

I didn't expect sexting to be the catalyst for my return to sanity. When Tony and I connected over LinkedIn, he admitted to developing a crush on me during our early text conversations when we'd worked together at a local news station eight years before. Back then, he was young—nineteen. He worked behind the scenes in the control booth. I was twenty-six, and though he'd joined our weekend crew for parties and after-work hangouts, I didn't take a romantic interest in the pimply-faced teen. He was tall and lanky, standing more than six feet tall, had wide eyes and a crooked smile, and when he walked, his shoulders led the rest of his body.

He didn't stay at our station long, advancing quickly to higher markets.

I was two years into my communications desk job, and loathing each morning I woke and drove to the office. I sat at my desk with inflated daydreams of escaping a world of loneliness and boredom.

In my office at the administration building, I was sitting at that same desk the first time he sent me a picture of his dick. I suppose, to his credit, he did ask permission before he sent it.

Not even considering it when he'd asked, I fired off a *No!* It was an abhorrent proposal. I reminded him that I was very married.

*I'll respect your cho*ice, he wrote back.

But he didn't.

We'd exchanged flirty texts for weeks. It feels like a cliché to say that I got caught in the Venus flytrap of his flattery, but I did. He'd tell me I was beautiful, how talented he thought I was and that he thought my muscular arms were one of my sexiest features.

In the beginning, I steered the conversations away from flirting. I'd bring up former co-workers or Everett or some random sports topic I thought was benign enough to justify continued communication. He called us "friends."

But feeling desired and the danger of venturing into forbidden territory began to excite me even if I had no honest attraction to him. There was something tantalizing about the thought of sex outside of my norm. I'd been married for four years, and though Charlie hadn't been conceived yet, Everett and I had settled into a banal, isolated routine. Tony became a break from reality, a disconnect from my wretched life that I'd been craving since I was a kid.

Talking to you makes me feel so good

I like talking to you too.

I convinced myself it was a harmless remark, not an invitation for things to progress.

But on the day of the dick pic, he began to tell me that talking wasn't the only thing about me that made him feel good.

I've been thinking about you

Yeah?

Thinking about your body, how sexy you are

I looked at my office door. There weren't many people who worked in administration, and my office was in the back corner of the building, next to the bathrooms. Most people only ventured that way after lunch for digestive reasons.

I could take the bait, or I could end everything. I considered telling him that he was out of line and that we couldn't keep talking to each other. I felt a yearning to say no. But I found myself without a voice. I found myself acquiescing to his sexual whims. Every time he texted, even if he wasn't standing in front of me, a part of me felt muted, ignoring my own emotions and obliged to comply. Or, I chose to disregard my moral values entirely for a few cheap thrills and continue the relationship.

When I didn't write back, he sent another text.

I've been thinking about you. Stroking myself.

I felt a heat rising in my core, an aching between my thighs. Not harmful, just needy. I looked at my office door and into the hall—all quiet.

Yeah?

Do you want to see?

I dropped my phone on the desk, my fingertips flying to my lips. I think this dramatic display was for the audience of one in my office: me. I was pretending to be shocked as an out. Oh my God. How bold of him! How dare he!

Then, I rolled my eyes and picked up the phone. My body was warm, like the start of a fever. I was intrigued, enticed, lured. I found myself typing the opposite of what I was thinking. My body told my brain, *Let me have this.*

Yes.

A shaky breath emitted through my nose. The phone bobbled in my trembling hands. I put it down and stared at my open office door, aimlessly swinging side to side in my computer chair.

Five minutes later, my phone chimed. One picture came through, then a second and a third.

He was in his bathroom, a sink, toilet, and bathmat visible in the frame with his long, thick erection. The tip was red and swollen in the first picture. In the second, his hand was wrapped around the base, squeezing. The third showed semen in the basin of the sink, his cock still hard in his hand.

I felt awe and amazement. Not because of his considerable size. I was stupefied that I had agreed to this. I felt a dampening at the junction of my work slacks.

And then I felt shame.

Turning my phone screen down, I sat it away from me at the corner of my desk and spun my chair towards my computer. I opened the least sexy thing I could think to start working on—an Excel spreadsheet.

Then my phone chimed.

The sigh that came from my lips was one of irritation. My lips became an equal sign, pressed together in disdain. Suddenly, I wanted him to go away.

Chime.

"Dammit," I grumbled and wheeled my chair around and picked up my phone. I opened the conversation.

You made me cum so hard. You there?

I scratched at the crinkles that had formed between my brows.

I'm here.

What do you think?

As I scrolled up and looked at the pictures again, I had to admit that he had something to be proud of.

You're really big. I hit send before my inner voice could talk me out of it.

You like it?

I do...

I've got to get cleaned up. Talk soon?

My lips flapped as I blew out a raspberry.

Yeah. I've gotta get back to work.

Thanks for making me feel good.

My head tilted as I considered his reply. I had made him feel good, but I was steeped in guilt like a teabag in scalding water.

I didn't reply, instead returning to the spreadsheet and data.

That was the first time we had a sexting relationship. I didn't reciprocate the sending of pictures. Not then.

We began swapping sexy messages and talked about the things we liked in bed. We daydreamed about places where we thought it would be erotic to go at it: an empty warehouse, a bathroom at a stadium, or maybe even on a road trip, pulling over to the side of the road and climbing into the backseat.

I didn't know how to stop it. I didn't know how to speak up for myself and say that I wanted it to stop. I was conditioned to keep going. It may sound like an excuse, but it was how I felt, stuck in a wheel in constant motion. Life felt like it was happening by chance rather than by choice.

I didn't know who I was, so I became what everyone wanted me to be. In his case, as with so many other men, I became his arousal.

One spring afternoon, I closed the door to my office and wept. I covered my mouth and held a tissue to my eyes and nose to catch the droplets before they wet my clothes.

I told him about the weeping. This was wrong. I couldn't manage my fear and shame any longer. Even as I told him how upset I was, I didn't say the word "stop."

I don't want to cause you trouble

Thank you

I dared not leave my phone more than two feet away from me at home. I kept it face down on countertops, switching the ringer off. I shoved it into my pockets when wearing pants, even to walk through the living room.

The thought of Everett seeing a picture or a text made me nauseous. It would end us. I asked myself how I'd feel if he was doing the same thing with someone else. The hurt and betrayal that something like that would cause me would be grounds to leave. Everett and I may have become the couple we had vowed we wouldn't, but he was a good man. My soul was connected to his, and I couldn't imagine living without that half.

I hid in the bathroom, pretending to be on the toilet, or I'd linger in the garage to text Tony. I encouraged Everett to spend time with his parents, so I could be at home alone to sext and masturbate.

After the weeping, I wished Tony well.

I'm sad that we have to stop talking.

It's for the best, I wrote like the ending to a greeting card. Then, I blocked him.

I opened LinkedIn, Facebook, and Twitter on my phone and unfriended him on every platform.

May 16, 2015

The sliding glass doors have barely cracked open before I slip between them. A long, winding line has formed and reaches the back of the stanchions. I hear the beeping of security wands and the buzz of hundreds of conversations carrying on at once. Before anyone can approach the end of the line, I scurry into place.

I move my phone to my pocket and check the time twice. Waiting with the rest of the herd, I'm impatient to make it through TSA screening. Stepping from one floor tile to the next, I peek over the heads of passengers ahead of me. The taxi had been forty-five minutes late to pick me up. When we arrived at Dallas/Fort Worth International Airport, the driver had scarcely braked before I hopped out to jerk my suitcase from the trunk and sprint to the baggage check-in.

One TSA line that is moving faster than the others becomes my target. I tap the screen of my phone to look at the time once more before I drop it with my purse and shoes into a bin. I sprint to the short line, and soon the conveyer belt and X-ray machine are in front of me.

I blow out a long, meditative breath when I reach my gate eighteen minutes before boarding.

It is a small crowd for a short flight. I drop my purse onto one of the vacant, blue vinyl chairs and place my Max Lucado inspirational Christian book in my lap. Sunlight streams through the spotless airport windows in tandem with the fluorescent lights overhead, washing the small sitting area in extreme brightness. The windows give a view of the American Airlines plane connected to the gate. A crew on the ground is loading luggage onto the plane.

A young mother sits in a chair across from me, arms folded across her chest as she watches her toddler daughter roll on the carpet. The girl's little blonde ponytail is mostly free from the elastic that once bound it together, a mess of hair shooting out in all directions. The remnants of something pink and sticky frame her mouth and cheeks. The little girl has a cookie in her hand, and most of it crumbles as she clutches it and rolls back and forth. The crumbs scatter on the carpet, but she reaches for a chunk to shove into her mouth.

"Nungh ungh!" The young mother shouts and reaches out, swatting the child's hand away from her mouth with a whack.

The child erupts into a fit and begins to kick her legs as she continues the theatrics, letting out one high-pitched shriek after another.

"Serenity!" her mother shouts at her. "Serenity, quit it!"

The other passengers watch the tantrum, horror etched onto their faces. We all know we are about to get on a plane with that.

I look at the aghast faces and then back at Serenity and her mother. There is more screaming. I lower my head and cover my mouth. My shoulders began to shake as I fight off laughter. It seems to me little Serenity should have been named Hell on Wheels.

Of course. Of course, I'm heading to treatment with an unruly toddler on the plane. There had to be one more reminder of what I was leaving behind.

The previous afternoon, I loaded my suitcase into my SUV and stepped back into the kitchen. Everett summoned Charlie to his side, where I knelt to look my almost-two-year-old in the eyes.

I'd been mentally going over what I would say to him as I packed the night before—time to deliver my address as calmly as possible. There was a sinking in my gut at the thought of leaving him—leaving my home—behind.

"Mama's going away for a little bit," I said. "But I'll be back soon." I paused and gulped hard before continuing. "I love you very much."

I tried to hug Charlie tightly. I kissed his curls and then his cheek as he fought to pull away. It broke my heart that I couldn't squeeze him closer and let it linger. He wiped the kiss I placed on his cheek away as soon as he wiggled free.

"I'll be back soon," I repeated after he crossed the kitchen and put some distance between us, making sure I couldn't grab him again. I inventoried his little features, taking a mental picture I could visualize for a few days at least.

My knees crackled as I rose from my stooped position, my weary body trying to stand tall before Everett. There was a fleeting second of eye contact before I looked down at the tops of my sneakers. He pulled me into a hug, wrapping his broad arms around me. I felt the warmth of his chest pressed to mine and slowly lifted my hands to hug him back.

"Go get better," he said into my ear.

I moved the side of his head with mine as I nodded. I had no idea what "better" looked like, but I knew things couldn't get much worse. I was committed to trying—trying to get better.

He held me at arm's length, his hands on my shoulders as he tilted his head to meet my eyes. "I love you."

"I love you, too," I replied sincerely.

"Charlie and I will be okay. Don't worry about us." He gave a little smile and squeezed my shoulders. Everett was always so rational and hopeful; opposites truly attract.

"I'll call when I make it to my folks' house."

I stepped back from his touch. Charlie ran off to find one of his toys.

Everett trailed me to the garage. We didn't have anything else to say to each other. The old gears of the garage door screeched as it lifted, and I cranked up my car. Everett took a few steps forward when I backed down the driveway and waved goodbye. The corner of his lips lifted in a soft smile. I tapped the car horn lightly twice and was on my way.

As I drove away from my life, I didn't feel tears coming on, but I felt deep sadness nonetheless. In forty-eight hours, all contact with everyone I cared about and everyone who claimed to care about me would be cut off for six days.

I'd driven to Garland to spend the night at my parents' house to be closer to the airport for my flight.

Dinner was solemn. My parents and I didn't talk much. No one wanted to address why I was there or that I was leaving for the Shades of Hope treatment facility in the morning. I found sanctuary in the guest bedroom, where I scrolled on my phone most of the night until I popped a couple of muscle relaxers Mom gave me and fell asleep.

Seventeen hours later, I was in a metal tube soaring through the sky. Goodbye, Serenity.

When we land at Abilene Regional Airport, I schedule a cab to take me to my hotel. Rolling my suitcase outside to the front of the airport, I find a bench to sit down and wait. It's the middle of May, and West Texas threatens to be too hot. It is still pleasant enough to sit in the shade, but a few minutes in the sun and beads of sweat will roll down your back.

My suitcase is loaded into another cab, and I am on the road again with another driver, heading toward my hotel. It is my first time in Abilene, and it is a bigger city than I expected.

"What brings you to Abilene?" the woman driving the cab asks. Her hands are on the steering wheel, and I stare at her over-processed brown and blonde hair in a French braid. The volume on a Christian radio station is turned down low.

I balk at the invasive question, but the lie is quick. "It's a work trip."

"Oh, yeah? What do you do?" she asks, our gazes meeting in the rearview mirror.

Could you please drive the damn cab?

"I'm a sports reporter." Only half of a lie.

"Covering our Wildcats? So proud of our teams." She beams over the local college's athletic program.

"Yup."

Graciously, there is no more small talk, and soon I'm at the hotel and in my room.

I'd been perspiring in the plane, tensing with each of Serenity's wails and sweating in the May heat. I squeegee my jeans down my legs and toss my accursed bra and its soaked underwire over the hotel desk chair, and my T-shirt drops down onto the geometric shapes of the crimson and gold Marriott Courtyard carpet with a whack.

I'm naked and unbound as I set the room up for my comfort.

The portable air purifier I travel with was too large to pack in the one suitcase I was allowed to bring. I set up the little USB fan that I had purchased at the grocery store and placed it on the nightstand, tilting it and aiming it so it would push out a stream of coolness over my body on the bed. It's the only way I can fall asleep without drugs.

I enjoy my nudity until I'm refreshed. Minutes later, I'm in sweatpants and an oversized T-shirt, stretched out on the bed, pillows stacked behind my back. The air conditioner hums with an occasional knocking noise. I wonder if it will keep me up tonight. The half curtains shield enough of the window that only a slit of light streams through their juncture, and they wave flag-like from the blowing of the air conditioner. Phone in hand, I unlock the screen and tap. The message thread I open first is not that of my husband.

Hey, I made it.

How was your flight? Tony replies.

Screaming kid the whole way, but fine otherwise.

That sucks. What are you up to tonight?

Resting.

My breath hitches. I'd put this conversation off for two months ever since I'd been onboarded with the treatment center.

Look, I have something to tell you.

?

I hadn't mentioned it before now because I wasn't really sure how to tell you. But the trip I'm on, it's not for work.

I watched the ellipses on the screen bounce before his reply came through.

?

I'm here to enter treatment. It's for all the stuff I told you about, you know, with the PTSD? I'll be here for six days and I won't be able to call or text once I get there. They take our phones.

I read my own text message over and over for several minutes before the ellipses jiggle in the lower left corner again.

So I won't be able to talk to you?

No. I clasp my phone.

Well, it's good you are getting help.

I read the message on the screen but doubted the sincerity of its sender. Then comes the question I'd been expecting.

What does this mean for us?

I stare at the screen and lean my head back against the headboard.

This was my second online affair with Tony. Five months ago, at the start of 2015, I was in bed watching TV at home when I checked LinkedIn. I'd come home and poured myself a glass of wine that led to a second glass of wine that I was gulping to ready myself for Charlie's refusal of bedtime. It was my night for the battle. Another distraction was waiting.

I had a new connection request. It was Tony again. I tapped the screen to open the headshot on his profile. His face had matured, the acne was gone, and I was looking at a handsome, stylish and brilliant young man.

"Things will be different this time," a voice whispered in my ear. I knew better, but I accepted his request.

The next morning, I had a new message in my inbox.

Hey! Hope you are doing well! Would love to catch up sometime soon! What's your number?

It was the same, but I knew I'd have to unblock him to allow him to call. A few taps on the phone and the line was clear. I messaged him back with the number.

He called me one evening before Everett got home from work while Charlie was playing on the floor and watching TV.

"So good to hear your voice," he said cheerfully. "That sexy voice of yours."

"Everett would kill you." My husband wouldn't. He hadn't even played football like most Texas men. He'd never been in a fistfight. I offered the threat in hopes that maybe this time, things would remain platonic. But I knew I was lying to myself again as soon as I accepted his connection request.

"That's only one of the reasons he'd kill me?" Tony laughed.

"You know exactly why," I replied, my tone incredulous.

He laughed a full, sly laugh. Although I could only hear it through the phone, it seemed to come from his belly, and I imagined his entire body was shaking.

The sexting resumed three days later. It didn't stop when I was looking after Charlie alone. It didn't even stop when I found out Tony had been lying to me about the casual girlfriend he said he had. In our acts of deceit, I had also been deceived. He was married.

The text messages, pictures, and phone sex became more frequent and intense. We would call each other right when we reached our orgasms to let the other hear our moans. Then we would hang up and go on about our day or our evening as if we weren't two sexual deviants latched onto each other.

Tony was one of the reasons I was going into rehab.

What does this mean for us?

I reread his text.

I don't know.

The truth was, I wanted this time away to be the end of "us." I wanted it to be the end of all my online relationships and sex chats. I wanted, as Everett said, to "get better."

Will I be able to talk to you again? When you're out?

I run my hand over my face and lick my lips.

I typed and hit send.

No.

Chapter Seven

Pandora's Box

1989

I was balanced on the edge of my tiptoes, one hand pressed against the metal railing below the white, wooden top shelf of dad's closet. I braced myself, the imprints of wire hangers embedding into my palm as I considered the wobbly stool below my feet.

Feeling around on the shelf, I didn't know exactly what I was looking for, but I was looking for *something*. Something I knew I was not supposed to have access to.

It had been about a half-hour since Uncle Melvin had dropped me off at home after school. I was bored with *Disney Afternoon* cartoons. I often ventured into my parents' room where I spread a buffet of off-brand Cheetos and bagged chocolate chip cookies on a paper towel on the floor and munched away until Mom came home from work two hours later. Dad wouldn't be home until almost sunset. This day, I wanted to explore. JJ had a car, was in high school, and was rarely home in the afternoons.

I was in the fourth grade and was starting to become more and more intrigued with the idea of the woman I'd be someday. I would open the double doors to my mother's closet and look over the rows of dress suits, feel the silk fabric of her blouses or wool of her sweaters, and look for something interesting to try on. I would try to balance in her four-inch heels, teaching myself how to walk across the carpet in them, my little feet pressed against the toe of the shoe, a massive gap between my heel and the shoe's heel. I would sway my hips and attempt to switch, but it came across as a clunky march as I walked back and forth in front of the mirrored paneled wall in my parents' bedroom.

One day, I found a sheer black robe with a feathered boa stitched around the collar at the back of mom's closet. I stripped down naked and wrapped it around my sixty-five-pound frame. I slid my feet into a pair of her black pumps and twisted and turned in front of the mirrored wall, trying to imagine what I'd look like one day when I had breasts and hips and, with any luck, much more of an ass.

I was outed for my wardrobe changes when Mom found one of the black feathers left behind by the robe on her country blue carpet.

She asked, "You been trying on my clothes?"

With fear of punishment, I softly confessed. To my surprise, I wasn't in trouble. Mom was more amused by it than anything.

This particular day, my taste for my mom's exquisite wardrobe had soured, and I was looking for something new, something much more provocative. So, I had gone into their bathroom and retrieved the sitting stool, a contraption with white vinyl over the padding and green, uneven metal legs. I was relying on it then to help me find whatever my little hand sought. I felt around until my fingers tapped against something hard that felt like cold plastic. I grabbed it, still holding on to the rail and balancing on my toes.

Holding my retrieval in front of my face, I found a black VHS tape. There were no markings and no label on it. I knew what it was. I would love to tell you exactly how, but I knew. I knew it was something I wasn't supposed to watch. I knew it was something for adults, which is why it was hidden behind various old shirts and my dad's mementos on that shelf. Maybe it was the same way I always knew when a boy was interested in touching me.

I balanced my nine-year-old self again as I bent my standing leg and lowered the tip of my toes on the other until I felt the carpet underneath them, examining the tape in my grip.

There wasn't even a flicker of hesitation as I headed to the silver, top-loading VHS player on my parents' entertainment console. By then, it was about six years old and had been brought with us from the old house to the new one. I pressed the

Power button and then the Eject button as the cassette cradle lifted with a buzz and a robotic whirring. I put the tape in and pressed the cradle back down until I heard it click. I grabbed the TV remote and watched until the screen glowed. Switching the input, I pressed Play on the VCR.

Tanned, naked, pixelated bodies writhed on the screen, and a woman's incessant moans and gasps for breath blared loudly through the speakers over a generic, thumping soundtrack that reminded me of the Muzak I heard at the department stores. She was between two men, lying on her stomach as one pounded away at her from behind. She was giving the man kneeling on the bed in front of her face a blow job, a term I had become familiar with at school. I don't think I watched what unfolded on the screen for more than thirty seconds. The man kneeling began to shoot jets of something across her face, and I was too young to understand it was semen.

In all my instances of abuse, I don't recall ever having been formally introduced to the bodily fluid. Thinking it was pee, I was horrified and slammed my hand against the Stop button. I carefully but mindfully rewound the tape to where the scene had started before ejecting the tape.

I climbed gingerly back atop that stool and made sure to flip the tape over and put it in the same position in the same spot where I had found it.

If the disgust I felt at that moment had been enough to force me to stop the tape, that feeling of repulsion didn't last.

Over the next few weeks, I would think back to the tape and inquisitively began to wonder what other forbidden items I might find on another search. My investigation began after school once again. The pair of hours I had alone in the house became my inquisitive time to delve into sexuality, which, looking back, was already much more advanced than it should have been for my age. I was entering a time when my mom would take me to purchase my first training bra from JCPenney. It was an AAA, the smallest possible size for a chest that barely had the bumps produced by mosquito bites. Some girls at school had started their periods, and all I had was a starter kit tucked away in the cabinet in my bathroom with tampons and maxi pads ready to go for the big day.

Yet here I was, searching for more porn. On the floor of Dad's closet, underneath a row of clothes, was a brown leather attaché case my mother had purchased for him as a birthday gift. I can only remember him carrying it to work a few times when she first gave it to him before it settled into its home on the floor of the closet. It had faux brass closures and a dual combination lock. Again, I wasn't sure how, but I knew I'd find more of *something* in that case.

I sat cross-legged on the floor and pulled the case into my lap, eyeing the combination lock. I memorized each number's position. I thought for a few breaths about what the combination could be. I wouldn't say it was any amount of intelligence that led me to use my dad's birthday, much more that it seemed like the obvious choice. So, one column at a time, I pressed and spun the numbers around, a clicking sound with each turn until I had put in the date of his birthday. Holding my breath, I pressed in on the sides of the two buttons, and as they shifted to the left and right, the clasps popped up. Bingo.

I lifted the top of the case, and there were at least four more unmarked, black VHS tapes inside over a stack of magazines. I pulled the tapes out and sat them on the floor beside me before pulling out one of the magazines. *Hustler.* On the cover was a woman with big, teased brunette hair, crisp-looking from all the hairspray in it. She was wearing a headband and a big smile. Her breasts were exposed, but she wore the bottom of a bikini and leg warmers. My breath quickened as I flipped open to the first few pages with heightened anticipation. I remember vividly a cartoon of a man masturbating as he sat in a chair in front of a TV showing a woman also masturbating. Above the television was a fan with fish dangling from it, blowing them out and wafting a scent toward him. I scrunched my nose up at the lewdness of this but continued to flip through the magazine.

I stopped when I came to a section that had the lady from the cover. She was not alone. She was fully dressed in the first image as she stood with a man who seemed to be her aerobics dance partner from the way he was also dressed. A pole extended from the ceiling to the floor in this scene, and in a couple of shots, she was spinning over him. As I turned the page, a feeling of recognition washed over me. The man in the photos had pulled down the waistband of his biker shorts to reveal an erect penis. She was staring at it, her mouth slightly opened, her eyes wide. I knew that she knew. I knew what he wanted her to do, and as I looked to the next page, the scene unfolded in some familiar ways, but also in some I'd not yet known.

I went back to that magazine a few more times over the years and studied those photos. I'm not exactly sure why. There was a level of arousal I felt from them but also a level of shared experiences I felt *with* the woman on the page. She was to be his plaything, and he had revealed himself to her with an air of dominance. Even as a child, I already related to what I saw.

I put the tapes and the magazine back into the case, closed it, returned the numbers on the combination lock to their previous position, and ensured the handle was exactly as it had been before I slid the case back into the grooves it had left in the carpet, leaving it to appear untouched.

I returned to the case, to the tapes, and to the top shelf by balancing on the stool repeatedly. I continued to find something *new* for quite a long time. Each time I returned and dug a bit deeper, I found something different. There were porno books with stories I thumbed through and read like a school assignment. The combination would be put into the case, the closures released, tapes popped into the VCR. In the instances that I ventured deep into the contents, I would remember the timecode on the VCR when I started each tape to make sure I rolled it back to the exact position before returning it to the case or the shelf.

Around that same age, I have my first memory of masturbating.

I hadn't experimented with providing myself pleasure before then, and quite possibly, the videos, magazines, and books had tempted me into experimenting with self-stimulation. I didn't even know what masturbation was before seeing a woman touch herself on one of those tapes. I had slept with my hand in my underwear as a child, a fact my mother had pointed out to my "Ainty" during a sleepover with my girl cousins. I had been pretending to sleep when I overheard the conversation and felt the covers shift as my aunt peeked to see if my hand was indeed inside my pajama pants, which it was. But that was never about any type of feeling. I may not recall it clearly, but I have the thought that someone at some point told me to do that when I didn't know what to do with my hands while I slept. It's an odd memory to have but one that is concrete in my mind. After the night of the sleepover, I didn't do it again. It felt like something I was not supposed to be doing, even though there was no gratification in it. My hand simply was inside my own underwear.

When I first experimented with masturbation, I was still a kid imitating what I had already seen and what I had already felt with Nathan. I used the edge of my mattress and moved in the way that was familiar to me for a few minutes, feeling a brief tingle but nothing earth-shattering. It would be several years before I tried again and took it much farther.

By the following school year, Nathan had moved to East Texas to attend an HBCU. When Dad first told us Nathan would be heading off to college and living a two-hour drive away, a sense of relief ran through me like my entire body. I could finally exhale.

His visits during the summer months were shorter and fewer as he became older and more interested in the things older teenage boys often are interested in. Which certainly provided me with a respite from feeling like a hostage in my own home from June to August when school was not in session.

It was the end of the fall semester, and we were picking up Nathan and his belongings from the dorm and moving him back to his mother's place for the winter break. The only reason I can think that my parents wanted me to tag along on this outing was not for any extra set of hands to help carry things, but rather for exposure to the campus and a glimpse of the college experience. They were always trying to provide me with some type of life experience to spark more interest in a successful future, not realizing I was already fully invested in education, a career, and carving out a bright future.

Still, Dad and I headed east under gray skies. We stopped at the Dairy Queen in a town called Big Sandy. I found the name hilarious because it sounded more like it was named for a portly woman than for the sandy creek bottoms that cut through the forest of its East Texas pines. In the rented van, we parked, and I ate buttery Texas toast and chicken strips, dipping them in white, creamy gravy, swallowing the food down along with the anxiousness rising like bile in my chest. I'd had two hours to think about the greeting I soon had to make and play the part of a dutiful and loving little cousin.

When we arrived at the college, Nathan's bags were packed, and we loaded up the minivan to the point where Dad had enough space to see out the back window. I moved from my position of shotgun to one of the empty seats in the back not packed with Nathan's stuff.

I was quiet the entire way home, letting them chat as I tuned out the conversation, listening to the radio and watching the passing rows of evergreens as we moved like a chess piece from one patch of Texas back to the Metroplex.

It was neither the upcoming Christmas break that I feared, nor the occasional drop-in visit on a three-day weekend, like Good Friday. It was always the summer months that I came to dread when Nathan had the idlest time and the most opportunities to put his hands on me.

Even those instances had dwindled in number by then. There was an afternoon at home when Dad had brought home a huge box from work, like one used to ship a refrigerator. I had a sweet spot for those plain, cardboard boxes and would transform them into my playhouses in the spare room of our new home that was mostly empty except for a television and my Nintendo NES on the floor. I would take those boxes, cut out shutters and doors, use extra flaps to make a windowsill, and add flowers along the windows of my creation with markers and construction paper. One afternoon, I was giving Nathan a tour of my estate inside that box when he slipped his hand between the legs of my shorts and pressed at my center. I froze like a statue and waited until he simply took his hand away. We continued the tour as if nothing had happened.

When school let out for summer, it was usually a few days before my birthday—our birthday. There were many times of joint birthday celebrations. Polaroids show us leaning over a homemade cake, blowing out candles together. Mom would make a special dinner, and we would dine and open our presents together.

It was, as my mother would later describe it once she was aware of the abuse, "torture." I was smiling and laughing and trying to enjoy gifts on what should have been a special day for that little girl, but instead, I was putting up a front of happiness as I sat down to break bread and cake with my molester.

My tenth birthday was different. My tenth birthday became the first celebration that truly felt like my own. By then, Nathan had met a girl at college, and she had become his girlfriend, eventually becoming the mother of his children. They moved in together, and his visits home either saw her coming home with him or were day trips, and he would return home to her. Her appearance in our lives became my salvation.

On my tenth birthday, I celebrated at home with five of my closest friends from school. We ate salty chips and salsa and cupcakes on the back porch before coming inside and watching my favorite film, *Willy Wonka and the Chocolate Factory*. I opened their gifts and thanked them before seeing them out the door. I felt for the first time like my birthday had been about me.

"You know," Mom began after I had walked my friend Callie to the door and waved goodbye to her, "you were acting awfully fast."

The elation of the celebration withered.

I tilted my head but knew not to question her. Any Black girl in the south knew there were two things you didn't want to be labeled by the older folks: fast and dumb. Being called fast was the equivalent of being called a hoe. Simply put, she thought I was acting too grown, too mature, and not like the obedient, passive child she normally saw at home.

I wasn't quite sure how to take it. I was behaving with my friends at the house the same way that I acted with them at school. They all seemed fine with it and liked me for the funny girl that I was known to be. That girl was at odds with the subdued good girl my mother expected me to be at all times. All I could think, all I could feel, was a sense that somehow my true self was bad.

During a time when I was discovering my sexuality and exploring what sex meant, the message seemed to ring clearly in my ears that I was no good.

Chapter Eight

Scrambled Porn and Dial-Up

1996

I sat cross-legged on the sky-blue carpet of our living room and pulled the knob on the wooden box television. Grabbing the remote control for the satellite, I punched in the coordinates and listened. Outside, the C-Band satellite that stretched above the roof of our house rotated with a slow grinding as the TV screen flickered from one blurred image to another while the satellite moved towards its destination.

I felt the all too familiar pull to go back to what I knew. Porn became my bottomless bucket of Halloween candy. I couldn't grab a piece or two and savor it any longer. I was salivating for more of what became my sweet goodness.

Cauldrons of sebum-filled pimples encircled like witches by tiny blackheads discolored my cheeks and forehead. Monuments to my youth. My period had become a painful monthly reminder of my ascent into womanhood. Joyful outbursts were censored these days. My brain monitored moments of glee with the attention of a prison warden, ensuring that my lips would not stretch wide enough to reveal the metal brackets behind them. Sweet sixteen, as they called it, was cruel. I found sanctuary from the discourse of navigating high school by withdrawing into the chimera of my teenage fantasies and worlds of pleasure.

I happened upon the channel a few days before. Occasionally, some of the premiere movie channels would bleed through the blocks of the providers, and I could catch a movie from HBO or Showtime on a clear day (no way my cheap parents were paying for those). Instead, as I channel surfed, I came across scrambled porn.

I'd still been sneaking into the same, unaltered porno stash of Dad's into puberty and beyond. But this chance encounter with an adult channel was a locomotive veering off the tracks with me as the hapless conductor, both too weak and unwilling to slow it down.

The satellite stopped moving, and I pushed the channel button a few times with the type of heart-thumping anticipation I'd previously only known when I walked in the opposite direction of my class for a glimpse at my crush. There was a fluttering in my belly. I stopped at the channel information I had memorized.

My brown eyes were wide and shining like bronze medals. Yes. Still there.

The green glow of the clock on the stove would flip from one minute to the next until a full hour had passed. My eyes, tantalized by lewdness on-screen, flitted to that clock periodically despite my deep disconnect from my other surroundings.

No one would be home for quite some time. You see, my solo afternoon playtime continued even after I had started high school.

I had my own car by then. JJ had graduated from high school four years earlier and moved out. Dad often worked overnight shifts at the warehouse, sleeping during the day when I was at school and leaving the house at the same time I was exiting campus. Most evenings, it was me and Mom and her dinners of liver or some variety of Hamburger Helper. She and I didn't talk much by then.

On afternoons when I wasn't tied up with school activities, I came home and assumed the same cross-legged position in front of the TV. Over time, I would move the satellite around to the different coordinates I had discovered that offered up the scrambled carnality.

My four-leaf clover days were when the porn came through with the clearness of Sardinian waters. On those days, at first exposure to the vivid quality, I felt a sudden flush of warmth that spread outward from between my legs.

I unzipped my wide-leg jeans or took my pants off entirely and slid my hand inside my underwear, rubbing at my center. My heartbeat pounded like a double-bass drum as I shivered. My fingers rubbed and tweaked, stroking up and down the inside of my dampening folds.

But I always stopped. Despite my years of dedicated porn viewing (training videos, as I would later call them), I never could grasp how long I was supposed to touch myself for. I knew there was supposed to be a payoff in the end, but what exactly was it? The women on the screen would thrash their heads around and scream, but I had no idea what they were feeling. Touching myself felt good, of course, but there had been no fireworks. No big bang.

Not until one afternoon, solely by accident. I watched a clear feed, a scene with a blonde and a man in a fake alleyway. I felt the building of the tingle between my legs. I didn't stop. I continued to rub, a little harder and faster. My back arched, my lips parted as I let out a gasp and then a groan that seemed to start its journey from my sensitive sex, making its way up my belly and heaving chest before it leapt from my mouth in surprise. I yanked my hand from between my thighs and slammed them shut. Eyes bulging, I looked at the TV screen as I gulped down breaths and tried to stop the dizzying faintness.

Oh my God. Was *that* it? Was that what I was supposed to have been feeling all this time?

I had given myself my first orgasm. The world felt like a tornado swirling intensely around me, but I was still seated on the living room floor. I turned away from the porn, reaching an unsteady hand that smelled of musk towards the satellite remote. I typed in the channel for something benign like one of the sports networks and waited until I was sure the satellite was off the forbidden channels before I turned it and the TV off.

Beads of sweat had formed over my lip. No calmness settled upon my limbs. I'd lost control.

After a few shaky breaths and a return to my senses, I gathered myself up off the floor and headed to the bathroom to wash up, taking what my mom called a "po' hoe" bath in the sink to wash between my legs. I slid back into my jeans.

Fifteen minutes after washing between my legs, I hopped in my '89 gray Sentra and returned to school for a student council meeting.

"'Sup, Maya." My buddy since middle school lifted his head and nodded at me when I arrived in the way that popular boys coolly greet their peers.

"Hey." A meek smile spread over my closed lips, cloaking my braces.

We were selling Blow-pops as a fundraising effort to support our homecoming dance. I'm pretty sure the blonde on the screen had been giving a blowjob when I orgasmed.

As our student body president droned on about sales of those suckers, I muted his dialogue as my internal voice grew louder in my ears.

"That was amazing," the back part of my brain cajoled. "No need to be frightened. Let's do it again."

It was too much and not enough all at once. It was the peak of Mount Everest stretching out over a horizon of clouds. There was much more below the surface to explore.

I've read that some who try cocaine know almost immediately that they will use it again after that first hit. I had my cocaine now. As much as my little body could handle, it craved an endless supply. I didn't fear an overdose. I had no idea of the fallout that was brewing.

Mentally, I was a teenager immersed in sexual longing, not unlike many others.

I had at least a dozen crushes on boys at school. Secret crushes because I thought my Blackness hindered them from returning my feelings. I was often the only Black student in my Advanced Placement classes.

I sat behind Noah Oliver in AP Spanish IV. My eyes traced every strand of blond hair down to the nape of his tanned neck to the collar of his Polo shirts. He wore a necklace of a leather strap and seashells. He wore khakis and leather sandals even in the winter. His eyes were Pacific Ocean blue. Noah seemed to be more of a fit for a surfboard in Malibu than in a Texas suburb.

"Toni Braxton is so fine," he said, half-turned in his desk chair as those blue eyes met my anxious gaze.

"You think so?" I steeply arched an eyebrow. I could feel my neck burning and the heat rose into my cheeks like a love-sick thermometer.

"Hell yeah." His head jerked. Our teacher walked the room, licking her index finger as she handed us a worksheet no one was bothering to begin work on.

Timid as I was to express my feelings, I was never too shy to interrogate someone. "Do you like Black girls?"

He lifted and dropped his shoulders casually. "Yeah."

I began to list a few classmates, young Black women who were popular, including our school's lone Black cheerleader who was dating his best friend.

"Toya?"

"She's cute, yeah." He nodded.

"Tiffany?"

"She's cute, too."

There was a long pause—the silence filled with bravery.

"What about Maya?" I asked. It felt like a whisper, but I'm sure I was speaking at normal volume.

Noah's Hollywood smile showed every white tooth in his mouth. "Maya's cool. For sure." He bit into his lip as the smile held and didn't fade for some time.

I didn't reply. Or if I did, it was inconsequential to the feelings I had inside me right then. Somewhere a heavenly choir was singing. I thought I would slide right out of my chair and onto the buffed linoleum floor.

As if he knew my thoughts were swirling, wondering if I truly had a chance with him, the corners of his lips turned down as if he tasted something sour. "My parents wouldn't be cool with it, though."

There was another expansive silence. His desk was right in front of mine, but he seemed far away now. I must have flinched when what felt like a dagger of ice embedded itself in my heart, and he turned away from me in his seat.

I fantasized about Noah and a secret sexual rendezvous with him. I dreamed of even being able to date him, away from the hawkish gaze of my strict parents. They did not allow me to date. I often reflected on the fact that they believed I was old enough to operate a three-ton speeding vehicle on the streets of a major city but not go to a movie with a boy.

I listened to R&B and pop ballads about love and believed that only intense, unrequited love was all that was available to me. I watched Angela Chase pine over Jordan Catalona on *My So Called Life* and identified with a girl that obsessed over every detail of every interaction and wanted so desperately to be noticed by that one boy. Sitting in the Laura Ashley decor of my bedroom, I rolled on my bed and listened to my stereo or Walkman and repeated heart-wrenching ballads as I dreamed of interactions with Noah, others, and celebrity crushes like Leonardo DiCaprio and Brad Pitt. My vivid imagination would place us in romantic tug-o-wars that always left me in anguish, blinking back the tears I felt from my daydreams.

In my head, I could be with Noah or Brad or whoever the hell else I wanted to be with despite our parents.

I defy you, stars! I remember wiping at my snotty nose with a napkin greased with theatre popcorn butter as Leo's Romeo collapsed to his knees in anguish. I had a longing for the type of toxic love that only exists in cinema. With an emphasis on books, not boys at home, I had only one way to find intimate pleasure.

I watched and read porn whenever the opportunity presented itself. There were times in my room alone or in my bathroom when I would masturbate three or four times a day. Compulsive, the treatment center would later categorize it.

I would even sneak to Dad's closet, grab one of his books and read it as I touched myself. My parents were always in other rooms, each in their corners of the house, and never popped into my room to check on me.

Like with cocaine, watching and reading porn wasn't enough to sustain my high. I grew increasingly bored with Dad's stash and the distorted satellite images. My parents' rigid dating rules began to backfire. I became obsessed with finding some way to connect to the opposite sex, though I would never have outright defied my parents. I feared the repercussions far too much.

Technology brought innovation to my desire. Looking back, it was as if I'd had eight years of erotic programming uploaded into my cerebellum. My operation was wired for sex.

Then, blessedly, a thing I'd been enjoying for about two years provided me with a new hit. AOL allowed Americans to connect with information and each other with a few taps on the keyboard.

After a tedious day of navigating the dynamics of high school, at home once again, I sat down at our family computer and listened to the rapid dialing of a number before it was followed by several buzzes and a shrill squawking.

"Hello and welcome to AOL," the worldwide web greeted.

Using the only username we had available, that of my parents, I searched around for something of interest. The satellite porn channels had begun advertising new additions called websites that were dedicated to viewers wanting to see more from their computers. I tried to access a couple of sites, but our dial-up connection was slow as frozen molasses. The most I saw was a banner with a half-naked woman across the top of the page. I closed it and then noticed one of the icons for chatting. All I had to do was click it, and I would be connected with other humans sitting at their computers. I watched the chat scrolling in the main room. It was mostly single people looking to hook up with other single people. I knew I had no business talking to strangers looking for a good time on this new internet, but the more requests I saw for chat partners, the more intrigued I became.

I thought of something to say. So, I wrote. "Hey, any guys want to talk?"

The response was immediate, and Lord bless me, was I dumb.

"IM me," several users responded.

"IM me?" I wrote back and laughed. "Of course, I'm me."

"Instant Message me," someone further explained.

I grimaced, and my ears burned hot.

I picked one of the names at random. I don't recall his username, but it was enough for me to want to reach out to him. I had to ask how one IM'ed someone else and felt all the dumber for it. The instructions came through in the main chat, and I double-clicked some guy's name, and a little gray and white box appeared at the top corner of my computer screen. His username showed up in red.

Hi. I wrote and chewed my bottom lip as I watched my cursor flash next to my parents' username in blue.

Hey there. A/S/L?

I had no idea what that meant.

Sorry, I'm new to this. Could you explain what that means? I asked, picturing myself sitting in front of the computer in a dunce cap and clown makeup.

Age, sex, location, he wrote back. I memorized those letters, their order, and their meaning. They would become a part of my lexicon for three more decades.

Novice that I was, I was mindful enough to know that I couldn't admit to my real age. I wrote back *18/female/Texas.*

Cool. 29/M/New Jersey.

Cool. I'd no idea what to say or do next.

Do you have a picture?

I gripped the mouse, feeling tightness radiate from my hand and bicep into my shoulder. I knew this was a big no-no, even if the dangers of the internet hadn't (yet) become part of one of those preachy school assemblies we had to attend. AOL was still so new at the time we weren't yet being coached about stranger danger online.

No, sorry

Want to see mine? He wrote, seemingly unfazed by my lack of sharing. It couldn't hurt for me to get an idea of who it was I was talking to. I didn't expect to see Jason Priestly on the other end, but hey, you never knew.

His picture was average, an out-of-shape man with blonde hair shellacked to his head with too much gel. He wore a basic blue and white striped polo in front of one of those Owen Mills standard backgrounds.

I remained as polite as possible.

It's a nice picture. Which, it was. I just wasn't attracted to the person in it. Again, that didn't matter.

What are you wearing?

It escalated rather quickly, but I was game. I looked down at my baby doll dress with the spaghetti straps over a white T-shirt and my fake Doc Martens.

T-shirt and panties. The lying started to come out effortlessly.

Mmmm. That's so sexy.

I noted the little moan he typed out at the beginning. I was studying, learning. Hard hair from New Jersey was my first teacher in this online sex arena. Moaning even by text was acceptable?

I found control. I admit, I was manipulative and a liar. I rotated between different names like different personas in the chat. Sometimes I was Victoria, a biracial 27-year-old and theatre actress. Other times I was Em, as sweet as honey with the skin color to match, a college co-ed.

In those early days, I was much more powerful there than in the real world. Not in the oversexed, pedophilic idea of a Lolita but in the way that I realized how far men would be willing to go for sex. Even a hint at helping them orgasm, and they would almost fork over their social security numbers, though my intent was never anything nefarious. I found a kingdom where I could reign.

I didn't feel I belonged anywhere else. I didn't fit. Online, I could be whoever I wanted to be. How would they ever know any different?

The femme I would become during cybersex wasn't on par with the girl in real life. Emotionally, when I entered high school in 1994, I physically and mentally felt my immaturity. It had been pointed out too many times to count in middle school, but even I recognized the elementary mindset I seemed to be stuck in.

My friends weren't engaging in precursors to sexual activity any longer; they were having full-blown sex. They were attending parties and drinking, and I was often stuck at home with my parents watching *Dateline* when there wasn't Friday night football. I turned my nose up at their behavior. I was determined to be the exception, not the status quo. I was abiding by the house rules. I was a pious girl, holding steadfast to the church lessons that sex was "bad" and being promiscuous was sinful. I'd even decided that I would save myself for marriage, even if I wasn't still sure that I was actually a virgin.

"I don't get it, though. I do want to make love the first time I do it," I declared to my mom on the car ride home from church. Our pastor had admonished us in a sermon for saying we were going around and claiming that we were "making love."

"God is love," The Reverend berated us. "The Bible declares it. So how are you capable of going around and making God?"

This drew some "hmmm's" and "well well's" from the congregation. It hit me extra hard. I believed that making love was the sensual act between consenting, loving adults, while sex itself could be rougher and disconnected. At least, that's how it looked in the videos.

Again, according to my pastor, I was sinfully wrong.

Mom pursed her lips at my statement and added with disdain. "You're too young to even be thinking about that."

Yet, I was fully invested in porn and sex chat.

Physically, I was the same awkward Black girl from middle school, only taller. My discomfort in my skin was made more palpable by the hormonal changes in my appearance. I was still flat-chested, and my hips seemed to be more angular than rounded. The acne left behind pigmented, discolored spots that never seemed to fade. I felt I was scarred forever (in more ways than one) and was too self-conscious to lift my head and reveal my face. I wasn't allowed to wear makeup, and my exposed, bare face was in direct contrast to the painted country club princesses around me.

The transition from elementary to middle school had been rough, but middle to high school was even rougher.

South Garland High School was a school steeped in the Garland community's resistance to integration when it opened in 1964. Four years before I walked the halls, there had been a public outcry about the school's use of the Confederate flag and the mascot's gray uniform. After making national news, the school board changed the mascot's uniform from gray to blue, and the stars and bars were replaced with two crossed swords. But *Dixie* remained our fight song. Our cheerleaders threw their fists in the air and shouted, "The South Shall Rise Again!" at the student body when we trailed in games.

The wheels had broken and flown off the Maya super student express my freshman year. During that first semester in the fall of 1994, my grades plummeted as I sank into a deep depression. As my grades dropped, my parents thought I was becoming another distracted and unfocused teenager. One home luxury after another was stripped away: my bedroom phone, my digital Walkman, my stereo, and finally, my TV.

Mom and Dad thought I needed to concentrate more on my schoolwork, and that I'd become lazy. Sitting on my bed, next to the light of my lamp, schoolwork was all they had left me with to pass the time.

With a blank stare, I transported myself outside of those rose-pink walls. Noah's arms would wrap around me on a summer trip to his family's cabin by the lake. His parents welcomed me and embraced me as their future daughter-in-law. Or, Ethan and I would share a kiss after the team lost the big game. I would cup his sweaty face in my hands as I rose onto my tiptoes and placed a tender, comforting peck on his lips, and told him he was still my champion. More often than not, I turned heads, and the cameras flashed as I looped my arm through Brad Pitt's on the red carpet to the sound of a hundred camera shutters clicking rapidly and the blinding bursts of white lights leaving me unfazed as I turned my head and looked into his heartthrob eyes. I wasn't a failure then. Even when sitting at the dinner table with Mom in silence, I was still more than a disappointment in my head.

Along with the sense of being a failure came actual failure. I flunked freshman Algebra I by one point, earning a 69 in the class. The rookie teacher wouldn't change my grade either, not even when Mom called and appealed to the principal. I found myself with a very new, foreign activity: summer school. I felt like a loser after excelling for so many years. I was embarrassed for anyone even to know I had to attend it.

When my sophomore year began in 1995, I joined the Southern Belles drill team as a manager and made two new best friends who remained so for the rest of high school. I was finding my footing on that slippery, adolescent slope.

Despite this, depression stayed as close as FBI surveillance. It watched and waited for the joy to come before it put a bag over my head and threw me in the back of a van to rush me back to the land of the downtrodden.

Spring of sophomore year, I wrote a poem—not a very good poem—and submitted it to be a part of the South Garland High School collection of student creative works known as *Libertas*. It was titled *House of Sorrow*:

The walls are painted a cold, dark black
And the shutters outside the windows are tightly latched
The doors are locked from the inside and out,
A house once filled with screams and shouts
House of sorrow, life of pain
So very different, so much the same
Long ago there was once a life of children running and playing about
But the shadows of the walls have now cast those memories out
Just as the life I had is gone,
This house of sorrow so easily lives on

Any teacher, administrator, parent, or even fellow student who read that poem might have given pause at the writer's intentions. I was afflicted with a silent, inner plea for someone to know the truth about me and my childhood. I wanted someone, for once, to ask me if I was okay, to open the door for me to speak honestly and without inhibitions. I remained the little girl in the car, wanting anyone around me, those who had their hands on the steering wheel, to see that I was hurting and guide me to a new, happier course.

My muted implores never received a response. So, my desire to be seen and heard went unfulfilled through most of my high school career.

I turned again to the only prescription I understood to remedy whatever I felt was lacking in me. Daily doses of perfectionism were gulped down as I joined the student council and became a class officer. In addition to the drill team, I joined the speech and debate team, Ecology Club, Mu Alpha Theta (the advanced math club, which I found funny, considering I'd failed Algebra), Future Homemakers of America, Texas Association of Future Educators, and was the bookkeeper and a manager for the boys' varsity basketball team.

My happiest accomplishment up until that point was when I became a ball girl for the Dallas Mavericks and got to meet Michael Jordan, Dennis Rodman, Charles Barkley, and one of my crushes, Jason Kidd. Sports was always my refuge, my safe spot to land and devote energy.

In our yearbook, each member of the graduating class of 1998 had a list of accomplishments and organizations attached to their name. The paragraph beside my name is eight lines long.

One more organization became my saving grace. In Texas's University Inter-scholastic League Theater, I felt the happiest I had ever been. The stage was where I was comfortable. Pretending to be someone else wasn't at all hard for me—I did it every day in real life. On stage, I was finally seen and heard by all.

1998

His lips were on mine, soft and warm. I had begun to relish their feel when a new sensation hit. His tongue slipped over the seam of my lips. I eagerly granted him entrance.

"Dang ya'll," declared one of our theater classmates, a blonde sophomore girl. Her disembodied voice was ignored, along with the crowd of voyeurs standing around us.

I didn't care about the onlookers. All I wanted was for that feeling to contin-ue—the feel of his lips and his tongue moving wet and warm with mine. I had watched enough romance movies to get a general idea of what I was supposed to be doing. From the intensity and force with which Christian reciprocated my movements, I definitely was doing something right.

I'd wished for that moment the whole of senior year. Seventeen years old, and I finally got the first kiss that counted in my book—my first consensual kiss.

We stood in the dark shadows behind the stage curtain of the Little Theatre where we had class. Our teacher was out for the day, and we had a substitute who couldn't have been any more disinterested in what we were doing. It was a couple of weeks before the end of the school year when I would graduate. The spring show was in the books, and with nothing to rehearse, the horny theatre kids were idle and restless.

Teenage minds decided a game of Truth or Dare was the best way to pass the class period. The sub stayed in our teacher's office while we played in the dark.

I had liked Christian in simple crush form since he had dated my friend Thao in the sixth grade. But senior year, when the handsome varsity football player joined our competitive performance theater group, a girlish crush transformed into the desires of a girl on the brink of womanhood. He had hair as black as raven's wings, blue eyes, and the types of lashes people pay money for.

I asked our friend Jimmy to dare me to kiss Christian. Jimmy didn't blink, hesitate, or seem at all surprised by my request. Instead, he nodded in the affirmative with a playful smirk. It was a scheme on my part, but it was the only way I knew I was going to get what I wanted.

So, when Jimmy said, "Maya, truth or dare?"

I sweetly replied, "dare" with doe-like innocence.

"I dare you to kiss Christian," he said with a Cheshire grin.

The dozen classmates standing by *oohed*. Everyone in class knew we had a thing for each other, though we had never acted on it. Hours of rehearsals together, weekends at competitions and post-performance parties, and a seven-year friendship climaxed at that moment.

As we became the main event, I felt Shakespeare and Keats in his lips. It transcended my most elaborate fantasies. The realness of it all—the warmth, the longing—was a lover's sonnet.

When we finally pulled apart, gasping, I opened my eyes, lids heavy still and blinked into focus a set of curious eyes that were stunned and frenzied. The kiss ended, but the physicality of our relationship had begun.

When the bell rang, and we stepped out from behind the cover of the curtains, I reached for my backpack at my desk in euphoric bliss. I didn't feel my feet as they moved one step after another. Christian reached out a hand, gripping my bicep, and stopped me.

"I feel so much closer to you now," he said and then wrapped his arms around me for a tight, lingering hug.

"Me too," I replied and squeezed him back.

All of which would have been fine if he didn't have a girlfriend.

The gravity and weight the kiss carried began to sink in as I walked through the halls to my third-period history class, clutching the extra books that wouldn't fit in my backpack to my chest. People spoke to me, and as I looked into their faces without giving a reply, I wondered how long it would be before the whole school knew about the kiss.

Sure, I had gotten my first real kiss, and it was with a boy who I was positive I was in love with at the time. But it was sullied by a new type of wrongness in my life, regardless of how incredible it had been. He had a girlfriend for four years, Ginny. I wasn't exactly sure of what our friendship would look like after that kiss, either.

The more I thought about the kiss, the more dread replaced elation. It was an intimacy I had not experienced before, but he was not mine to share it with. I'd taken control of a situation to get what I desired, but I walked away from it with the relentless weight of my demonic friend, shame.

Part 2

Chapter Nine

Shades of Hope

Journal Entry

May 17, 2015
   11:29 a.m.
   I wanted to open with something deep, something profound so that when I look back at this journal when I look back on this day, I'll have some great reminder of the moment my life was about to change.

   Truth is, I'm scared. I'm scared of what will happen open over the next few days, scared of what I will feel, scared of who I will see and who I will be with, scared of the person I will be on the other side of this.

   As much as I'd like to think my life will remain intact and I can shed the emotional baggage that has dragged me down and held me back like sandbag weights on a hot air balloon, I'm worried my transformation will be so complete that I shed all that is familiar in the name of self.

   I want to not just be a better wife, a better mom, a better friend, I want to be a better person. I want to be the woman I dreamed of as a girl. I want to be the woman God wants me to be, unsoiled and faithful, happy and loving rather than bitter and cynical.

I want to rid myself of shame and secrets. I want to feel the freedom to be who I am and who I want to become without feeling shackled, trapped, anxious, or even hopeless.

I am reminded of the young Liberian athlete I met during my documentary trip who said, "Where there is life, there is hope." There is life in me. Flowing in my veins, pounding in my heart, taking in the world with each breath. Therefore, there is hope, Maya. Rather than fearful, God let me be hopeful. Let me feel your arms of care wrapping me, enveloping me with Your love and mercy. Just as You have forgiven me Lord and given me second chances time and time again, let me put forgiveness in my heart and the past of yesterday away to no longer be a cancer in my life today.

I maybe said it once out loud, but it should be repeated that I have forgiven God.

The unmarked white van pulls up outside of the highway-side hotel. The roar of nearby traffic settles in my ears as I stand under the awning to the hotel entrance, suitcase in hand.

The aged van is a carryover from the last production of Astro vans almost a decade before. Its dented, white paint is peeling away from each ding in its body to reveal the dull gray of metal underneath. I'm certain I saw a similar van in a hostage scenario porno.

My eyes are so intently focused on that archaic van as I ponder its safety that I hardly notice the driver's door open until I hear it slam. Through the windows, I can see a pair of aviator shades and blonde hair walking around toward the back of the van until the blonde hair and aviator shades are standing in front of me.

The toffee skin of her arm is covered in a full-length, colorful, tattoo sleeve. Not what I was expecting from a ... nurse? A counselor? An intern? I wasn't sure, but when the Shades of Hope Treatment Facility called about a half-hour before to tell me a driver was on the way, I'd imagined Nurse Ratched would be picking me up, or at least someone far more clinical and sterner in appearance than this woman.

"Maya?" Her voice is even and calm. I realize the nerves vibrating all around me are confined solely to my body. She's done this hundreds of times.

I force a small smile and clear the bristling from my voice. "Yes, hi."

"I'm Juana," she introduces herself. "We've got to pick up one more, and then we will head to the center. There's an afternoon flight arriving with the others," she explains. *The others*. I shudder. Juana reaches for the handle of my suitcase.

"Oh! I can help!" I rush to offer. She either ignores or rejects my statement because she picks up the weighted-down bag, unburdening me. She carries it to the rear of the van, and I watch as the kimono she wears over a tank and jeans billows behind her. I'm at least half a foot taller than her, but she lifts my luggage as if it weighed not more than a down pillow and sets it into the back of the van. She slams the doors, and I take it as my cue to enter the van.

There are three rows of tan, cracked vinyl seats, foam-stuffing peeking out from some of the tears, but despite Juana being the only other person in the vehicle, I choose to sit in the very last row in the back passenger corner.

My back is straight. I twist the hairs on my arm, watching Abilene outside rush past the van window in a long centipede blur. There is no chit-chat or small talk between Juana and me. We ride in silence for almost ten minutes before we arrive at a moderately maintained motel.

A woman with silver threads woven through black waves of hair is standing with a tattered suitcase at her side. As Juana eases the van to a stop in front of her, our eyes meet for a frame as she inspects the other travelers on this sobering trip. Juana hops out again, adjusting her aviator shades. I discern their muffled greeting outside the van before Juana repeats the motions of grabbing the woman's luggage and carrying it to the back.

The back door opens in unison with the sliding van door as Juana puts the old suitcase next to mine, and the woman laboriously lifts a foot onto the van's running board. I feel the van lean downward as she uses it for support. She grunts, and I can hear the gasps and wheezes for breaths. I try not to observe this cumbersome dance, but I find myself staring at her bulk as a swollen hand wraps around the inside door handle, and she pulls herself inside. Tendrils of dull black and silver hair are becoming wet from her exertion to enter the van. She turns her flushed face towards me, breathing strenuously, her chest heaving. My eyes move from the dark vacant gaze peering back at me to the beads of sweat on her forehead. With one more hard yank on the handle, she fully enters the van and plops down onto the front row of seats.

From behind, I watch as she adjusts her sagging denim blouse, pulling at it where sweat has already stained the back and collar. She pulls at its bottom and moves it in a wave-like fan to soothe the perspiring skin underneath. Before Juana is fully settled into the driver's seat, the new passenger asks, "Can you turn up the air conditioning, please?"

"Sure!" Juana obliges, and there is a whoosh from the front vents that, after a few seconds, causes me to hug my elbows and retreat deeper into the crook of that vinyl seat for warmth.

That is the last bit of conversation for fifteen miles. I'm not one for small talk, but it would have been nice to hear something other than the sound of the woman's breathing and the narration of stories I'm constructing in my head. Images of yoga and horseback riding flicker like a montage with thoughts of shock therapy, gurney straps, backless hospital gowns, and syringes.

Abilene's surprisingly urban retail hub gives way to what I had pictured of west Texas in my head. The land is flat but green. April and May's rains have quenched the thirsty earth, and late spring has bloomed into waves of grasslands as we head up Highway 84.

My eyes move from the window to the back of the nameless passenger's head. I can see the rainbow refractors of Juana's aviator shades in the rearview mirror before I look past them both, and my hand reaches out and clutches the empty seat in front of me. I brace myself and lean forward.

"Wow," escapes my lips, but given the air conditioner is on the highest setting and my distance from everyone else in the van, no one else hears it. When I'd filled out the multiple questionnaires for Shades of Hope, I noted that the physical address was a place I never knew existed. It was a town called Buffalo Gap, and, in the distant horizon, I became mesmerized by the source of that name.

On either side of Highway 84 sat two ridges, once as mountainous as the rest of the Rockies they had been a part of, now as flat as two stacks of playing cards. Layers of eroded limestone, shale, and sandstone created a mosaic of reds, yellows, and browns that seemed pancaked atop one another.

I pull out my phone while I still have the ability to do so and look up information on Buffalo Gap. According to lore, the Indigenous tribes would startle the buffalo roaming those grasslands in between those ridges. Tribespeople armed with bows and arrows and spears would rain down their weapons to capture only the number of buffalo needed to feed and clothe their tribe. Birthed from that history was the town's name.

From the parted clouds overhead, rays of sunshine strobed over those ridges, calling to me in a moment when my spirituality wasn't so jaded. If millions of years could transform the majestic sight ahead, then surely there was hope that nature could work a miracle in me in six days.

Nothing is as I'd expected. I'd Googled some pictures of the place but thought the manicured lawns and homey buildings were for curb appeal, like the glossy brochure for a resort that is actually only two stars. I was convinced buildings in the photos were nothing more than front offices, a literal front, and I was really going to be trapped inside some room without any sharp objects, blunt edges, and with bars over the windows. But when the white van stops on a gravel driveway, what is in front of me reminds me of my grandparent's home. There is a wooden sign in the front yard outside a white picket fence that says, "Shades of Hope Treatment Center."

A jeep and a small silver Airstream RV are parked next to the house. As I, No Name, and Juana climb out of the van, the door to the jeep opens. A thirty-something blonde with a short bob steps out in jeans, a T-shirt, and sandals. Her shades are pushed up into her light hair like a headband, and as my shoes shuffle over the gravel, she offers a warm smile. She shuts the door to the jeep, not bothering to lock it. We leave our luggage in the van.

There are other houses and other buildings, all of which are part of the treatment center. The treatment center sits in a neighborhood, where the neighbors became cohabitants of the wayward souls that drift in and out and sometimes back again to these Shades of Hope buildings.

The light spring breeze lifts our hair, and the rustling leaves draw my attention to the grove of oaks and Texas ash trees throughout this neighborhood. Where the boughs and branches of one tree end, another begins, creating an arc of shadows and peace along the clay roads. We are canvassed in the protective shade, a shield over the three of us, as we follow Juana up the creaky wooden slats of the stairs to the long porch. There are white rocking chairs spread across it, the wood dipping and crying a bit under our feet as Juana unlocks the front door and lets us all inside.

The dank smell of the room has the scent of hundreds of home-cooked meals and old books in the wood paneling. The space is clean and furnished with plush leather sofas and throw pillows that welcome some of us to a place that feels like the home we never had. A closed-off fireplace sits beneath a mantle decorated with knick-knacks. The walls display scenic paintings of the Texas Wild West and Big Bend National Park, where those ridges mark its entrance.

"We have box lunches for each of you," Juana says and guides us into the dining room. We move like school children forming a line on the way to the cafeteria. She motions towards the rectangular wooden table that seats six, and we each pull out a chair, scraping the feet over the old hardwood floors. Next to the dining room, we can see through an open area a large kitchen, more industrial than anything you'd find at a residence.

Juana grabs a stack of Styrofoam boxes and places one down in front of the three of us, along with some glasses and pitchers of water.

She finally takes a seat, grabbing a box and some water for herself.

"Does everyone want to introduce themselves?" she asks.

I open the Styrofoam and look down at a clump of tuna salad sitting on top of a single romaine lettuce leaf. There's something white and round sprinkled with seasoning that, after moments of musing, I determine are chickpeas along with some slices of red apples.

"I will," the blonde says. I lift my eyes from the curiously-seasoned chickpeas to her smiling face. She gives a big wave, using her entire arm, and leans her elbows on the table. "I'm Rebecca. I'm from Missouri," she begins. "I drove down and stayed in my RV at Big Bend for a couple of days."

She looks directly at me, her smile widening, and I can feel the friendly wafting off her. It feels like I should speak, so I go next.

"I'm Maya," I announce. My voice and demeanor are both oddly meek for someone accustomed to commanding the room's attention. "I'm from Tyler, which is in East Texas." I have nothing further to add.

Rebecca and I both look at the woman who has remained silent. "Hi," she says in a flat tone like a telemarketer reciting a prompt. "I'm Jean. I'm from Maryland."

"Hi," Rebecca and I say simultaneously, like sorority sisters. This draws a huge grin from Rebecca.

"I'm Juana," our driver re-introduces, though it's not necessary. "I'll be staying in the house with you over the next few days. I keep watch at the house, make sure everyone stays safe and healthy." She nods and smiles. My eyes move to the dragon curled around a dagger on her arm.

"You're our house mom?" Rebecca smirks.

Juana laughs. "Basically."

I reach for the pitcher and pour myself a glass of water.

"Before each meal, we start with a prayer, specifically the Serenity Prayer. Does anyone here know it?" Juana looks at each of our faces.

I twist my lips and shake my head no.

Rebecca lifts her hand like a star pupil. "I do. I can lead it!"

Juana nods back, and Rebecca begins. I bow my head and listen. "God, grant me the serenity to accept the things I cannot change, courage to change the things I can, and the wisdom to know the difference."

We lift our heads, and I'm already struggling to retain the words of this prayer.

Juana digs into her food, and I pick at the tuna, taking small bites. I ignore the chickpeas. The crunch of the apple resounds all too loudly in the quiet room. I pick up on Rebecca's chatty energy, but she restrains it and keeps quiet as the rest of us do. My senses are infused with too much newness: the new sights, the new sounds, the new smells, and even the taste of the food. If there is any comfort to be found, it's that the clock is ticking down. I've arrived. Now I had only six more days until I could go home.

When Counselor wrote "Shades of Hope" on a sticky note ten months before, I never thought I'd be here.

Last night at the hotel, I tossed a few of my life crutches away. I considered ordering *Fifty Shades of Grey* on pay-per-view but watching a story so steeped in sex seemed wrong when I was entering treatment for sexual addiction in almost twelve hours. Instead, I headed down to the lobby and got a hard apple cider from the bar. I sipped it and watched a basketball game before I finally popped the only two sleeping pills I had brought, turned on my little fan, and drifted to sleep.

After a mostly quiet meal, we are back in the van and headed to the airport in Abilene. Again, the van ride is quiet. Rebecca sits beside me in the back row.

When we pull up to the airport, Juana is on her phone. We are there to pick up the two others who will be part of our intensive group.

A young man is the first to make our trio of degenerates a quartet. He is 6'2," with dark brown hair sheared down into a buzz cut. His brown eyes dart about the van as Juana adds his suitcase on top of the others.

"Hey." There is a small waiver in his voice. It's not baritone or authoritative. He sounds like a high school senior.

"Hey," each of us says back in a staggered chorus. He slides onto the middle row of seats and gives a sigh before rubbing his palms on his thighs. Juana steps onto the sidewalk and paces as she talks into her phone. We watch and wait as she walks to and fro until she waves her hand at a young, petite, red-haired woman.

Another bag is added to the back before the door slams. The redhead joins the young man in the middle row.

When she begins to talk, I have trouble placing her heavy accent. At first, it's so thick that I think it's British cockney. She's talkative, saying hello to each of us.

"I'm Julianne." She gives me a tiny smile, her head swiveling on a neck that seems too thin for her head. It's then I realize this heavy accent is very much that of a southern debutante. Slow, low, but not with a hick's twang. It's the drawl of a society woman, someone I'd picture twirling a parasol and wearing a hooped petticoat if it weren't 2015.

"Maya."

"Sorry ya'll," she apologizes for the delay, and each word out of her mouth seemingly has an extra syllable in it. "My flight was running late, and they took *for-ev-uh* at the baggage claim."

"I'm Lucas," the lone male member of our party says.

The southern belle's arrival changes the dynamic. We begin to converse more on the drive back to Shades of Hope. Jean is in the front row, Lucas and Julianne are in the second, and Rebecca and I sit in the back. Julianne is from Virginia, and I imagine a plantation-style home with dulcimers and the three young daughters she mentions running around the lawn with a team of landscapers constantly working on it. As she speaks, I notice the back of her head. There is a small bald spot, and her red hair is thin. When she turns to the side, her brown eyes have faint dark circles under them, and there's a hint of peach fuzz on her chin, illuminated in the sunlight. At some point in the conversation, she mentions an issue with her thyroid.

Lucas is the only fellow Texan from the group, born and raised in San Antonio. He's an attractive young man, although I wonder if he's even of legal drinking age.

When we get back to the Shades of Hope main house, the smell of hot food welcomes us along with a cook. Misty is a young brunette hustling around the kitchen. She greets us with a "hey ya'll" hoisting pots around the kitchen like her babies. Juana leads us to a hall between the serving window and the dining room.

"You each get the same kind of cup." She holds up a tall, clear plastic cup for us and taps at the line under the rim. "You can fill it up to this line or measure it on this scale." She pointed to the table in the hall lined with silverware, plates, and a measuring scale. "Either way, it's exactly eight ounces of milk for you to drink or to have with your cereal in the morning."

A few looks are exchanged. Juana puts the cup down. She grabs a plate. On the counter of the kitchen window are the meal items for the night. It includes some baked chicken breast. Juana places a white ceramic plate onto the scale. "Zero out the weight first," she taps a button until the numbers return to zero. "Then add your protein." She uses tongs to place a chicken breast on the plate. The scale numbers move, but she grabs a knife and fork and hacks into it. "You get exactly four ounces of protein with lunch and dinner. With breakfast, you can either have a hard-boiled egg or two turkey sausage patties," she explains.

There are slow, quiet nods—Julianne shifts from one foot to the other. Wrinkle lines form around Jean's puckered lips. Rebecca doesn't at all seem surprised. Lucas and I look at one another and then back at the food. There's the chicken breasts, some sauteed vegetables, watermelon chunks, and salad. We are required to eat all the food items for a balanced meal, Juana explains further.

When I had looked up the information on Shades of Hope, it touted a number of disorders and addictions it treated but primarily focused on binge-eating, compulsive eating, or anorexia or bulimia. I didn't think I had a problem with any of the above. So, the prospect of eating all this food, three big meals a day, seemed like a lot. Especially for someone who spent most of her career eating McDonald's out of the bag in the news vehicle as she sped down the interstate from one stadium to the next.

Julianne folds her arms in front of her belly, hugging herself. "We have to eat all of it?"

"Yes," Juana says, looking her directly in the eyes.

Julianne's head lowers.

The assembly line of the food pyramid on our plates begins. I hacked into a piece of chicken, and when it stopped at 4.2 ounces, I looked at Juana, who simply shook her head, and I hacked away at it again until it was exactly 4 ounces. The little chunk I had to discard was placed back with the other leftovers on a plate.

We sat down at the table. Juana laid out a few more rules. No one was allowed to go to the bathroom immediately after or during the meal. This seems to bring a heaviness to our quintet. Rebecca again recites the Serenity Prayer for the rest of us still ignorant of its verses.

As I taste the chicken and vegetables, already feeling quite full and wondering how I'll manage to digest a salad as well as the watermelon chunks that remain, I look across the table at Julianne. She is twirling her food around on her fork, and tears are cascading down her cheeks as her shoulders tremble with silent sobs.

I watch each tear track roll out, only to be chased by another. The soft crying eventually turns into loud sniffles. I look to Juana. She says nothing. Shouldn't someone do something? Comfort her?

"Juana?" I question, lifting my brows. I toss my head in Julianne's direction.

Juana shakes her head at me. "No one intervenes. When someone is feeling their emotions, we let them experience it."

Damn. That feels cold. I look to Julianne. I don't understand her tears, but I want to at least give her a hug. I want to provide her with some comfort, rub her back, and say it'll be okay. But Juana meant what she said. So, we sit and chew our food while Julianne's sobs fill the dining room.

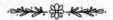

Juana stands closely by my side as I unzip my suitcase. I imagine the colored ink from her tattoo sleeve transferring to my forearm. My panties, bras, T-shirts, and leggings pile up on the twin bed. Before I have fully placed my intimates and personal belongings on the faded, floral comforter, worn as flat as tissue paper from time, Juana's hand slides into every pocket and crevice, even unzipping the lining of my suitcase, scouring for any type of contraband.

"What are those?" She points to the hardcover book and glittery gold and black journal I'm clutching against my breasts.

"These?" My head jerks back. "One is a daily Christian meditation book. This other is my journal." There is a wondrous awe in my answer. I don't see how these could in any way be offending items.

She extends her open hand towards me, summoning these books into her grasp. I slowly hand them over. She opens each and thumbs through a few pages. She holds each by the cover and shakes the pages loosely, aiming towards the floor should anything drop out. The books are handed back to me. Her hand returns to the suitcase, fingers probing before she ruffles through my clothing. She lifts pairs of my panties to see if anything may be wedged between them.

"Meditation books and journals are okay. No other kinds of books, though. No headphones or iPods," she recites. "And what is that?"

The little USB fan sits on the bed next to my shirts. My shoulders tighten. I can feel the three pairs of eyes on the other side of the room watching my inspection, waiting their turn.

"It's just a fan." I seesaw my head. There is a plea in my voice. "I can't sleep without one." I lick my lips and wonder if my right to sleep with a fan will be overruled.

"I'm the same way," Rebecca chimes in. "I brought something too, a sound machine. Unless it will bother everyone?"

I look over my shoulder at Rebecca, Julianne, and Jean. All stand with pursed lips, arms folded over their chests. Rebecca looks around, eyes attempting to meet each of our gazes for approval.

"I'm fine with it!" It's out of my mouth quickly. My genuine hope is that I can keep my fan if she can keep her sound machine. It's a small luxury, a balm in an abrasive situation.

I'd taken the twin bed by the window in the corner that provided some distance from the others. All four women would be sharing a room, a jarring discovery that contradicted the fiction I had drafted of my six-day stay. I'd pictured the bars and, yes, the gurney, but never roommates. How was I supposed to find a breath of solitude if this group of misfits constantly surrounded me? The toilet came to mind. Maybe at least a few minutes alone in there?

Jean and Julianne grant their approval to the sound machine, so it and the fan are not banned. I give them a grin of gratitude.

Juana begins to inspect my toiletry bag and asks me to hand over the prescription pills I'd listed on my intake form. I move a hairbrush and toothpaste around as I dig.

"If you brought any mouthwash, it's not allowed," Juana announces to us all.

I balk. "Mouthwash?"

"Yes. Some people will drink it for the alcohol content."

My hand is suspended in the toiletry bag. I look into her brown eyes as she nods, demonstratively answering the question I hadn't voiced. Jesus. *What kinds of people come through this place*, I wondered? My body flinches when I realize I *am* one of those people. By comparison, how sick was I really, if even truly sick at all?

I think of those other souls who have stayed in this house.

After dinner, we finally headed to our home for the next few days. The sign in front of the house only marks it with the Shades of Hope logo and Residency Unit. I suppose this lets the neighbors know that if they see anything suspicious around the house or one of us hightailing it out of a window, to call the center or the cops.

I think of the other bodies that have slumbered or found themselves restless in the same bed I'll try to sleep in tonight—all of us, every last one, broken by darkness.

My rummaging continues, and before I locate the pills, I graze a little piece of home that slows my heartbeat.

I hand Juana my allergy medicine and the Celexa I have been taking since I was first diagnosed with postpartum depression. She sits them on a chest of drawers before she tells me I can put my belongings back in my suitcase.

But before I do, I take out Charlie's little red sock. It had become my travel companion by chance when I first began flying across the country as a consultant. I was dressing in a Chicago hotel room one morning when Charlie's infant sock dropped to the floor as I unfolded the blouse it had been tucked away in. Since then, I'd kept that sock with me on trips for almost all the two years of his life so far. I caress the fire engine red cotton, marveling at its tiny size, and am reminded of the tiny feet, the miracle I'd created.

I had called home before leaving my hotel room, checking in with Everett and saying I love you to him and my distracted toddler for the last time for almost a week.

The sensory assault of another new place creates more longing for home. It culminates into wariness and a desire to retreat. So, I busy myself. I put my clothes away as Juana moves around the room, inspecting luggage and gathering more pill bottles. I set up my fan on the nightstand beside the bed. It's not ideal, but again, I'm not jutted up too closely to the others. A set of vertical slat blinds separates my bed from the neighboring window. It overlooks a covered back patio. Easing a slat aside, I survey a pile of dried, dead leaves in the corner outside the window and a spiderweb spanning from an iron chair to the window glass. I imagine snakes, snails, slugs, and all other manners of repulsions under the carcasses of leaves. I look down under the blinds on my side of the window and eye the remains of at least three spiders, shriveled legs curled in around their abdomens in a suspended death grip. I think of spiders crawling all over me as I sleep and let go of the blind.

Juana exits the room, arms cradling bottles of pills. As the others begin to put their things away in drawers, there isn't much conversation. Juana returns. There's a monologue about short showers because the one water heater in the house takes light years to reheat, and we don't want the last of our inpatient group to receive an arctic blast from the showerhead. As she speaks, I wonder if a few cold showers may end up as part of my treatment plan. That's what happens in the movies to the crazies and what people always suggest as a remedy for the "hornies."

We diplomatically agree to limit our showers to no more than five minutes and to rotate who gets to go first over the next six days.

"I need your phones." Juana's directive isn't callous or delivered as a drill sergeant but expectant and calm. It is what we all knew was coming, what we committed to when we put our signatures on the agreement. Mine had already been off since the first van ride. I think of powering it on once more before I'm forced to relinquish my second child, but I'm halted by sudden fear. *What if he has messaged me again?*

The phone remains off as Juana takes it and four others in her hand. She disappears again. I'm not tempted to see where these things are placed, but I can hear the opening and closing of a cabinet in the next room and the metallic clinking of a lock.

We are summoned to the living room. When we first arrived at the house, my jaw went slack at the blueness of it all—a blue carpet, two blue sofas, and a blue recliner, all in the living room. Blue is said to be a calming color, bringing about tranquility and a sense of order. How screwed up were all of us that we needed *this* much blue in our lives? But the living room would become the common area, a shared space, where we had to be when not sleeping or washing up for the day.

Lucas was staying in a smaller guest house out back alone. Juana explained that we were supposed to have been a party of six, but a last-minute cancellation had left Lucas as the only man. As each of us sat down on one of the two sofas, I found myself inventorying the young man. I crossed my legs, hinging forward at my hips, fingertips stroking the flesh of my throat. He was young but still a man,

with an athletic build and broad shoulders. He was also quite tall. My gaze flicks
to the man spread of his knees in his basketball shorts.

A thick object flaps in front of my face, interrupting my observations. I don't
look up at Juana as I take it from her. It's a book, bound in blue (more blue).
I read the letters imprinted into the vinyl cover: Alcoholics Anonymous. Juana
distributes the books, and I pretend to flip through the more than 500 pages, not
out of interest in the contents, but anything to avoid mindless banter.

I hadn't considered my drinking to be an issue. After I undressed from picking
up Charlie from daycare and a stressed day at the office, a glass of wine took
the edge off. It made the nights, cooking dinner, bath time, reading stories, and
tucking him into bed manageable. But we all get a copy of the book.

"You guys are lucky," Juana's voice breaks into our rampant book perusal. All
eyes lift to her. "You've got the dream team for your intensive: Tennie and Kim.
They are mother and daughter and incredible counselors. They're going to help
you so much. All the counselors are great, but you're really lucky you're going to
work with them."

Lucky wasn't the word I'd use to describe my presence at a treatment facility,
but Juana's words take a chunk of the fear coiled inside me, and it releases with a
trifle of optimism.

There's a wide smile as Juana nods her blonde head. "They'll be here in a
minute."

She sits down in the blue recliner. I look over at Julianne. No one asked her if
she was okay after dinner. It bothers me, and I want to ask, but I glance at Juana
like she's a guard watching inmates, and I sit in a hush, placing that thick blue
book in my lap.

The storm door opens. The first to enter is a tall and thin woman wearing
wire-framed glasses with shoulder-length hair the color of a grey tabby cat. She
wears not a bit of makeup but is naturally pretty in the way that women in health
ads seem to glow. Her eyes turn up at the corners before her lips do. She holds the
door for an older woman with short hair dyed as black as charcoal. Her dress is
that of a distinguished older woman, the type of clothing my grandmother would

get from Neiman Marcus. Her all-black outfit is accented by a silk scarf knotted around her throat. Her leather loafers look soft but supportive, and her lips are painted Christmas red.

"Hi!" Her voice sounds like tires on a gravel back road. It wobbles with her age and Texas accent.

She is small in stature, made even smaller by the slight arch in her back that seems to cause her to stoop. The large leather attaché case she carries seems to further weigh her down.

"Hi." Our greeting is in unison, and I am again struck by a likening of us all to school children meeting their teacher on the first day of class. Juana grabs two chairs from the kitchen table and sets them in front of the window. Our visitors take their seats and look back at five apprehensive faces.

Their eyes don't dart or attempt to find somewhere else to land as mine do. The older woman settles against her seat back, lifting her chest now. She rests a hand on her knee, and I note the wad of tissues she twirls before lifting it to her nose and sniffling. The younger woman hooks her arm over the back of her seat and adjusts her glasses as she crosses her legs. She nods at the other woman.

"I'm Tennie McCarty, and this is my daughter, Kim." The older woman gestures. Kim says a curt hello before her eyes fall directly on me, and I look away. Tennie bends slowly, and I watch how age has slowed her movements like swimming in honey. She pulls a manilla file folder from the attaché case and spreads it across her lap. After licking her thumb, she flips through several pages.

"Welcome to Shades of Hope," she says. There's a breath before her brows steeple. "We read over each of your profiles. You all need to be here."

Chapter Ten

Angelfire

Fall 1998

Three hours away from home. Close enough that, in a tricky situation, I could make it back with a car ride up the interstate. But far enough out of reach of the necromantic clutch of my past that eighteen-year-old me was boldly dodging like Freddy Krueger's metal nails.

That's the real reason I chose Texas A&M University.

I'd gone potluck, a term used for the random assignment of a roommate. After my early admission, I was determined to live the true college experience. A few high school classmates were heading to A&M, but it was a short list, and none of them were appealing as roommates.

Hurdling up the stairs to our front porch one hot June afternoon, the mail truck had just pulled away from the house as I ripped open the envelope with the A&M seal stamped in maroon on the front. According to the letter, my roommate's name was Kate. The irises of my eyes widened as I skimmed over the details about where we were to live on campus. Kate's full name, address and phone number were marked in bold in the middle of the page. She was from an affluent part of Texas known as Lake Travis.

Kate arrived at the dorm the day before I moved in, already selecting the bed and desk on the far-right side of the room. I'd wanted to look studious when I arrived on the college campus, dressing in formal khakis and a knit top, despite moving in during an August heatwave. Kate mistook me for my mom when she opened the door.

"Are you Maya's parents?" Her voice rose octaves as my face fell. I was standing next to Dad outside the door, and Mom was still huffing her way up the stairs to the second floor of Neely Hall.

Kate was nice enough, but her collection of fantasy posters and a menagerie of black dragon candles had sent my visiting aunt and uncle back to Dallas to report to the church and everyone they knew that I was rooming with a demon worshiper.

Kate didn't worship demons, but she did fall at the altar of the charming and attractive male of our species. After our first week living together, we'd gone to IHOP after a football game and eaten pancakes at two in the morning. A rough-looking guy with a neck tattoo and a pack of cigarettes tucked into his shirt pocket gave her the come-hither eyes from across the restaurant. As we were leaving, he stopped her and got her number. He wasn't a student but a local with a nine-to-five construction gig. Three weeks later, she abandoned our shared dorm room to sleep at his place every night.

I had a roommate for three weeks, and then I was on my own. In our short orientation period, I learned that Kate's butt-length black hair left strands everywhere on the white area rug my mom forced us to buy. And that she drove a brand-new silver Mustang, the very car I dreamed of owning myself. Kate gave me a taste test of something I'd soon consume en masse.

"Oh, that's that group; they have that one song, 'I Want You Back?' Right?" I asked as she tossed the clear plastic CD case over to me. I looked down at five black and white portraits seemingly eyeing me directly, one face, in particular, drawing my attention to it more than the others. *NSYNC.

She pulled the metal frame draped over all that hair away, and her ears reappeared from under two foam pads. "Seriously, they have this one song on here. It's so beautiful. Like, its lyrics mean God put more time into creating her than anyone else. It's the sweetest thing I've ever heard! Listen!" She untucked her legs from the top of her black comforter and stepped towards the stereo framed by wax dragons. She punched a few buttons and then turned the volume knob up as the melody started to play.

I sat crisscrossed on the floral navy and rose-pink comforter mom had bought for me one day on her lunch break, my back against a rose-pink bedrest pillow. My parents had also bought me a twin-sized mattress. We'd sat mine on top of the plastic-covered mattress provided by the university. I dropped a good three feet down to the floor each time I swung my feet around to get off the bed and had to use my triceps and forearms to push myself up into bed.

The strumming of a guitar and the tinkling of a triangle began to play before a low, slow, thumping beat. We'd gone to Sam Goody earlier that day at Post Oak Mall and bought a few CD singles and albums. I'd selected R&B tunes, and Kate chose the *NSYNC album. I'd seen their video on MTV throughout the spring and summer leading up to my first semester at A&M, but I was too busy fantasizing about Christian and being a senior to put much thought into a boy band.

When the chorus kicked in, Kate spun around from the stereo, one hand to her heart, another covering her mouth. I pearl-clutched at my clavicle, and we swooned.

"That's so romantic!" I cooed.

When the second verse kicked in, I heard what I believed was the most beautiful voice I'd ever heard. Kate skipped across the room and hoisted herself up onto my bed next to me as we looked at the CD case together and pulled out the insert. We reviewed the names of each member. There was Justin, Lance, Chris, Joey, and JC.

"Chris seems like a bad boy." Her eyebrows wiggled as she let out a chuckle of naughty intrigue.

I looked at a chiseled jawline with black hair and blue eyes and, from that moment on, declared I was a "JC girl." We listened to the CD every day together until we returned to the mall and I bought my own copy. In the mornings, as we prepared for our first week of classes, MTV played "Tearin' Up My Heart" half-hourly, and Kate and I would stop what we were doing to watch Justin Timberlake sing to us as he straddled a bed.

It may have been one of the few things we bonded over. My first college football games, I attended with Kate. We stood on the third deck of Kyle Field, up so high in the student section that the birds were flying below us. We mocked high-fiving Jesus anytime the Aggies scored. I'd gone to my first college party with Kate the night after my parents had left. She sipped a flat beer. I declined to drink mine as we watched a girl taking shots from an ice block. Then, Kate met Jacob at IHOP and became a gone girl.

I had three weeks of the college experience before my life became no more than my class schedule. I chose to major in Journalism at the College of Liberal Arts. They put the aspiring reporter, liberal arts kids in the dank basement of a fifty-year-old building. After my days as a ball girl with the Dallas Mavericks, I'd decided I wanted to break barriers as a woman in sports.

So, I woke up, went to my 8:30 a.m. political science course, an even more unfortunate way to start the day, and returned to a quiet and dark dorm room. Sometimes I'd grab lunch, choosing to get it as a carryout rather than sit in the cafeteria by myself. I'd take my meal back to the room and turn on Kate's computer since I hadn't brought mine. In class, I flipped the lectern over my lap and plopped down on the back row. I'd watch my classmates furtively, listening to their conversations about sexual conquests the night before or plans to head to a party on Thursday night. I crossed from one end of almost 4,000 acres of campus to the other on foot with my head down. Eyes concealed behind baby-blue lensed shades and my Walkman in hand as my backpack jostled with each step over the concrete, *NSYNC songs played in my ears, muting the world around me.

In college, I became aware that I was not special. Everyone else had also been straight-A or Advance Placement students. Everyone else had been in student council, cheerleading, or drill team. Everyone on that campus had been accepted at college because they had achieved at a high level. I learned that I was ordinary, average at best. Anything I had once believed had made me unique, so easily validated in high school, was a hallmark of mediocrity on a college campus.

Now, I know that the same reason I chose Texas A&M became the same reason I wandered campus as a wraithlike spirit, a Charles Dickens character—the ghost of a once popular, fastidious high school student.

There weren't many brown faces either, and where I had been comfortable with that in high school, I was greeted now by the occasional sneer or eyes that followed me with displeasure. The students from small country towns that weren't quite accustomed to the sights of integration found themselves sharing a campus with the likes of a small percentage (seven percent to be exact) of Black students.

Two months into the semester, I made a tearful call home that I regretted for weeks after.

"I don't know if I can do this," I sobbed as my hopes of a new vibrant life crumbled.

"Do you want to come home?" Mom asked too quickly.

Given my hopeless outlook, it was an enticing offer, but of all the things I'd done in life, I'd never quit. I would stick this out and find a way to make it through.

"No," I said in a stronger voice as I sucked up the snot bubble forming in one nostril. "No. I'm staying." I nodded as if she could see me through the phone. But then my voice became weak again. "This is just so hard."

The girl in high school who wouldn't have been caught on campus for a millisecond without makeup—once she was finally allowed to wear it—struggled to pull her hair into a bun some days. Washing my face and brushing my teeth felt like a chore. My vacant stare greeted me in my dorm mirror each morning, the only face I would look directly into for days at a time. The girl who had done everything she could to stand out and be seen now just wanted to camouflage into the crowd, wave her hands, say abracadabra, and vanish.

When I was the loneliest, when the melancholy and the grief of this failed attempt at independence felt suffocating, I had the boys.

One night I sat down at Kate's computer and went to the official *NSYNC website. From there, I found in the browser other suggested sites, sites created by fans just like me. In a blink of an eye and faster than I could right-click, I wasn't alone anymore. Others like me, girls who loved the band, founded a message board on an Angelfire website. There were various sections, one dedicated to discussing each band member individually or the group as a whole. Still, there was also a section for something I had never heard of before called fan fiction.

I clicked the link and was immediately ensnared by the first tale I read. These fictitious scenarios using the real singers as characters were the types of fantasies that I had already been daydreaming about. I dreamed of what it would be like to be in a relationship with JC, and here were the words glowing with deliverance.

I lurked silently on the message board for a couple of weeks. Some writers were more popular than others, and I read their interactions with their dedicated readers. These girls were the Stephen Kings and Jane Austens of the fanfiction world. I began to comment on their stories, praising them for their work. When they responded, our connections were forged.

I couldn't simply read their work and encourage these girls to write more. I wanted to be one of them. I wanted people to read my stories and glow over my ability to write Joey Fatone like Mary Shelly. I made up a username to write under, Em02.

My very first story was a love triangle trope. Justin met a college girl in Texas, made her his girlfriend, didn't appreciate her, and in swooped JC, her true love who had always admired her from an arm's length. There was a gross amount of angst, an unreasonable wardrobe for a college student (this was before Sarah Jessica Parker convinced an entire generation we could wear Prada and Jimmy Choo shoes), touches of emotional and even physical abuse, and, ultimately, sex.

Some other writers included sex scenes in their works, but it took me months to build the mental fortitude to write about sexual acts for the entire world wide web to read. I was also writing about something I hadn't truly yet experienced. For all the abuse and the multiple sets of hands that had molested me over the years, I didn't know if I had experienced penetration by a penis. I dissociated so intensely during those experiences I had no memory of blood or severe pain. I had no idea what the sensations of intercourse felt like. When I wrote about orgasms, the gallons of semen spilt by the boys I wrote could have powered a vehicle. I wrote with the idea of making love in my mind or with what I had learned from watching porn. The scenes started with very little description, abstract, glossing over the shared intimacy. But as my confidence and readers grew, words like "cock" and "pussy" were written and published without batting an eyelash.

Through the Angelfire message board, I met Min, Christina, and Wendy. They became my new best friends as my real-life friends were now scattered across colleges in the south. But the friendships, online or not, were just as real to me. I spent every waking free minute and hours into the night with these girls.

Wendy was a very reserved, devoutly Christian girl from Kentucky who lived at home with her parents and worked in a candle store. Her father would taunt her about her weight and about her lack of direction in life. He teased that she would become an old maid and live in their mobile home long after he was dead. I got the feeling that sometimes Wendy hoped his death would come sooner rather than later.

Christina was one of the first girls I knew to not only embrace her insatiable sexual outlet but to flaunt it openly. She was blonde and seemed to live by the creed that they did in fact have more fun. She was one of the few of us to have a boyfriend, and she talked openly about the things they did in bed. She wrote her erotic scenes with the same ease of conversation.

Min was an Asian-Pacific Islander living in California. Her use of words like "hella" and "sick" worked their way into my vernacular the more she and I talked. "Bitches are crazy!" she would call me and shout whenever there was drama on the message board. My personality mirrored hers.

I could have joined one of the many student clubs at A&M. I could have put some effort into striking up a conversation with other students, but I had done the tap dance for so long since elementary school I was tired. I preferred to develop these friendships because there was no shame with these girls. We didn't judge each other for our obsession. I would find it too difficult to explain why the band meant so much to me. The girls online understood and welcomed me as I was.

I began to water the seeds of those friendships and cultivate those connections more than retaining my connections to my friends from back home. We would phone each other occasionally or email, but it was a decimal percentage of time in comparison to the hours I spent online chatting with the *NSYNC girls.

I would exceed my monthly allotted long-distance call hours from my dorm room by talking to Min in California. When I hit my limit there, I ran over the small eighteen-minute allotment I had for my Motorola cell phone. Mom screeched in my ear for five minutes when a $234.08 bill arrived.

It didn't stop me from calling my friends.

My heightened fantasies and the increasingly graphic content of my stories had a byproduct. As Britney Spears sang about loneliness killing her, my wish for the power of connection became stronger. I still had never had a boyfriend. Kate popped back sporadically, usually when she and Jacob fought. This made for a sleepless night for me, as he called repeatedly and I was charged with relaying that she didn't want to talk to him and "she says you're an asshole." They always reconciled, and she always left for another couple of weeks until the next fight.

One night Kate returned to the dorm with Jacob and his cousin, Anthony. I'd met Anthony before, one night when Kate invited me to join the three of them at the movie theater. I supposed I was there that night to keep him from feeling like a third wheel. He was cute, thin and lanky, with floppy blonde hair he had to toss out of his eyes continuously; he had the skater boy looks with an Adam's apple that bobbed when he talked.

I'd spent the better part of that week preparing for a midterm that required me to submit 5,000 words on dramatic irony in Shakespeare's plays. I had gone to class that morning and spent an afternoon unmoving from Kate's desk chair, determined to submit my paper the day before the deadline rather than the day of. In my haste to finish the paper, I failed to eat.

When Kate, Jacob, and Anthony showed up, they had a bottle of Jack Daniels with them. The same girl who had refused even a beer at her very first college party threw back two shots of Jack (that she can remember), although there were certainly more, on an empty stomach. Two hours later, my back was pressed against the double-stacked mattresses of my bed as I sat open-legged on the floor. Memory serves as a flicker of an image of a piece of brown wheat bread with the corner nibbled away resting on my lap. It was Kate and Jacob's offering to help me sober up.

"Put some bread in your stomach," Kate's voice said through my fog. She and Jacob went downstairs to smoke in front of the dorm building.

That left me alone with Anthony. As quiet and as shy as I had become in college, I was a talkative drunk.

I don't recall the nature of the conversation or what led me to speak these exact words; the liquor from that night still puts my memories into view like I was swimming in the brown liquid. I can, however, recall quite clearly looking at Anthony and saying, "Yeah, I am a virgin. But I'm tired of it. Thinking about just giving it up." I still wasn't sure of the accuracy of that statement. I didn't know if I even still had a hymen.

The words slurred out, and the rest of the night is black.

The next morning, I retched the Lucky Charms and the tea I tried to drink. There was red mixed into the vomit, and I knew it was blood as I looked down into the bowl of the toilet, gripping its sides as another wave lurched.

After attempting to eat breakfast and pulling my head out of the toilet, I winced my way back to my bed, taking every ounce of energy I had left to make it into it. Kate had been decent enough to stick around. The blinds were shut mercifully, and Kate turned down the fluorescent light in the bathroom that may as well have been a spotlight.

"We put a mirror under your nose to make sure you were still breathing," she said as I groaned when I woke up.

"For real?"

"Yeah. We got pretty worried. You weren't responding to anything we said."

If I wasn't responsive to sounds, had I been responsive to touch? Anthony popped into my head as I covered my eyes from the bathroom light.

Kate was at my bedside. I looked down, and I still had on my socks and jeans and my sweater from the day before. How I had even gotten onto the bed was a mystery.

"How—"

"Jacob," she explained.

Jacob called and told me to drink some orange juice and take some aspirin or Tylenol. "You probably tore the lining in your stomach. If you throw up more blood, you probably need to go to the doctor," he advised. I didn't know if any of that was true, but Jacob seemed like the kind of person who knew about hangovers. I hung up with him and groaned as I lay back down.

"You okay?" Kate asked, still by my bed.

"I will be," I said. Her voice wasn't very loud, but the decibels at that moment in my head were like that of a death metal concert.

"No, I mean like ... are you okay?" Kate lifted one shoulder in a weak, timid shrug as she tiptoed around her real question. "You like, never drink, and last night you drank so much you blacked out." I could hear the concern, which I resented. What did she really care? She was never there.

"I just wanted to let loose, is all. I'd been working on that damn paper, and I wanted to have some fun ..." I went still and suddenly felt very sober as the words I spoke played back to me like a recording in my head. *"I'm just going to give it up."*

"Oh, God." The horror hit me, and I looked down at my button and zipped jeans. I threw my forearm over my forehead and closed my eyes.

"I think I said something to Anthony last night that was out of line."

"Oh." Kate chuckled. "We know."

Forgetting the sharp pain in my head and my light sensitivity, I whipped my face toward hers. "He told you?"

"Yup," she popped her lips as her eyes went wide. "Gotta say, you're probably lucky Anthony is a good dude."

"We didn't—"

"No."

I was relieved *and* disappointed. Part of me wanted to get what could or could not be my first time over with. The abuse and dissociation left me uncertain of that status.

Kate stood by my bed, lingering as if she wanted to say more, but I rolled over onto my side and closed my eyes. She left me to rest before I attempted to go to class that afternoon.

Then she was gone again.

My night away from the group had left them all in a panic, wondering where Em was. Min left a voicemail message. I replied once I could hear the sound without feeling like my ears were being stabbed. When my eyes stopped burning, I went back to my haven and back to obsessing over the band.

I wasn't entirely alone or without friends. I had two consistent non-sapient partners with me, shame and guilt, as old as sin and guiding me evermore.

The hours at Kate's computer and the internet connection's speed made access to porn easy. I'd open multiple tabs to the sites that offered free thirty-second to one-minute clips, my eyes taking in as much of those snippets as they could before I'd move on to another site.

Like with the band, I found message boards for specialized interests. I found special websites just for sex chat, where strangers could virtually meet, stimulate, and vanish. I also learned about kinks and fetishes, wondering if I might like to try a few.

My masturbation went from two to three times a week to two to four times a day. If I wasn't talking about the band or writing fan fiction, I looked at porn on Kate's computer.

In class, I daydreamed of sexual encounters. Sometimes with celebrities like JC or a cute guy I saw on campus from time to time. Sometimes with the strangers I met in chat. My grades didn't suffer entirely for it, but they could have been better. For the first time in my life, at the end of the semester, I received a D in business math and had a pair of C's on my report card. I isolated myself, retreating even more into that dorm room to masturbate. I attended class with the thought of returning to the dorm just to touch myself and find that delicious tingle.

It wasn't just that my orgasms made me feel alive, they kept me from grieving my lackluster life and feeling alone. I began to worship what felt good—avoiding reality. I was repeating in me what was not healed. In the sex chat sites, I found myself tolerating more requests from men that I found intolerable. They violated my morals, but I went along with them, still not finding my voice to say no. When men wanted to play out fantasies of non-consent or asked me to call them Daddy, I did so even though I found it repulsive.

The weak trifle of faith I had held on to since my baptism at 11 was now challenged by knowledge and science. As I took geology and biology courses, I had a hard time believing that God had created everything down to the particles and atoms. Earth's continents moved on plates, and science explained to me how this was possible.

I'd been skirting along a fault line most of my life, leaping from one seismic shift to another without ever regaining balance. Again, I wondered, where was God in all of this?

Chapter Eleven

Hello and Welcome to AOL

October 1999

Maya u have to tell them

Min's black words charged into the gray-bordered chat box like a rodeo bull in a chute. The thought of thrusting open the gate on my long-kept secret felt like bucking my entire existence, hanging on to two-thousand pounds of rage, still clutching to a rope for survival.

I sat still in my desk chair on a quiet Sunday afternoon, blinking as my eyes read Min's message over and over. In my second year at Texas A&M, I lived in Hobby Hall on the first floor in a room near the front entrance. Hobby was a co-ed dorm, and you'd often hear the fellas from the second and fourth floors hurtling down the stairs that neighbored our dorm room wall, sometimes using mattresses or plywood like makeshift sleds. This year, I was living with one of my former high school classmates who still wasn't high on my list of amiable cohabitants, but after Kate, I wasn't keen on going potluck again. My roommate had gone home to Garland for the weekend, and with the Aggies on the road for football the day before, most students living on campus had taken advantage of the away game schedule and returned to their hometowns or party destinations.

The entire dorm was as quiet as a library. I may have been so focused on the impending task Min had given me that I failed to remember any of the usual noises and chatter that were a constant with our room so close to the front door. Maybe, I noticed how quiet it was in the dorm because my senses were so acute at those moments.

I'd just confided in Min at some point during our interactions that I had been molested for a number of years by my cousin. I'm not sure of when, but I had built up such a strong bond with her that I trusted her with the secret that only he and I knew. It helped that she wasn't someone I had to see face-to-face each day. I trusted her in part because thousands of miles away in California, I'd never have to see the look of judgment or concern in her eyes that I feared so greatly from others.

Nathan had returned to my parents' home. He and his wife had separated, and during their split, he was living in one of my folks' guest bedrooms. Even a three-hour car ride away, he was still too near.

He was a father of three—a six-year-old boy, a two-year-old girl, and a seven-month-old boy—by this time. His daughter's birth and growth into toddlerhood broke one of the locks on my overstuffed suitcase of secrets. Nathan and his soon-to-be ex had named the child Layla in tribute to my moniker, a decision that made me cringe with grotesque horror. It was an honor I did not want from a man I found repulsive. It was even more sickening when I thought of him labeling his child with a name so close to the girl he had abused and corrupted.

When Nathan moved in with my parents, I returned home less often. There was one three-day weekend when avoiding home couldn't be helped. Mom and Dad expected me to return over Labor Day weekend. That Saturday night at home, I found myself in the room where the family computer was held, typing away to the girls.

Nathan came into the room, not bothering to knock. I didn't turn to look at him, instead pretending to ignore that he was there. I stopped typing. He placed his hands on my shoulders, and they tightened as he bent down. I could smell the sulfur again. He placed a long, lingering kiss on my cheek, and I held still as a shiver of disgust ran down my spine. I felt my stomach churn and fought back the urge to retch.

"Goodnight," his voice was flat as he stood up and let me go.

He walked out of the room and closed the door behind him.

Hello? Min wrote after several minutes had passed, and I still hadn't replied.

I took Min's words and transformed them. If the situation were reversed, what would I tell her? What would I encourage her to do? For once, I decided to be a friend to myself. I decided to love myself enough to defend myself.

But how? How did I begin to formulate the words about atrocities no loving parent wants their child to experience? I knew my mouth was still unable to speak it. Writing was my outlet. So, I let my fingers do what my lips could not. I let my typed words tell my story.

I thought back to that moment in the computer room as I looked at Min's words. I thought of Layla, the petite catalyst for strength in my world.

ur right brb

My index finger pressed the enter button with determination, but as I rose from the chair, I realized the moment of conviction had been fleeting. I climbed up onto my bed, stacked with two mattresses just as it had been my freshman year, and reached over to the phone on the chest of drawers. The beeping tone of each number echoed in my ears slowly. My fingers did not dial the same number I had been calling for almost fourteen years with as much eagerness to reach an answer on the other end. The bells rang in my ear four times, just one less than when the answering machine would pick up, and my mother's authoritative voice came through.

"Hello?"

"Hey," I replied, the greeting clipped.

"Hey!"

I rubbed my hand over my pant leg and bounced my knee as I sat at the edge of the bed. "Are you busy?" The words were cut again, like mincing vegetables for the perfect recipe. I had one chance to do this. The perfectionist waved red pom-poms in my head and sinisterly cheered that I had one chance to get this right or screw it all up.

"No, what's up?" I think my mother could hear something amiss in the way I spoke.

"Uh, could you get online?" A trembling breath left my body. "There's something I need to tell you."

Mom paused. "Is everything okay?" Her voice lifted, an attempt to sound gentler and tender, which was hard given the depth of her voice.

I didn't answer the question. "Could you just come online? There's something I need to tell you?" The plastic phone receiver was pressed so hard against my ear the cartilage began to ache.

"Yeah, sure!" Mom returned with the same theatrical cheeriness. Still, I could tell from the wobble in her "sure" that she was worried. "Just give me a minute to turn the computer on, okay?"

"Okay. Talk to you in a minute." I didn't say goodbye and put the phone back down on its base.

I walked back to the desk and pulled the chair back, feeling nothing at all. I was numb, the way I always was when I faced something difficult.

I was outside of myself now and became a voyeur of one of the biggest moments of my life. I watched as a young woman sat at her desk. The pads of her hands rested at the edge of the keyboard as she stared at the computer screen. The desk lamp lit only half of her face, the other side in darkness. It gave her the appearance of having two faces: one in the bright, waking world, the other in the shadows.

The young woman rolled her shoulders as she waited, fingers hovering over the keys. She sat so extremely still, like a doll someone had set up at a computer and desk to appear as a student. Were it not for the rising and falling of her chest, picking up in rhythm now, I would not know she was alive.

When the computer speakers make the sound of a door opening, I am back in my body and mind.

Hey

Mom's words appear.

Hi. What's going on?

There's something I need to tell you, and it's really hard for me to say

Did something happen

Yes, but it was a long time ago

Did someone hurt you

My mother's early determination of the situation brought relief and a sliver of cynicism. If she could detect it now, why hadn't she detected it for all those years?

Yes

Somebody at church?

No

Somebody at school?

No

Who

"*Who.*" I knew the one-word answer would create a Chernobyl-like fallout in that house. I was grateful to be away from the blast zone.

As had been the case with so many pent-up feelings and emotions that I could never vocalize, my fingers moved to deliver the response.

Nathan

On the other end of the conversation, I had no idea what my mother was feeling, saying, or even doing. It was better for me that way. I tended to latch onto her emotions as if I were a marionette with her pulling the strings. What made her rageful made me angry. What made her panic caused my own anxiety. Through the computer, it finally felt safe to tell her.

Still, even hours and hundreds of miles apart, I sensed the disillusionment descending on her and our family in the questions that came one right after the other.

Did he touch you

Yes. It started when I was five. It went on for a long time. Years.

I did not feel vindicated as I typed. The unloading of decades-old secrets did not take the weight off my shoulders. I did not feel lighter. I was conflicted. When this Sunday began, I am sure my mother never expected to learn by that afternoon that a family member had sexually abused her baby girl.

Yes, now, Mom knew. Someone in the family finally knew. I was embarrassed, relieved, panicked, but most of all, uncertain of what would happen next. As the tsunami of feelings rolled from my belly upwards, I used every ounce of mental fortitude to hold back the waves and returned to the extreme feeling of nothingness.

I can't say for sure that I began to cry, although I feel that I must have. Part of my memory tells me a cathartic outburst came, but it, like the other unpleasantries in life, is shut away in a lockbox in my brain.

Thank you for telling me. We will take care of it.

Mom's reply had the efficiency of a customer care representative making sure I'd be happy with the outcome of a transaction gone wrong. It also had the ominous undertones of a mob boss. Nathan would be "taken care of."

Thank you

After fourteen years of keeping that secret, I was thanking one of the people I had diligently kept it from.

Are you okay?

Now felt as good a time as any to continue letting the truth serum sprinkle over my keyboard.

No

It's going to be okay, sweetheart. Do you want me to tell your dad?

Dad. When I had called the house and spoken only to Mom, he had faded into the background like an extra. He had brought Nathan into the house, into our lives. I couldn't bring myself to tell *him.* At this point, I am certain I was crying.

Yes, please

Okay. We will talk to you soon. You get some rest. I love you.

I love you too. Goodnight.

I watched the screen until I heard the sound of the door closing coming through the speakers, and the chat box on the screen went dim.

A good thing my roommate was gone. I needed to be alone.

Yet I also needed arms around me. I needed the warmth of a protective body shielding me. That need would remain for decades because it was rooted in my soul and left unfulfilled since I was five.

My fingers had spoken for me. I told my mother that Nathan had been molesting me not only for me but to protect Layla. I wasn't trying to be a hero or display some great courage. My fear that he would hurt another child had eventually outweighed my need for silence.

I didn't know it, but a part of me began healing that day.

I went to the bathroom sink and grabbed a washcloth, turning on the faucet until a tepid stream of water flowed. I wet the cloth and then pressed the rag to my nose and red eyes as I sniffled and wiped away my tears. I hung the rag back on the towel rack and flipped off the bathroom light, unable to look at my reflection again.

I did it

I messaged Min back, who I can only imagine had been in a frenzy for the last half hour. It had taken less than five minutes to change the course of the rest of my life.

How did it go

Mom was supportive

It was the truth.

I'm proud of you

I told myself the same thing. *I'm proud of you, Maya.*

I said goodbye to Min, explaining I needed a little time, and logged off for the rest of the night. I turned to my escapes. I rested on the bed listening to my *NSYNC and 98 Degrees CDs on my Walkman. I put in a VHS in the VCR my roommate and I had purchased at a pawn shop and watched a compilation of NSYNC concerts and MTV's Total Request Live appearances I had recorded over the last two years.

I didn't eat dinner.

I showered, scrubbing my body with the bar soap and letting the water rinse the suds away, cleansing me.

That night I slept. I slept more deeply than I had since I had left home.

What I'd believed all those years, that I'd get in trouble if I told, it didn't happen.

Instead, Nathan did.

Chapter Twelve

The Truth Will Set Me Free ... And Then All Hell Broke Loose

December 1999

A graveyard in a small English village at two a.m. was a livelier scene than my parents' home that Christmas. Not so much as a single snowflake, pellet of sleet, or a dime of hail had fallen in north Texas, but it felt icy nonetheless. There was about as much warmth and cheer as the deep freezer at a slaughterhouse.

I was a spectator to the slow dissolution of a twenty-year marriage. I watched as my father, who I once believed to be so tall his head would hit the doorframe of any room he entered, withered and depleted to someone frail and stooped. He seemed to border on 102, not 61. We'd never been big on hugging as a family, but my father became emaciated to the point I thought to hug him would be to break him—physically and emotionally. All within two months.

Mom's stern face was even more dour, as if she'd smelled something consistently unpleasant lingering in the house. The house itself was a giant, holiday snow globe and my admission had shaken it up, stirring up the picturesque existence of the residents as slowly all around them the debris began to settle. Screaming would have been preferable to the silence. I don't remember enough words to fill a thimble being spoken between Mom and Dad, not even as we opened presents joylessly on Christmas morning.

The best thing I could do, in my head at least, was to stay out of both their ways. JJ was still living on his own in an apartment, so it was just Mom, Dad, and me at home again.

My old bedroom became my hideout. I ventured out to grab a snack or a small bit of dinner that Mom made (when I actually had an appetite), and then I made my retreat. I slept till noon or two o'clock like most college kids, but it wasn't just from late nights online. I'd brought my computer home from college and the stacks of VHS tapes with recordings of the band. AIM and the videos became my constant comforts again.

Sleeping also gave me a bit of a vampiric existence. I avoided my parents during the day while I snoozed and did not have to face the blue norther of tension floating through each room of the house. I slept during the day and ate and encountered people, *my* people, at night.

It may be the only period in my life I don't remember masturbating, watching porn, or engaging in online sex chat. The thrill of sex in any form had temporarily lost all appeal.

I had another bone to pick with the scriptures. I'd been taught John 8:32 growing up. *The truth shall set you free.* The truth itself may have been freed from the bondage I'd kept it in for the last fourteen years, but what followed my admission was nothing like freedom. I'd traded one set of shackles for another.

My parents did not blame me. I was fortunate that I was believed the minute I'd typed those words about what Nathan had done.

I don't know what immediately followed my computer conversation with Mom. From October to December, almost forty days passed before I was home for winter break.

Nathan vanished. All signs of him—clothing, furniture, photographs—were removed, wiped clean like giving me a refurbished model of our home. Gone as he was, the evil he had done lingered and took its toll on all of us.

I heard things but did not ask for details. Even now, I could have asked Mom. I thought about sitting her down and asking what happened with Nathan after I'd told so that I could share it with you. All these years later, I still don't want to know. So, I can only tell you what I do.

One night, while home from college over the Christmas break, I was sitting at my computer desk, chatting with friends in my pajamas, the home phone rang. I answered it the same way I'd been doing since I was seven.

"Hello?"

The curt reply requested my father by his full name and hissed "please" at the end.

Ms. Lovely. She sounded as if there were boar bristles lining the center of her panties and she'd forgotten and sat down too quickly.

I held the phone. People talk about the sensation of your blood running cold. My blood was hot and churning like motor oil in my veins. It was my nervous system that turned itself off. There was a little switch that I could flip on and off and select to be present or not, and sometimes it activated without my control. My brain immediately told my body this was something I did not want to deal with.

Dutifully, I opened my bedroom door and covered the phone receiver.

"Dad. The phone's for you," the voice of a nineteen-year-old girl said in my head.

I put the phone receiver up to my ear and listened until there was a click and my father's baritone voice answered.

I set the phone down on its base.

I had not been back at my computer desk for any longer than five minutes when I could hear hurried shuffling and raised voices outside my door.

The megaphone that seemed to be built into my mother's throat amplified every word loudly, but I only discerned *JJ, Nathan, house.*

I opened my door to a fire drill, but no one was exiting. Dad was moving faster than I'd seen him move in days, and Mom was following him.

No, my brain said. I stood in the doorway to the living room but didn't cross the seam in the carpet at its threshold. I wanted to ask what was going on, but my brain kept telling me it was best that I didn't. My spirit returned to the safety of my computer desk but my body remained in that doorway.

Mom finally stopped rushing around for no understandable reason that I could see. She wasn't changing clothes or gathering her purse and her keys. She was moving because the situation told her to move.

She stopped and looked at the body standing in the doorway.

"JJ showed up at Ms. Lovely's house and threatened to kill Nathan. He tried to attack him." I saw her relay this to me like a Western Union telegram reader from the 1920s. Her head swung from side to side with each word as if the syllables required force to create them. She spoke with astounding efficiency.

"Oh," the body replied. It turned and shuffled to its bedroom and closed the door. It rejoined its spirit at the computer desk and resumed the conversation about a boy band.

There was a pinewood table for toddlers and, on top, one of those bead roller-coasters that challenge and frustrate your brain.

Part of me grieved. That little table was for a kid in a psychologist's waiting room. What traumas and crimes had they endured that brought them through this same door? I grieved more when I realized many of them had likely gone through what I'd gone through at about the same age. I was now the adult that a molested girl had grown to be. How different would my life have been if I had received help at an age when I was small enough to sit at that wooden table?

A man with a thick, 1970s police officer's mustache and thick brown hair opened the door for me, Mom, and Dad. He wore a gnarled, crocheted sweater vest over a too-large, button-down shirt, buttoned to the top and loose-fitting khakis.

He called our last name, and we stood in unison like our family had been called in the draft. We were ushered from the waiting room to an office with a wall of bookcases filled with thick, bound manuals, past editions of the *Diagnostic and Statistical Manual of Mental Disorders*, and books on family relationships and trauma. The three of us took a seat on a sofa that looked like a carryover from the 80's, in front of windows covered by metal blinds from the same decade. The rumble of cars and diesels on 635 filtered in from outside. The room smelled like old books. It was comforting, as my olfactory connected it to visits to Nicholson Memorial Library on Saturday mornings as a kid. The familiar smell helped me to sit back on the sofa.

"You're Maya?" Dr. Jones looked directly at me and took a seat in a metal and vinyl chair that creaked as he rolled it closer to us.

I nodded.

He took a deep breath and offered me a closed-lip smile. "How are you doing today, Maya?"

I let out a sardonic laugh. "I've been better."

The brown mustache lifted, revealing teeth and a bottom lip but concealing the upper. Dr. Jones was the first psychologist I had ever met intentionally. The office and stacks of books lying and leaning in all directions conveyed not only a busy schedule but the complex intellect of someone who studies minds.

He thanked me and said something to the effect of, "Great job completing the forms; I know it's a lot of questions, but it helps me to understand what you are feeling."

I nodded with understanding, having sat on my bed and filled out question-naires and surveys about "trauma," a term that was not a part of my everyday vocabulary until that first office visit.

Dr. Jones asked my parents questions about their family histories and the generational traumas that were gifted to all of us, twisted little genomes we had inherited.

"I can work with both of you together," the doctor said to my parents. "But her," he nodded at me, "she's going to need to be treated by someone else on her own."

That's how I entered therapy for the first time.

Dr. Jones recommended that I see the psychologist in the neighboring office. Much to my comfort, it was a woman, and her name was fittingly Dr. Goode.

I wanted a female therapist. Telling my most intimate details to a man felt like the opposite of safe.

"My diagnosis for you is that you are suffering from severe depression," Dr. Goode said after my second session. I would stare at her striped, multi-colored socks during every visit and at her worn brown leather loafers when she talked. Her brown hair was straight, and she wore cardigans even in the summer months. I don't remember her laughing or smiling when I spoke, but I looked at her more like a friend I was opening up to.

She wouldn't let me gloss over the hard stuff, though.

During an early session, I rattled out the details of the first molestation by Nathan when I was five. "And then another time—" I began.

"Wait, hold on, wait, wait." She put up a hand like a crossing guard to halt me from going any further. I huffed. I realized I'd been recounting the events in my head the same way for years. Flipping quickly past one memory to the next in a rush to get past it all. No matter how quickly the words came out, the impact wasn't going away in a rush. It was going to take years to unravel the twine of mental wounds that were knotted and twisted inside me.

Dr. Goode and I spent the rest of the session talking about that first time. She asked me how I felt. She asked if I was frightened. She asked if I felt anger toward Nathan. I would answer, and she would jot down notes on a yellow legal pad. I wondered what notes she was making about me. Behind her, on her cherrywood desk, there were files and similar legal pads stacked high. Stacks of life details reduced to manilla folders and yellow legal sheets in what looked like a cluttered mess.

Yes, of course, I was frightened and angry then. I still was.

I began to see Dr. Goode until it was time for me to return to college and begin the next semester right after Y2K. The world had not ended as false prophets had predicted, but my life as I had known it before was, in fact, dead.

There was a temporary stint with another therapist that could see me locally in College Station while I was attending classes, but when summer rolled around and I made the trip back home, I returned to Dr. Goode's sofa.

She was the therapist who told me that pills and alcohol mostly led to brain damage rather than a successful suicide.

There were pills at the time I was assured were helpful. Dr. Goode referred me to a psychiatrist who put me on an antidepressant. I was warned about abruptly stopping them, told this would make my depression and "illness" worse and could enhance suicidal thoughts. I listened as the side effects were listed, a list that sounded longer than the benefits.

I began to wake each morning and swallow down the bitter white pill as part of my daily routine. It took some time, weeks, maybe even months, before I could tell if the therapy and pills were working.

My parents went to see Dr. Jones together a solid two additional times before Dad tapped out. It wasn't for him, he claimed.

If there was a divide between my parents going into the Christmas season, it had widened to a chasm going into the new millennium. My father's reluctance to seek treatment only worsened my mother's animosity.

"Are you and Dad going to get a divorce?" I finally asked one night as she and I sat in the living room watching TV. Mom was on the sofa, and I was in another one of her winged backs diagonally positioned from her. I pulled both feet up into the chair and hugged my legs.

"Whatever happens between your dad and me, happens," she said, her tone cool.

I watched my mom watching the TV, lips tight after delivering her reply. A combine's auger began to spin inside me. It harvested all the emotions and feelings my brain had been disconnecting from. As it spun, the turmoil, confusion, guilt, fear, and regret were chopped up into bits and released as a startling wail. Mom's head whipped towards me as I sobbed.

"I feel like ..." I began to cry so hard I was choking on my own words, my nose clogged, my throat battling to let words and breaths and sobs out all at once as my eyes dripped salty pain over my cheeks. "I feel like it's my fault."

"And," I put a hand to my heart and gulped in air that wasn't there, "I feel like if I hadn't said anything, everything would still be okay. You and Dad would be okay. Everyone would be okay! I shouldn't have told." I dropped my forehead onto my knees.

Mom didn't get up from the sofa. She stayed seated while I cried and lamented the fate of my family. Dad was somewhere in the house, but he never appeared. I'm sure my cries could be heard from any room, but neither parent came to me. When the tears finally slowed to sporadic twitches, convulsions, and sniffles instead of full-body tremors, I lifted my face to look at my mother.

I saw her wipe tears away from her own cheeks without a word to me.

Chapter Thirteen

Day 1

Journal Entry

May 18, 2015

Alright, so, I'm here. I've met our crew and we are all a beautifully dysfunctional pack. There is Rebecca, 33, who works for a brokerage firm in St. Louis, who is a compulsive overeater; and Jean, 51 of Maryland, who suffers from food addiction and depression; Julianne, 30, a mother of three toddlers from Virginia who is a bulimic, and Lucas, 24, from San Antonio, a mechanical engineering student, Longhorn, sex addict and alcoholic.

It's freeing, not that we have labels, not that we are all some type of freaks, but that there are others. There are others who appear greatly normal but suffer on the inside. There are others who deal with guilt, shame, and a feeling of being out of control, and at times helpless to their addictions.

Today we had our vitals taken, were issued meds, went to breakfast with Tennie and Kim in group, went to lunch, read a chapter of the AA book, had a *lecture on addiction and co-dependency, had dinner, worked on meditation practices, then returned for individual writing, snack and group reading.*

Today has been eye opening, mostly informative. One of the biggest things that came out of today was the suggestion from Tennie and Kim that Everett may be a love addict. This has me concerned about our growth as a couple and his willingness to work on any issues, as a couple or by himself.

I hadn't shared a bathroom with anyone other than Everett since I lived in the dorms at A&M almost ten years ago. My cautious parents had never sent me to an overnight summer camp, nothing more than a few church retreats here or drill team excursions there, so I'd never truly had the experience of sharing a bathroom with three other people.

It *was* like being at camp, if camp were designed not for theater kids, athletes, or missionaries making Biblical arts and crafts but a dysfunctional camp for people who had achieved five-star addiction status by hitting rock bottom.

The four of us had claimed various spots in front of the mirror, places that would become our territory for the next six days, brushing our teeth, swiping on foundation and lipstick and twirling mascara over our lashes. I had not expected to put on makeup. I wanted this experience to be the one place where my bare face could be free without judgment. When I saw the other women swirling powder brushes over their noses and popping their lips to secure their pouts, and with the presence of Lucas, I felt a push to add the cosmetic enhancement.

There wasn't much in the way of conversation. The uncertainty of the day ahead brought with it a nervous silence that pulsed in each of us. Small talk and chit-chat covers the surface, but lurking beneath is a fault line of fear and solicitude. I slip away from the bunch, carrying my clip-on ponytail in my fist. I monitor the bathroom door from my bed as I throw the hairpiece over the bun knotted in a scrunchie on my head and pull the elastic string until the metal teeth dig into my scalp. *Secure.* The metal raking over the sensitive flesh provides a constant discomfort, a biting reminder that this is all very real, I am very much alive and, try as I might, I'm not completely numb to it all.

I'd slept the night before. It came as a surprise given the new place, new sights, new smells, new people, new (old) bed crammed into one room. The submersion into the new had left me so tired that my eyes closed, and I was asleep not long after I'd adjusted the little red fan.

When Rebecca emerges from the bathroom, the ponytail swings behind my head.

About thirty minutes before, Juana had knocked on the door to our room as the sun's rays tickled the ridges of Big Bend and moved into the valley where Shades of Hope is located. We'd not been given time to brush our teeth, comb our hair or wipe the "sleep matter" from our eyes.

Lucas steps in through the back storm door and joins us as we take seats on the sofas and chairs.

We are to read from page eighty-six of the "big blue book" for Alcoholics Anonymous. Juana instructs that we are to read this passage every morning, not always as a group, but at least on our own before we begin the day.

"Anyone want to volunteer to read?" Juana asks.

Rebecca raises two fingers in the air. "I will." She flips the book open to the exact page without any trouble locating it.

"On awakening let us think about the twenty-four hours ahead," she begins. We listen to her relay the passage that encourages us to trust in God and lean into the universe when feeling uncertain or fearful rather than fall back to old habits that no longer served us. After completing the required reading, she presses the book closed.

"I need everyone in the kitchen," Juana says.

We line up, facing a little hallway towards the garage that is lined with brown cabinets, each with its own lock. A white scale sits on the floor. Juana pulls out brass keys and opens a cabinet. She pulls out a small plastic tub filled with the small orange and yellow bottles we'd forked over the evening before. She distributes our medicines, all of us receiving antidepressants, as we step forward one by one.

After we each take our pills and are given a glass of water, we step forward into the little hallway, some distance between us and the rest of the group. Juana instructs us to step on the scale.

Jean lifts bare feet and places them on either side of the scale. The plastic creaks underneath her, and she keeps her chin lifted. If she ever looks down, I don't see it. It appears to me she's trying to avoid whatever number appears. She steps off it and moves away from the scale and from the group, to the other side of the room. Rebecca goes next. Julianne stands uncomfortably close to my back, and I glance over my shoulder at her. She hugs each of her elbows in a hand as she rests her forearms against her stomach. Her closeness makes me realize how tiny she actually is. It isn't just that she is short, maybe five foot two at the most, but her limbs are more like that of a seven-year-old girl than a thirty-year-old.

I step onto the scale and look down. One hundred and fifty-five pounds. I shrug it off as something to neither lament nor rejoice. Julianne moves forward, still hugging her arms, and Juana instructs her to put them down by her side to get a good reading.

I look away and lean against the kitchen sink as she steps off. Lucas is the last of us to go.

After the assembly line of medicines and weigh-ins, we began preparing for the day. Lucas returns to the guest house out back.

We climb into a Ford Expedition and begin the short drive from the house to the Shades of Hope center. The radio is tuned to a local pop station. I'm glad for what feels like the first connection to the outside world since we left the airport yesterday.

The music seems to put the others at ease as we find reasons to converse.

Ellie Goulding's "Love Me Like You Do" serenades us, and Julianne sings a verse of the song. Her voice is light and beautiful. I imagine her in a Baptist church choir in Virginia.

"I almost watched *Fifty Shades of Grey* the other night," I comment as Juana backs out of the driveway. "It was on pay-per-view." The song on the movie's soundtrack takes me back to the hotel and my last night off the wagon.

"I saw it at the theater with a friend." Julianne grins. "I mean, if you read the books ..." She hunches her shoulders and chuckles.

"Oh, I did." I nod. "I decided since I'm here getting treated for sex addiction, it may have been a little too on the nose," I respond dryly, and laughter moves through the SUV.

We pull up to the picket fence where we gathered for our meals the day before. We are informed that breakfast will be the same mixture of protein and fruit for the next few days.

"You can have either a boiled egg or two turkey sausage patties, along with rice cereal with eight ounces of milk or Greek yogurt and a bowl of fruit," Juana says.

Caffeine isn't permitted. Decaf is offered up for any who felt the shakes or headaches from the bean juice withdrawal, but none in our group partakes of this particular stimulant.

I grab the turkey patties, Rice Krispies, measure my milk to the top line of the plastic cup, and then select a bowl of freshly-cut chunks of watermelon.

Before we dig into breakfast, we recite the serenity prayer. I am a bit more familiar with the words at this point, speaking up loudly on the parts I had committed to heart like "the courage to change" and whispering the parts I was unsure of, like "wisdom to know the difference." I'd moved from a D- to a solid C+ in the memorizing area in the last twelve hours.

I still felt the tremble of disquiet within me despite the conversation that flowed much more amicably than it had the night before. I hardly ever ate breakfast and now I was pouring milk to the exact gradient. I wonder how Charlie and Everett are doing this morning without me. I look around the table at the five faces that were becoming less unfamiliar ... but I miss home.

During breakfast, Tennie and Kim arrive and greet us. They move through the house and out the back door, telling us to join them in one of the other buildings.

We put our dishes in gray tubs and then walk out onto the back porch to a humid May morning. The grounds are covered by the shade of trees, sunlight peeking around the branches and leaves, shyly greeting us as we walk on a path of circular gray stones and low-cut, dewy grass. We step inside a separate utility building where we are told the group meetings and healing exercises will take place.

It was mostly one large room, an open space with gray carpeting and undressed windows to let the natural light in. It does not have the dank odor of the house or the dining center. It smells of new wood paneling, and the eggshell white paint seems fresh on the wall, the tinge of chemical meeting my nostrils when I inhale. In the corner, there is some equipment piled up, and I notice that much of it is padded. Thumb tacked to the wall are a few charts and diagrams reminiscent of the laminate math guides in an elementary classroom. One is marked "Feelings/Emotions."

We sit in a circle, Kim and Tennie with us on the floor. A smaller hallway is behind the main room with the bathrooms.

The bathrooms. Since we had just eaten breakfast, we became aware of one of the many rules for the intensive.

"If you go to the restroom, you have to ask someone to go with you and stand outside the door," Kim explains.

My head swivels from one side to the other, making eye contact with each of the shocked faces.

"We've had those with eating disorders that try to vomit after their meal. It's a safeguard to keep you sober while you're here," Tennie added.

My eyebrows were surely brushing against the baby hairs along my scalp line. I try subtly to glance at Julianne, who is picking at the rubber edge of her shoe.

I am not interested in trying to puke up what I had just eaten, but a level of privacy is being crossed. If I have a case of explosive gas, I didn't need Rebecca outside the door hearing the tuba noises coming from my ass.

Still, we all nod with understanding and silently acquiesce.

We are given a green tote bag, with the Shades of Hope Logo in white. Inside are some spiral bound papers and a few stapled sheets, a notepad, and a pen.

Kim hands each of us a writing pad and a printed piece of paper. I read the top, "Shades of Hope Treatment Plan."

"Before we get started, we want each of you to look at your goals for this six-day intensive," Tennie says. "We primarily focus on issues with food, but there is space for the other areas of struggle you identified on your intake form. Take a few minutes and fill it in."

I drew a line through the pre-inserted number 1 and wrote a 2 over it.

Problem Number 2: Problem Identified: Eating Disorder Type-Binge/Purge.

Goal/Objective: To assist client in developing a healthy style of eating which supports health and mental well being: to be able to live free of eating disorder behaviors.

Strategies of Accomplishing Goal:

1. Client will write a history of Eating Disorder

2. Client will follow a prescribed meal plan.

3. Client will participate in all group sessions.

4. Client will receive nutritional counseling.

5. Client will participate in body image exercises.

6. Client will participate in family of origin work.

7. Client will learn the basis of 12-step recovery.

8. Client will have a defined aftercare plan
   before discharge.

In a free space below, I updated my primary problem.

Problem Number: I write in "1." *Problem Identified:* I write the words "Sexual Abuse."

Once I'm done, I pass the form to Tennie. She looks over it and scribbles something down before handing it back to me.

Under my self-identified problem, she wrote, "Client will participate in Family of Origin Sculpting and Shame and Anger Reduction Work."

It is signed, "Tennie McCarty, CS, CIRS."

I sign my name underneath hers, and we enter our covenant. This one-sided sheet of paper holds the key to my new life. I hand it back to Kim, who filed my form away with the others.

"As we told you last night, we follow the 12-Step recovery method here," Tennie says. "In your bags is a Step 1 worksheet. Over the next few days, when we have breaks, I want you to write out your most honest account of how you reached Step 1."

I pulled several stapled worksheets from my bag, each marked as "First Step Prep." I'd been given one each for sex addiction, alcohol, and codependency. Two of the three are surprising. I understood my sexual addiction, but I wasn't prepared to label myself an alcoholic. I also did not think codependency was in any way an addiction.

"If you have more than one, just work on the prep for the area you feel is your biggest struggle." Tennie had reached into my brain.

"One of the ways we work the steps is through our introductions and how we identify ourselves. For example, before we speak, we say our name and what we are struggling with. Hi, I'm Tennie McCarty, recovering compulsive eater, recovering bulimic/anorexic and adult child of an alcoholic. Before we go around the room and share, I want you to keep in mind how you identify because it may change as you learn more about yourselves over the next few days."

"It's important for you to know about Kim and me, but also to understand that there is power in the group. When we share as a group, the shame and guilt many of us feel vanishes because we feel safe with one another."

Tennie detailed her lifelong battle with an eating disorder, childhood trauma of watching her father commit a violent crime, and her codependent and abusive relationships. Kim shared with us how daughter became like mother, having suffered childhood sexual abuse and then mimicking the bulimia she had witnessed from her mother, as well as her struggles with alcohol, sex addiction and gambling.

And so, they came to establish Shades of Hope to help others.

After telling us each of their own struggles, Tennie opened a round-robin for us to share our rock bottoms and what brought us to their doors.

"Hi, I'm Rebecca, recovering over-eater. This is my second time here," Rebecca begins. Tennie and Kim nod with recognition. "I was about 140 pounds heavier when I was here the first time," Rebecca reflects. "I've been doing really well. Still eating properly and doing my balanced three meals a day."

"So why are you here now?" Tennie asks Rebecca.

Her cheek twists as she tightens her lips in a reluctant posture of admittance. "Lonely," Rebecca admits. "I'm lonely. I don't want to go back to the place I was before because of it."

"Rebecca, we are glad you are here," Tennie replies. "Lucas?"

His long torso leans over his crossed legs, his shoulders rolling inward like someone who bench presses often.

His voice is low, as if softening his voice will somehow make the things he's done come across as less severe. "Hi, I'm Lucas. I'm a sex addict and alcoholic." His eyebrows squeeze together. "About two years ago, I started going on Craigslist to meet up with people. At first, it was just random girls and women looking for hookups." One of his shoulders lifts in a casual fashion. "Then things started to get bad. I would meet people for hookups in the morning and then again in the afternoon or at night. I was having sex with strangers sometimes twice a day. It was just women at first ..." His voice trails off, and he clears his throat and looks down at his hands. "Then it started to be couples and threesomes. Sometimes, I would even meet up with guys that wanted to suck me off. I'm not gay. I've only had real relationships with women. I wanted to get off anyway I could."

His head drops, and he slowly begins to shake it with an unsteady exhale. I want to tell Lucas that I understand. I want to offer kind words or lean across the small space of the circle and pat his hand. Instead, I say nothing, feeling I might actually be accepted amongst this group for more than just my sense of humor.

"Sexual addiction isn't as uncommon as many people think. God made humans to create other humans. But because humans genuinely don't like having to do things that require effort, God made it feel good so that we would want to do it. Otherwise, we would all treat sex like doing the dishes," Tennie says. My laugh is louder than the others. "So, in order for humans to produce more humans, God made sex feel really good. Sexual addiction escalates quickly, just like drug use. After a while, the high of orgasm isn't enough. It's the thrill of the situation. You need more and more and more."

Tennie's words bring with them a feeling of recognition and understanding. I thought I'd been the only woman, the only human being, on the planet who struggled in this way. Now, I don't feel like a pariah. There was a medical explanation for this as much as there was a psychological factor. If for nothing longer than a millisecond, I am validated.

"Thank you for sharing with us, Lucas, and we're glad you're here with us. Jean?"

"Hi, I'm Jean, compulsive overeater. As you can see, I'm overweight," Jean begins and jerks the corners of her lips up in a tense smile. It falls as quickly as it appears. "My doctor says I am morbidly obese." There is a silence as she contemplates her words, as if, for the first time, she truly begins to wonder how she reached this point in her life. "I was raised by a single mom. My mom could do anything. She's my hero. She started her own company and was often very busy when I was a little girl. If I wasn't at school or helping her with work, I was often left to play on my own. I didn't have very many friends growing up, the neighborhood kids would tease me because I was already a little plump back then. I didn't want to go outside and be taunted, so I'd stay in and watch TV. Mom would make me treats and snacks to keep me occupied while she was working. I think I began to crave food the way I craved attention from her."

"A few years back, my mom got really sick and stopped being able to work. I had put on so much weight by then that I was only able to take on part-time work that I could do from the computer because it was hard for me to stand or move for longer than a few minutes. We had to cut expenses and sold the car. I was shut in with my mom. Food became more of an escape. I tried dieting, and it would work for a few weeks, and then I'd be right back to opening the refrigerator and eating an entire meal standing there at two in the morning. I stopped looking at mirrors. I stopped caring how bad it got until I started having chest pains. The doctor said it was both from stress and my weight and that I needed to consider surgery. Even then, he said I might benefit from talking to a therapist. So, I started seeing a counselor, and she recommended I come here for treatment." Jean runs a hand over the brown and silver strands on her head.

Tennie nods, her eyes empathetic. "Many of us who suffer from eating disorders didn't have a basic need met as a child. Recognition and belonging are two early needs for every child, and when we don't get those, we tell ourselves that we can't care for others or ourselves. We try to find ways to supplement the child's needs. Binge eaters gravitate towards what we call mommy and daddy foods. Mommy foods are thought of as the comfort foods that are sweet, like cookies, cakes and cupcakes. Daddy foods are often fried foods, French fries or fried chicken. They are called that because they become what we didn't have from our parents in safety, so they are replaced with food."

Jean says nothing and clasps her hands together, and places her arms over her thighs.

"Thank you for sharing with us, Jean, and we're glad you're here with us. Julianne? What brings you to Shades of Hope?"

"Hi, I'm Julianne," she pauses there and does not attach an identifier. "Well," her heavy accent breaks the word into two syllables. "I ... I have some problems with food, too." There is a hard, obvious swallow that proceeds; the words she's spoken are hard to digest also. "It really started after the birth of my first daughter. I bought one of those jogging strollers. I went out every day and at first, I told myself it was just good for the baby to get fresh air and help me lose the baby weight. I would jog for an hour or more. I guess my rock bottom was about six months ago. I was in the bathroom throwing up." She grimaces, and her hand flutters to her neck that is rising with red like mercury in a thermometer. "I was throwing up, and my daughter came in," Julianne's lip trembles and she blinks as she gasps. "She said, 'Mommy, what are you doing?'" Her voice lifts along with her chin as if she can keep the tears from rolling back by elevating her head. Then it breaks. Her voice is a combination of sobs and words uttered too fast, but we still comprehend each one. "She saw me, and I ... I didn't know what to tell her. I don't want my girls to be like me."

Seated next to Julianne, again, I want to lean over and hug her, but I remember Juana's warning from the previous night. We are to let each other feel the emotions, no matter how difficult it is for us to watch.

Tennie studies Julianne pensively for a moment as the young woman continues to convulse from the wave of tears.

"Thank you, Julianne, for sharing, and we are glad you are here with us. As a mother myself, and one with a daughter who has an eating disorder, I can say I understand."

Julianne gives a weak nod. Tennie's eyes turn to me, and my back straightens tall and long like one of the pine trees back home in east Texas.

"Maya?"

Everything about me that has the power to numb myself is channeled. I'm not Maya. I'm not speaking. The words coming out of my mouth are my story, but they seem to be spoken by someone else. "Hi, I'm Maya; I'm a sex addict and an alcoholic." Those clinical terms reduce my complex existence into something so small.

"My counselor recommended Shades of Hope because I've been in therapy on and off for the last fourteen years, and sitting on a sofa just isn't enough anymore." The second set of eyes that are present while the rest of me wanders looks around the room and notices all the heads nodding. "I had really bad postpartum depression after the birth of my son. It wasn't until then that I learned why mine was so bad. For the first time in my life, I was diagnosed with PTSD." A pair of hands attached to my arms gesture as the woman inside me continues to speak. "I was sexually abused by a close family relation from the age of five until I was about eleven."

The voice pauses, and I feel a wetness on the soft flesh of my lip as my tongue drags over it before I continue. "He wasn't the only one to molest me. There was a boy who lived across the street from the time I was about six until I was eight. Both of them were touching me sometimes on the same day, though neither of them knew it. There was a group of boys once on a family trip to Houston." The voice doesn't elaborate on more details. There will be time for that over the next few days, my brain instructs.

Then, I'm there again, fully. I untuck my legs and fold my arms across my chest as one of my legs bounces. I chew the inside of my cheek, tasting copper for a moment but unbothered by the sting or that I've drawn my own blood. "I watch porn pretty regularly, which I didn't think was that big of a deal, but according to my counselor it is. I compulsively masturbate, sometimes three times a day. I've gone into online sex chat rooms for as long as we have had the internet." The list of my sexual dysfunctions is rattled off like a review of the grocery list. "About six months ago, I started having what I guess you would call an emotional affair with a former co-worker. We were sexting. It got to where I felt so guilty about it all; I felt like such a bad wife and a bad mother ... a bad person ... that I was suicidal." I look up at Tennie. My gaze has a marksman's accuracy in connecting with a target. "So, I'm here."

Tennie looks at me and then at Lucas. "Maya and Lucas, I'm going to ask that while you're here, neither of you masturbates."

My head draws back quickly. "Oh." I stammer as my mind processes what she said. "That shouldn't be a problem. I'm sharing a room with three other women." I cock an eyebrow, and there is laughter from all.

"We will make sure you don't, too," Rebecca teases. This draws a sincere smile from me as I look at her, and we continue laughing.

"Lucas, you're out there by yourself. So, you really need to be mindful," Tennie directs. "Have you already?"

Lucas huffs and gives a sheepish smile. "After we got unpacked and were in our rooms, I was there for about five minutes by myself when I had the urge. I did last night, and I did again this morning when I showered."

"From here on out, I'm asking that you abstain." Tennie's raspy voice has the command of a schoolteacher.

"Yes, ma'am," Lucas replies.

"Maya, tell me about your husband," Tennie says.

"My husband?" Confusion weaves itself into my question.

"Yes."

"I blink rapidly. "Uh ... we've been married for almost five years now. Our son is about to turn two in a few weeks ..." I trail off, shaking my head, unsure of what she wants to know.

"Does he know about your history of sexual abuse?"

"Yes ..."

"Does he have a trauma history of his own?"

I shake my head no. "Not Everett. His mom and dad are still together, grew up in a small country town. Honestly, sometimes I don't even know why he's with me. I'm so fucked up, and he's—"

"A normy." Tennie grins. "Someone without a clear trauma in their past. Everybody has been through something, but there are a few who grew up pretty unscathed as kids."

"Yeah." I give an exasperated laugh. "I'd say he's pretty normal."

"Does he know about your emotional affair?"

I shake my head no.

"Does he know you chat with other men and watch porn?"

"The porn, yes. I mean, really, who doesn't look at porn? The sex chat? No."

"How do think he'd feel about it if he knew?"

"Angry. Hurt." I rub my cheek.

"You mentioned in your intake paperwork that you have a history with rage. Have you ever shown it to your husband?"

"I would say Everett gets the brunt of it, yes. I threw a vase and a tripod at him last summer. He's never put a hand on me. My mood can be all over the place, and he hangs in there with me. We need each other that way, I think."

"Have you ever considered that Everett might be codependent? Many people who fall for addicts are. Particularly men who have addicts as partners."

I lick at my teeth and think. "I ... I don't know ..."

"What would you say your relationship with food is like?"

We jump from one subject to the next. It feels like an interrogation and an opportunity to be heard.

"Oh." I dig through the green bag and pull out one of the intake forms I had completed. I read from it out loud.

"Typically, don't eat breakfast, maybe a smoothie or granola bar. Typically, I don't eat lunch, but will usually pick up fast food about three p.m. Dinner, we rarely cook, usually take out for dinner." I fold the paper in half and put it back into the bag. "I've done cleanses. I've taken colon cleansers and diet pills. I go through extreme periods of exercise, then no physical activity at all."

"And your self-image?" Tennie asks, prompting me again.

"I don't know." I seesaw my head. "I think I probably overspend, yes. If I'm going somewhere I like to have a brand-new outfit for an event or work functions; I need something new. I have to be the person all eyes are on when I'm in any room. New clothes make me feel special."

"Do you get a high from buying?"

"Well, yes," I say. "When I know I have something coming in the mail or I've bought new clothes, it feels good. It feels like new skin. I'm a chameleon. I want to look good. I think most women are that way." I glance around under the assumption this isn't extraordinary.

Tennie inhales sharply as she looks around the circle.

"We have some activities planned for you over the next few days, but today is helping you understand the process and getting to know each other. We said it before, but we will say it again, there is power in the group." Tennie makes it a point to make eye contact with each of us. "Before we get started with the next activity, we are going to give you some time to look over your First Step Prep. Then we will have lunch and get started again. Okay?"

"Okay," we reply in unison.

"You can sit on the patio, wherever you feel most comfortable, to begin writing, just don't wander off the property," Kim instructs.

Rebecca is the first to grab her green tote bag, and I look around as the others begin to follow her lead, shoving our papers and notepads into the bags as we rise to our feet. Rebecca and Jean head back towards the dining center without a word to the rest of us. Julianne, Lucas, and I form a trio and make our way to the back patio and the tables and benches placed there.

It might be muggy, but there isn't the buzzing nag and sting of mosquito bites that I'm used to back home. There's a breeze that's pleasant underneath the cover of the porch and the shade of the trees. The fresh air renews my spirit and my dedication to transformation.

The three of us take seats and pull out our stapled packets.

First Step Prep Sex Addiction

　　1. *I am powerless over my obsession for sex.*

I read the prompt. For the first part of it, I am to describe my "unacceptable, hidden or unhealthy sexual behaviors." *Unacceptable.* I look over at Lucas and Julianne, both skimming over the printed text with frown lines creasing their foreheads. I'm glad they are absorbed in their own pitfalls. Now, I feel like retreating, shrinking away from this entire scene. I crumple over the table, resting my elbows on the weathered wood as I bow my head. *I'm here to get better.* The reminder brings both the perfectionist drive that has gotten me ahead in life and also a defiant determination against my demons. I dare them to hold me back any longer. I am not only going to recover and beat this thing; I'm going to be the poster child for sobriety and recovery.

I skim the page again.

Recall when you were at your rock bottom, the lowest areas of your sickness.

I click my ballpoint pen and press it to my notepad. The worksheet encourages us to hold nothing back. So, I don't.

Chapter Fourteen

Day 2

Journal Entry

May 19, 2015

I am remembering things I had forgotten.

I am remembering instances of victimization and behavior that I had tucked away. I am also realizing just how angry I am. I'm still so angry about what happened and what he did to me then and the person I am now. I know I have to let that anger go, but how? How when it has been the thing to mold me and motivate me?

As for this process, I am becoming frustrated with the process of being told when to eat, what to eat, how much to eat, weighing what I eat and filling out forms. It's been so much control with so little control on my part; I'm finding that part difficult. However, I see the benefits of the work and the talking. I'm still waiting for my opportunity to discuss my story. I think that will be where a lot of my personal healing will come from.

On today's walk, I had a thought. I recalled that despite feeling like I've been in control of my sexual experiences, I've been a little more than just a sexual doormat for so many. The pleasure I thought I was providing was me just being used, and that thought in itself pushed up feelings of anger for me.

As Tennie said, if the act would be under God's approval, meaning between spouses, then it's pleasing to God. I have to change the way I view sex and the pleasure it brings me in marriage.

Today, we took vitals and medicine and we ate breakfast. Then as a group we did a meditation where we reached out to our inner child. We then drew pictures of our childhood selves and images of how we thought about our bodies. Then a group member traced our actual bodies. We discussed the lowest points of our disease, mine being my suicide plan in July 2014. We discussed our vision for recovery, then went to lunch.

After lunch, we wrote on our body images our life maps. We broke it down in periods of 0-2, 2-4, 4-6, 6-8, 8-10, 10-12, 12-14, 14-16, 16-18, 18-20, 20-25, 25-30 and 30 to present. I wrote about major life events and traumas, and influential periods. After this exercise, I noticed my mood change. I was irritable. I think it came from suppressing the emotions of what I wrote down. My natural response is to feel anger.

Humiliation was the first order of business on the agenda for Maya today—at least, it felt that way.

We'd started the morning with the same business as the day before with the scale, the pills, sharing the bathroom mirror and measuring milk. When we arrived at the center we learned we would be much more goal-oriented today.

Yesterday, we'd been given little sheets of paper to journal our thoughts, feelings and emotions throughout the day. A bin was on the counter in the kitchen back at the house where we could drop off our writings. I'd turned my log in before bed and thought nothing more of it, feeling it safe, to be honest. The only eyes I thought would view what I'd written would be Tennie and Kim.

As we sit down in our group circle after breakfast, I quickly feel an immense sense of betrayal.

Tennie thumbs through the pieces of paper, and recognition strikes as I can see they were our logs, each individual page with scrawled personal thoughts on several of the pages.

Tennie licks her thumb and uses the wetted digit to turn a page. She reaches for the reading glasses hanging around her neck, slides them over her ears and looks at me and then down at one of the pages.

"I hadn't intended on wearing makeup," she begins. The heavy weight of two days of food stored in my belly was joined by the sinking sensation of a boulder within me.

Tennie continues. "But I did put on powder and lipstick and some mascara, and as much as I don't want to admit it, I know I did so in part because Lucas is here."

I gulp and force myself not to lower my eyes but to make direct eye contact with my outer. I feel the others' stares moving along the sides of my face like Charlie's curious hands when he inspects his mama's features. I imagine myself as a cloud of smoke, snaking from the burning tip of incense right up to the ceiling of that room and out to the sky—away.

I hadn't consented to my writings being shared with the entire group. I'm betrayed. Violated. This is a breach in every ounce of security I feel at this facility.

I sit cross-legged, but I lean back from Tennie and the others as a light-headed-ness comes upon me. Then, as I'd done when I was hurting as a child, I go silent. I don't like the story or the situation, so I make up a new one. One where I am no longer safe, and the villain of the story is Tennie.

She doesn't read any other excerpts from my log. Seething in anger as I was, I don't remember if she even read anything from anyone else.

"Thank you for being honest about that, Maya," Tennie says.

I nod. It felt like the only thing I could do. Nod my head and accept the embarrassment and the disillusionment. I've been exposed so fully. It feels like I am sitting buck-naked on that gray carpet. I don't want to look at Lucas, but I finally track my eyes to his gaze. He seems to wear the faintest little smile, and his eyes dance with curiosity. I look away.

Now, I hate it here.

There is no mention as to why I've been singled out. No explanation of why my log had been pulled to read aloud like story-time. We just move on. At the time, I didn't see the lesson in it. Looking back, I can see Tennie's goal. By outing one of the two sex addicts in treatment, it lessened the likelihood of anything inappropriate happening. I had the group's attention from here on out. All eyes were on me in the room, and I no longer wanted that feeling.

We remain seated, and Tennie instructs us that we are to take part in a quiet group meditation. I have trouble keeping my eyes closed as we sit, the backs of our hands resting on our knees, palms open to the ceiling. I crack an eye open to scan the others and see if anyone is watching me. It didn't feel safe to be in a room with others with my eyes closed. Especially not now.

My mind is wandering. I wonder what Everett and Charlie are up to. I wonder if Tony has tried to call or text to see if I really can't answer. There's an ache in my stomach from the increasing pressure of constipation after two days of consuming more food than I normally ate in an entire week.

I try to focus on my inhales and exhales, but something begins to shift with each breath. They don't become deeper, they come shorter, shallow. A seed of anger begins to bloom in a new section of the overgrown garden that represents each of

Maya's life experiences. In this freshly tilled earth, there was a little wooden sign that says, "Shades of Hope." It was past the weeded spots that said, "Tony," and the junkyard marked "Marriage" and the disaster area that was marked "Family." This little slice of land was being fertilized by mistrust and contempt.

We are about two minutes into the meditation when Kim's voice gently breaks the silence. This meditation was to teach us how to be present, to sit in stillness.

"Try to be mindful and remain in the moment," she directs with a calm tone.

I inhale deeply again and mentally scold myself for not being able to shush the noise between my ears. I am here to get better, and I am already failing at something. Peace of mind also feels like a tall order given my brewing rage.

After ten minutes of being unable to produce more than four seconds of quiet, we move on. The "camp for degenerates" feeling is added to by the crayons and markers that Kim pulls out and places in the center of our circle.

"Think of a time when you were a child, a memory of yourself as a kid, a good memory that you have, a vivid memory of yourself happy and safe. Now take that image of yourself and draw it," Kim says as she walks around and hands each of us a sheet of white printer paper.

An image pops into my head as soon as I take the paper in my hand. It's from Christmas morning 1987. I remember a polaroid snapshot of myself, taken with the camera I had received as one of my gifts. I was standing in my bedroom, torn strips of hastily-ripped gift paper all around my feet with my haul of new toys from Santa. My hair was parted down the middle and in two pigtails that had started to come unbound from a restless period of tossing and turning before I rose to inspect what was under the cedar tree in our living room at 3 a.m. In the photo, a broad smile stretches across my seven-year-old face, my dimples deep like canyons in my brown skin. I was missing at least one tooth on the top row, and I had slept in an oversized pink T-shirt that had been Mom's. Snoopy was on the front of it, and my twigs-for-legs stuck out from the bottom of that large T-shirt with wrapping paper piled up to my knees. I don't recall who took the photo, but I remember the image vividly.

It was one of the most honest and pure moments captured of me as a child. The smile wasn't forced or faked, the learned habit that had followed me into adulthood. I'd genuinely been happy that Christmas.

The availability of crayons was scant, so I chose purple for my hair after not finding black. I draw the pink Snoopy shirt and my brown skin and I try to make my facial features as prominent as I can with a big smile, dimples and large eyes.

It is the first coloring and drawing activity of the day. The second immediately follows. Our task is to create an image of how we view our bodies. Tennie and Kim give each of us a large sheet of butcher paper.

"Draw an outline of how you think your body is now, then tape the image you made of yourself as a child to the big paper," Tennie explains. I grab the roll of masking tape, pull off a piece, and tack my first drawing to the large sheet and go to work.

Moments later, I stare down at my artwork. My feet are two large potatoes and my legs and hips are nothing more than straight lines jutting out from the vegetables that are to be my feet. My hands and arms are far too large and far too short, respectively, and I'd drawn my belly and chest in a barrel shape. My hips are irregular lumps at my side. My head is the size of a cantaloupe, and I hadn't bothered to add hair.

Charlie's pudgy toddler fingers and still-developing fine motor skills could have created a better likeness than the one I drew. I stare down at the visual representation of my body that more closely mirrors something like a *Peanuts* character. Snoopy's depiction on the child version of Maya's shirt seemed right at home.

"Interesting," Tennie comments as she walks around and looks at my self-portrait. Even on a six-foot-long sheet of paper, I had managed to draw myself about a foot and a half too short. Kim walks over, and they stand next to me, side by side. I'd chosen a purple marker to make the rudimentary likeness.

"It's childlike," Kim says.

"What, my drawing skills?" I half snort.

"No." Tennie shakes off my joke. "The image. The way you drew your body is almost identical to how you drew yourself as a child. You drew your body like you still see yourself as that child."

I silently look at the purple curves and lines on the paper. My eyes track from the taller image to the little single sheet of paper taped on top. *Maybe it's just the way I draw.* My skepticism that I am somehow a repressed version of that child is strong, but as my gaze goes back and forth, I realize Tennie is right. I am thirty-four, soon to be thirty-five. I feel no more an adult than I did on my eighteenth birthday, or even my twenty-first when I'd had my first legal drink. The things I love, the things that bring me joy, are the things I'd loved or been deprived of as a kid. My mind flickers to a memory of me screaming and laughing carefree during my dating days with Everett as he spun us around on the teacups as fast as he could twirl us at Disney World.

Tennie and Kim survey our drawings. "Each of you needs to pick a partner now. On the same piece of paper that you used to draw yourself, we want you to lay down and have your partner trace an outline of your body in another color on the same side of the paper you drew your own image."

I look to Julianne who was already looking my way, and we nod in silent commitment. Kim volunteers to help Lucas as he is the odd person out as the fifth. Jean and Rebecca pair up.

Julianne smiles at me as she runs over and hugs my arm as if we were the best of friends, claiming me.

"Do you want to go first or ...?" She looks up at me.

"Sure," I say with a shrug. I look around the room and see the others taking off their shoes, so I do the same. I gingerly place my body on top of the thin paper, careful not to poke holes into it with my bony elbows and from the weight of my heels.

"What color do you want me to use?" Julianne asks, looking through the markers.

"Whatever floats your boat." My reply causes her to chuckle, and she grabs the green marker.

"Alright, I'm going to start at your head." She tucks her lips, the tip of her tongue poking through them as she concentrates and begins to trace the outline of my body. The plastic is cool and the ink slightly wet as she tries to glide the marker along the edges of my skin. As I lay there, looking up with her circling my body, a memory comes to mind. I stare at the ceiling. I part my legs some when she reaches the area near my thighs and carefully maneuvers to not brush against my lady parts too intimately.

I do the same in return. Julianne lay flat on her back and against the paper she seemed tinier. I begin to trace her outline and hold my breath as I move near the junction of her legs, wanting to be careful and not wanting her to think I was some type of a pervert deriving sexual gratification from this experience.

I reach out my hand to her and help her to rise to her feet and carefully step off the paper when we both hear sniffles from another part of the room. We watch as Rebecca traces Jean's body while she cries.

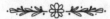

I open a spiral-bound set of card stock papers marked "Shades of Hope Weeklong Workbook" and wipe the back of my hand across my sweaty forehead.

We'd returned to the activity room from a group walk after lunch. Striding over the dusty, clay and gravel roads, my steps felt unnaturally slow. We were learning how to "walk." An activity that we were to learn we could do anywhere. No equipment, just solid ground, a pair of good shoes and minimal effort. Passing under the arching tree limbs and looking at the sandy yellow residue gathering on the tops and sides of my shoes, I realized I didn't know how to take it easy.

The workbook offers further insight into what I didn't know about myself. Inside was a page marked "The Addictive Personality Profile." As I read each bolded, printed entry, I realize I couldn't just check one or two lines here. I could check every line. There were twenty lines, and I ticked off each one: Emotional extremes, Need for Intensity, Need for Immediate Gratification, Extreme thinking, Lack of

Identity, Lack of boundaries, Lack of moderation, Overreaction, People pleasing, Perfectionism, Inability to express feelings, Low self-esteem, Attraction to pain, Assumption, Projection, Isolation, Need for excitement, Poor impulse control, Poverty mentality, Super sensitivity.

I was an addict.

It hit me in the same way that my words had put me in a chokehold in Counselor's office two years before. Here it was in black and white. Addiction had been there when I felt like I was losing control, fighting with an unseen enemy that was leaving me battered and mentally bruised.

"Addiction is like that," Counselor said.

There was a heartbeat where I dismissed the word. I heard her say it, but it was not applicable to Maya.

"I feel out of control." I'd looked to her for an answer.

She provided it again. "Yes. That's what it's like to be an addict."

I'd rejected it. I chose to disconnect from the conversation. This was another person's life she was referring to. Clearly, even as the licensed expert in the room, she did not understand my struggles.

The symptoms, being stuck, read like a checklist for my life over the last twenty-nine years. Every box has been checked, the list is full, the therapy bills have been paid for years, and, at this point, I want off the merry-go-round of crazy.

I didn't want any labels on my life. "Victim" was hard enough to accept. It stung like a wasp, pricking my skin and leaving me blistered and aching. I didn't want to be a victim. I certainly didn't want to be an addict.

Now, at Shades of Hope, every part of my identity is wrapped up in labels and medical jargon. It was the opposite of what I wanted. Labels boxed me in.

We line up against the wall, standing shoulder to shoulder. Tennie and Kim stand in front of us. This reminded me of the scoliosis test in middle school, but instead, we are all facing forward for some type of inspection.

We are to discuss our addictive behaviors and our rock bottoms, again.

"Hi, I'm Maya," I introduce myself for the second time that day. "Sex and love addict, alcoholic, bulimic, adult child of an alcoholic, adult child of a bulimic."

Yes, my list had grown after completing my life map.

"Maya, tell us about your rock bottom," Tennie guides.

I cast my eyes down to the floor. My hands clasp behind me. I begin to tap against the wall, the little bit of white on my index fingernail starting to scrape over and rake up the sheetrock.

"It had gotten to the point where I was coming home, seeing to my son having dinner, having a glass of wine or two to unwind, and then I'd go take a bath. I'd lock myself away in my bedroom most of the night. Some evenings, I'd be on my phone." I pause and run my tongue between my tucked lips, feeling the taste buds against my flesh, tasting the remnants of lunch still there. "I would enter sex chat sites and talk to strangers. Or sometimes, there was one person that I met from one of those sites, and we talked over Yahoo Messenger. I was even chatting with him while I was at work. Discussing sex and what we would do to each other if we could. I sent him pictures from the work bathroom stalls. I had no idea who this man was." I clear my throat, my eyes still locked on the dusty top of my shoe.

I review the emotional affair, postpartum depression while battling PTSD, the media days trip. Then, Elmo. Like the overture in a tragic opera, the crescendo of emotions swells, and my tears begin to fall in a rhythm like Paganini: weeping chaos.

"I felt like the worst human being on the planet. I felt like I was a bad wife and a bad mother and all of the things that happened to me happened because I ..." I point at my chest and look into Tennie's eyes.

She appears in front of me like I'd sunk below the surface of a pool and opened my eyes. Water clouds the surroundings. Despite the hostility I felt earlier towards her, something in me wants to share. I want to open up now. Maybe it's the proximity of being shoulder to shoulder with others who struggle; maybe it's that I'm not sitting down but able to stand up that helps me to finally speak up. All of the silence was breaking.

"There was this song." My shoulders move violently up and down as I lower my head and cover my face. "Elmo said that a person believes in you and I thought of my son and of leaving him. Then I looked up, and we were passing a barbecue joint, cause this *is* Texas." I snort and give a small laugh and the rest of the group laughs with understanding. "And I saw a sign and it said," I gasp and can barely get the words out and I nod at Tennie, "It said 'God sees you.' So I didn't kill myself that day."

Tennie stares and lets the emotions pass through me. "That, that is the God of my understanding," she says.

"I think God stopped listening to what I had to say a long time ago."

"You're here now," Tennie reminds. "That's for a reason."

Kim hands me a tissue. I blot at my face and blow out the mucous plugging my nostrils. There's no charm. This is everything that was underneath.

"Your struggle with sex is in part because it doesn't fall in line with your moral values?"

"Yeah, I guess." I sound as though my mouth is full, still wiping and blowing my nose.

"We talk to addicts about considering sex in a way that God would give approval to the act. If the act is between two partners who share a vow. Sex between spouses is meant to be enjoyable. It's when it is outside of that, that many find themselves at odds with what they are doing and what they believe."

This feels like a lecture. I understood from the church-goer concept of sex being between a married couple, but what about the times I had really felt empowered to explore my sexuality as a woman? Everett had become my husband, but the sex we had when we were dating was part of the manifestation of the love we felt for each other. At that moment, I remembered the "books not boys" lectures I was given as a kid and teen. Somewhere along life's route, that was supposed to change just for the purpose of one man? I was to go from good girl to some sexual goddess as a wife? How, without experience? How, without knowing what I liked? Pleasing to God? How was I to know what kinks God was okay with? I didn't want to hear scripture. It didn't seem fair. Most of the boys I'd known weren't receiving the same messages growing up; quite the opposite.

"Do you love Everett?"

I nod, but I'm angry.

"You don't want to do anything to jeopardize your marriage. I can hear it when you've spoken about him and your son. That's what you really care about."

I wasn't going to argue otherwise. It was true. Still, there were times when porn was more fun to watch and feel an orgasm rip through my body than sex with Everett. This was no knock against him or his ability in bed. It was what I felt I wanted sometimes. There were so many contradictory messages for women about sex—anger and confusion. Where is the line between exploration and self-care and pleasure? Then I think of the list. Those twenty lines.

I'm an addict.

Aluminum foil is wrapped over what appears to be a bowl at the kitchen table preset for us at dinner. I take a seat behind one of the wrapped bowls, a glass of water, and a bowl of grapes. The kitchen light is off in the other room, the stainless steel industrial appliances faintly shimmering in the dim light of the evening sun.

"We're doing something different with dinner tonight," Juana explains. "They say that you're eating too fast." She walks into the room carrying a little black boom box that has a CD player on top.

"We eat too fast?" I squawk.

She gives me a nod of patience.

"Don't take the foil off your food yet. This will be a silent dinner, but you will be listening to a guided meditation while you eat." Juana plugs in the boom box and sits it down on the floor near the table.

The growing seed of rage is a sprout now. I don't try to hide my anger. I roll my eyes and lean back in my chair. Juana continues to fiddle with the boom box until a staticky sound from the speakers, and a male voice greets us with a "Hello."

"Today, we are going to explore mindful eating."

I look over to the boom box furtively as if the recorded voice would manifest itself into a person. A person I want to punch despite the tranquil cadence of the male narrator.

"Often when we eat, we do so quickly, our bodies and brains are set to cruise control. We eat in the same way we approach many other aspects of our lives: automatically. Mindful eating helps us with a full experience of eating, tuning into our senses of touch and taste, but also allowing us to slow down and digest each bite we take."

"Now, lift the cover on the dish in front of you."

I yank at the foil as it squeaks and crumbles in my grip to reveal a bed of green, leafy lettuce topped with tomatoes, blue corn chips, ground beef, and salsa. This is the big reveal: a taco salad.

"Now, take your fork in your hand."

I look around the table, but everyone else's eyes are cast down at their food. I am already over this experience.

The voice begins to talk us through how exactly we should eat.

"Feel the chair against your back and underneath you. Plant your feet in front of you on the floor and feel them pressing down. Feel yourself supported by the chair and the floor."

I want to reach over and press the stop button on the boom box. That is quite enough. I've been feeding myself since I was about six months old. I don't need anyone to tell me *how* to eat.

"Grab some of the food and place it in your mouth. Close your eyes. What do you notice? Chew slowly. Feel the texture of the food in your mouth. Notice the taste and feel against your taste buds. Take a moment to fully chew the bite before swallowing. Pause and bring your awareness to the food and your relationship with it."

"Note what you feel in your belly. Are you hungry? Do you crave more? As you chew slowly, do you feel more full?"

No. I feel foolish. Not only have I relinquished control of what I eat but now, *how* I eat. We aren't allowed to speak as we listen to the thirty-minute recording, taking us from the start to finish of our meal.

I can't wait until I have a minute with Julianne or Rebecca to express my discourse.

Even the opportunity to do that was restricted.

"We just want to go for a walk," I explain to Juana after we are done with the meal.

"I'm sorry, but the only way you can go is if the entire group wants to go," Juana says, her eyes sympathetic.

Julianne, Lucas, and I had told her we wanted to take a walk after dinner. The day had been spent working so hard through our detail of memories, stretching our legs and some fresh air felt like a nice break from the confines of the house that evening. Jean and Rebecca had no desire to take a stroll with us. It was three against two, but the two were winning out.

"You guys are sure you don't want to come? Just up the street and back?" Lucas tries to appeal to the two ladies who are sitting on the sofa of the house working on their Step 1 worksheets.

"No," Jean says without looking up.

I exchange a disappointed look with Julianne and Lucas and then turn to Juana for any type of intervention.

"Let me check something." Juana leaves the room. I huddle with Lucas and Julianne, ignoring any lingering awkwardness from that morning regarding him, as we seemed to unite together in a common cause: we just wanted to take a fucking walk.

Juana returns a few minutes later. She explains that we were given the thumbs up from Tennie. I sigh at the small victory.

"You can't jog or run; just walk. Down the street and back up in fifteen minutes," she dictates. I expect her to tell us to be back before the streetlights come on.

Inmates in the yard have more freedom than we do. Before another word can be spoken, I unlock the door and walk outside, Julianne and Lucas trailing.

My legs stretch long in front of me in a deep stride as I feel the evening sun on my skin, and my nostrils fill with spring. The warmth is nice after being in the cold air conditioning for most of the day. That, or I was desperate for some semblance of independence and a break from control, that I was basking in the moment.

"Oh my God," I groan. "I had to get the fuck out of there. I'm about to lose it. I've been okay the last few days with all the requests but that meal? That was the breaking point. Like, that was the first time I got mad-mad." I roll my head around; my nose makes a circle in the air as I stretch and try to lock into these few breaths of unrestricted freedom.

"Telling us not to jog?" Lucas holds his hands up and frowns. "What if that helps me? Running clears my head."

"They don't want us to do any type of exercise other than walk," Julianne says. "I got in trouble this morning for doing yoga in the living room."

"What?" Lucas and I screech in unison.

"Yeah, I couldn't sleep. It was like 5:30, and the house was still quiet, so I went into the living room and started doing some poses and stretches to focus—get the tension out. I guess Juana gets up early because she came in and saw me and snapped at me, 'What are you doing?' She told me I couldn't and to go back to bed."

"That sucks; I'm sorry," I say.

"I mean, I understand them not wanting us to overdo it, but yoga is what helps me to feel better. It's not extreme."

"That's how I feel about jogging," Lucas chimes in.

"I can't understand why Rebecca and Jean didn't want to come with us? I felt cooped up in that house. I needed out. You got your watch?" I look over at Julianne.

"Yeah, five more minutes," she nods.

"What do we have next?" Lucas asks.

"Some group meditation." We move down the middle of the street. It's not paved or even a gravel path. It's pure sand and clay, and tan chalk collects around the soles of our sneakers again. "I'm not good at it. Meditating. I can't focus, and then I get pissed off that I can't focus, so I just end up pissed." I huff, and Lucas and Julianne laugh lightly.

"I'm glad we got to get out, though. Even for just a few minutes," Lucas says.

"Yeah," I grumble, my mind still on the brainwashed meal and Jean and Rebecca's rejection of even a casual stroll. I don't want to think about Tennie or the log as I walk beside Lucas.

I look up at the sky, a mosaic of darkening blue, bright orange, violet and thick clouds that seem swollen. Their bellies are gray and full.

I count: five more days.

·❧❀❧·

One hour after our walk, we arrive in a room adjacent to the main dorms, the size of most living rooms. The lights are off, so only evening light comes in. Our group of five has gathered with three others. Some of us sit cross-legged, palms upward, and some lie flat on their backs on yoga mats. Tennie and Kim are not there.

A woman in the room bounces. All I can hear are her heavy sighs, the cringe-inducing rapid pops and open-mouthed smacking of her chewing gum, and the rubbery squish of the yoga ball beneath her as she bounces on it like a human bongo drum.

Mentally pushing these annoyances from my brain is like trying to lift a stallion over my head. The smacking, the clicking, and the squishing only grows louder the harder I try. She is what our group deemed a "long-hauler," a client there for a twenty-one or forty-two-day stay.

I am in the cross-legged position, and the amplified sounds all around me heightened as if someone had turned up the volume of a hearing aid to the highest setting. I can't think straight. I hear the pop, smack, and squish grow louder and louder.

One eyelid pops open to look at this disruptor of peace. She has mousy brown hair, and is in a T-shirt, neon-colored leggings, and is barefoot. Her eyes are not closed and meet mine before I slam the observant eyelid shut again.

If I could string together four seconds of quiet this morning, maybe now I can stretch them into five. I would be content that I was getting better at meditation.

Rustling and bouncy girl is now sliding off the ball onto the floor and spreading her legs as she sighs without consideration for the many noises she is making.

The rage sprout is growing into a plant thanks to her. The day's events had watered it and nourished it into fury in my being.

I begin to lose hope. I will not find quiet here or rest. I have come all this way to return home just another broken sack of bones and brain issues.

I try once more. I channel the mom energy I use to block out the sounds of Charlie's abundant noise-making sensory toys in the house. I know how to tune her out. My soul is connected with the universe in those breaths.

"I will use you." A voice speaks so clearly that I open my eyes to see if someone is standing in front of me. There is no one. I inspect the others in the room. All eyes are closed; even the restless girl is lying still.

I have a long list of symptoms for my mental illness, but hallucinations aren't one of them. I look around the room again, eyes searching, seeking the source of the voice.

I repeat the message internally to myself.

I will use you. My eyes are still closed, visions of me standing with groups of other women, giving out hugs and joining hands with them come to me.

I whisper to myself, opening my eyes and looking up. "God?"

Chapter Fifteen

Day 3

Journal Entry

May 20, 2015

Today was by far one of the most intense and emotional of my life. Today we worked with some of the group on their personal journeys with Tennie and Kim. Jean, Julianne and Rebecca went today and each had about an hour and a half to two hours with Kim and Tennie's guidance as the rest of us watched and played the necessary roles. Jean released quite a bit of her inner child's anger and I told her I both admired her effort and was in awe of the process. Julianne's was also difficult but she gained quite a bit of healing. I played the role of her inner child as the rest of the group played various family members. They each repeated hurtful things that had been said to her during her lifetime. With a padded bat, she beat a pillow, then a large punching bag as she screamed the things she wanted to tell them. We all felt joyful at the cathartic release of her tears. She revealed that she had been victimized *sexually on more than one occasion. Afterward, we hugged and I told her I was proud of her. This day has been emotionally tough for me, as I shed many tears and shared in their pain as well. When Jean shouted, "I needed you!" to her parents, I thought my emotions would overwhelm me.*

Tomorrow is my turn and Lucas's turn. I am fearful and nervous. I don't always express my emotions well and I don't know if I can fully let myself go. I pray to God, good and merciful, that I get the healing that I need. God, please let my feelings flow, without fear and without restriction.

I'd been unwanted. My aunt's unruly cackle accompanied the recounting of my mother's unplanned pregnancy at every cookout, every holiday gathering, and frequently after church meals like family lore. I can remember one Christmas family dinner, an occasion that was meant to be joyous for a five-year-old child, as we sat on the sofas and love seats and chairs brought from the dining room in my grandparent's den. The house still smelled of cloves for the ham, baked pineapples from the upside-down cake, and collard greens. My stomach was distended after sneaking a few more pieces of cake behind Mom's back, and I was feeling drowsy from my full belly the first time I heard my aunt tell the story.

It had started as many pregnancies: my mother had started to feel ill, battling nausea and a few dizzy spells that lasted over several days. A devoted hypochondriac, she was certain she had contracted typhoid or salmonella. She headed to a doctor's office, where they told her it was nothing more than morning sickness and she was pregnant.

In shock, she stumbled outside the doctor's office to a payphone and called my grandmother, wailing and sobbing. When my grandmother could finally get her calm enough to articulate a sentence without shrieks and cries, my mother blubbered out the words, "I'm pregnant." My grandmother hung up the phone and refused to take any more of her calls.

"Girl, yo' sister pregnant!" My aunt mimicked my granny's accent as heavy and thick as Texas crude oil. Then the laughter followed as the family joined her.

"They all thought it was funny?" Tennie asks me as I stand in front of my life map scribbled on butcher paper and taped to the wall.

"Yeah ..." I look back at the paper and the bullet points I'd listed under ages zero to two: Mom told me she cried when she found out she was pregnant with me; Mom and Dad married five months after I was born; I was told that neither of my brothers was happy about my birth; and I share a birthday with my molester. I press the end of a marker into my palm so roughly it leaves an imprint of a circle on my skin.

"How did that make you feel?" Tennie looks up at me from her seat on the floor.

"Like a joke. Like my being born from the very beginning was a joke. Like no one wanted me."

It is the first time I'd made that admission about those feelings. I am an adult now, looking back at my childhood through the lens of mature, psychologically advanced eyes. I have more perspective than I ever could as a little girl. Mapping out my life, it is the first time I've truly considered the impact of my family's words and actions on me at such a young age.

As I recount the event, it isn't my intention to demonize my family, only to understand that the bottom rung in my developmental ladder was askew. The feeling of not being good *enough* or accepted for who I was may have incubated with me as I formed limbs, a nose, and lips in my mother's womb. Floating in amniotic fluid, possibly through osmosis, this mindset became a part of my being.

I examine the paper. The two creations of my body, the one I'd drawn and the one Julianne had traced, bordered by the scribblings of major life events near every curve and fingertip.

When I did arrive, Mom treated her baby girl like a doll. I know because she told me over and over again years later.

"Not just a doting proud mother, happy to share her adorable bundle with the world. No, really, like a fucking doll," I say.

She dressed me up when we had nowhere to go just to see me look cute. She fiddled with my hair, smoothing and brushing it constantly. I was the 1980s American Girl version of her. She loved bath time because she got to give her doll a spa treatment, which would have been fine if she'd been using a towel to dry under my arms.

My chubby rolls of baby fat, creased lines of plumpness that were like sausages, didn't meet the fibers of a towel for several weeks. The dampness that settled into those fatty folds began to mold and cause rot, like bedsores on a neglected nursing home patient. I was only about three months old. Mom said she went to lift me one day, and I let out a "scream" of pain. Her hands had slipped under my arms to prop me up, meeting the sore, moist, decaying skin of my armpits. She said the only thing worse than my wailing was the smell when she pulled off my top, lifted my arms, and saw my wounds like some gangrenous canker from a World War I battlefield.

An antibiotic ointment from the pediatrician healed my baby flesh in time. Mom attributes the mistake to being a young mother, even if I was her *second* kid. The dark shade of scarred, hyperpigmented skin under my armpits is the only reminder of that parental misstep.

"That can be considered a form of abuse," Tennie remarks. "Dressing your child up like a doll is a sign of perfectionism and sets them up for perfectionistic behaviors as well. It's codependent behavior, and the child's need for approval and validation starts to be formed through praise from the parents and praise for their looks."

"I think I have to agree with that." I have full recognition of those symptoms that feel as innate as breathing.

It wasn't the only mistake that would have a lifelong impact. Mom had stayed home with me those first few years of my life and, like many anxious mothers trapped in domestication with a toddler, a glass of wine was her visit to the breakroom each afternoon. Although, on one particular day, she'd left the long-stemmed glass of dark purple liquid on the nightstand, just within reach of her inquisitive two-year-old. I'd tasted a medley of sodas, the sour after-pull of apple and orange juice, and my favorite was grape juice at that age. I may not have noticed the earthy aroma coming from the glass. I can't remember if the bite of it burned my little throat on the way down. I drank a full glass of wine, I am told, and I passed out.

No one called the doctor or the hospital; instead, Mom let me sleep it off.

The event became another comical tale in my family's lore. Something to laugh about once everyone knew I was okay. It, for me, became prophetic. My affinity for wine could be traced back to that afternoon, a perilous introduction for the granddaughter and daughter of alcoholics.

My parents' shortcomings may have influenced the rigid rules by which I was raised. Though my imagination was encouraged and cultivated, free thinking was frowned upon when it challenged their plans for me. I was raised to do what my parents' said, not follow what they did. The fieldstone of perfectionism was already mine to push up the hill daily, and it made me an anxious child.

I first became preoccupied with my appearance. Perfection requires a certain face and body aesthetic. I was naturally thin, like my mom, but the more people talked about how tiny I was, the more I began to equate thinness with beauty. The women considered to be the most beautiful in the world at the time were all thin: the Beverly Johnsons, Imans, and Christie Brinkleys of the world. When I grew up, I knew I would have to be thin like them.

One afternoon during that same infamous summer of 1985, after I had already been molested, I decided to play the part of being a woman. I was going to shave my legs.

There wasn't even a hint of stubble on my bare, pre-pubescent legs, but women shaved, and beautiful women in magazines had long, lean, shiny, oiled legs. I thought I had better start practicing in order to be one of those ladies someday.

My mom was home for some reason that afternoon and on the phone with Ainty's ex-husband, Cole, who was in prison, serving time for what I later learned was murder. He had stabbed someone, and when I asked Mom if it was true, she only said, "More than likely. He has a temper." Cole had been a high school friend of Mom's and her first husband's. So, a collect phone call with him kept her occupied for quite a while because he rarely had the opportunity to use a phone.

I closed the bathroom door and grabbed Mom's yellow and white Bic razor, ran some water from the sink faucet and hoisted my right leg up onto the edge of the sink. I put the razor down, grabbed a bar of soap, held it under the water and then lathered my leg up.

After rinsing my hands-free of soap and drying them on the hand towel dangling from the silver ring on the wall, I reclaimed the razor and held it towards my leg, no wider than the handle on a baseball bat. I was too young and too stupid to know you didn't have to apply much pressure. So with the full weight of my hand, I placed the razor against my skin and pulled upward.

An entire slice of my brown skin peeled away like the skin of a potato in a vegetable peeler. In horror, I pulled the razor away, looking down at the white meat revealed for what would have been a heartbeat if mine had still been functioning. The spot flooded with crimson that streamed down my leg towards my ankle.

With soap around the wound and the deepness of the cut, I should have cried out in agony, the cut stinging from the chemicals in the lather. An entire section of my dermis was gone. I should have howled in pain.

Instead, I remained perfectly silent. I didn't cry. I didn't shout. I stared at the blood pouring down my leg, muted, not with shock, but in terror of getting in trouble. I had done wrong, and I had to tell Mom what I had done, something that I had been doing quite the opposite of recently.

I lowered my leg from the sink and opened the bathroom door slowly. Mom was mid-laugh with the phone to her ear sitting on the edge of the bed.

I stood still waiting for her to acknowledge my presence.

She looked at me, and there must have been something in my facial expression that caused hers to drop. "What is it?" she asked, full of panic.

"I cut myself," I said in a weak voice.

"How?" Mom frowned.

"Shaving," I admitted and looked at the floor.

"You're lying!" she exclaimed in disbelief.

I shook my head no and then pointed down to my leg. The blood was now on the carpet. I don't remember what she said to Cole, but it was hurried, about me having cut myself, then she slammed the phone down.

I don't remember the care she provided while bandaging the wound or how we got my cut to stop spilling blood from my leg like red Kool-Aid poured from a pitcher. I don't remember a lecture from her, but I'm certain I was scolded about acting too grown up, too fast. I have a dark scar on my right leg to this day to remind me of that moment. The day when I wanted to test the perfection of beauty and instead left myself damaged. I struggled to be who my parents dreamed I would be and who I wanted to be.

It did not help that in the early stages of my budding struggle for authenticity, somewhere in the process of starting school, my parents decided to change the way my name was pronounced. Around my family, from birth, my name had been pronounced: "May-yuh." Parents, grandparents, uncles, aunts, cousins, all said it this way. But just before my first day of school, my dad held a sort of a conference with Mom and me to tell me they'd been saying it wrong all those years. My father had been the one to select my name, had signed the birth certificate, the whole nine yards. For some reason or another, he had gone along with my mother's desire to pronounce it differently.

"It's supposed to be *My-yuh*," he told us both. Maya, like the famed author, Maya Angelou. "It means the first flower of spring," he said. When Google became a thing, I found out that was bullshit, and no such meaning was ever attached to the name, but it's distinctly what he told me.

I looked back and forth between my parents. They did not give me a say in that conversation but had they, I would have had nothing to offer up. If Dad said they had been saying it wrong, well, then it was wrong.

I stepped into Club Hill Elementary School for the first time at the age of five, after years of being May-yuh, and I was introduced to my first schoolteacher as My-yuh. As I began to make friends with other classmates and they'd ask my name, there was always a momentary pause as I had to think about the pronunciation. My-yuh, I would introduce, and then give a shy smile.

But at home, with family, I was still May-yuh. I had two names to go with my two existences. I was one person at home, another out in the world. I took on the My-yuh name and persona so well that eventually, I would become embarrassed if my family would slip and call me May-yuh when one of my friends was over. I told a friend in the fourth grade it was just a nickname and shrugged it off, but it had irked me deeply when Mom called out my other name by accident. It was like a secret being outed. I was the Fort Knox of childhood secrets and did not stand for any breaches.

Little Maya was so nervous about her goals of achievement they spewed out of her mouth on the first day of school for five consecutive years. I'd apologize to my mom as she'd instruct me to go brush my teeth again, and she'd clean the vomit up off the floor.

The nerves, in the beginning, had just a few, typical focal points such as: Would I make friends and be liked? How was I going to adjust to being away from home for so long each day? I also wanted to please my parents, especially my mother.

During my first-grade picture day, I sat down, offering a closed-lip smile that was immortalized in a photograph. It was 1986, and Mom had dressed me up in a fashion I can only liken to the then first lady, Nancy Reagan. My hair was slicked up into a perfect bun on the top of my head, with a satin red ribbon tied around the base, not a strand of hair out of position. I wore a white button-down shirt with red trim around the crisp collar, a red sweater vest and a red tie. I became her walking Queen Anne chair.

So began my preppy fashionable ascent through grade school. My attire and even my selection of school supplies was, ultimately, determined by my mom. In second grade, while most kids ran up the steps to the front of the school, their *New Kids on the Block* or *Transformers* backpacks jostling with every leap and shimmy, I was carrying a plastic, red briefcase. It had been one of many stacked as part of a display near the back-to-school clothes as Mom and I shopped at the local Mervyn's a couple of weeks before the first day of class. She thought it was the cutest thing and would add to my studious and well-kempt appearance. I was going to enter second grade dressed as a scholar fit for Harvard or Yale.

While I would have preferred a Punky Brewster backpack to match the pink, green, and white Punky Brewster sneakers I owned, I wound up with the most inconvenient school bag a kid could carry.

First of all, the plastic stank like rotting, dried fish. When I flipped back the plastic clasps to open it once we got it home, the spoiled smell wafted under my nose like the green odorous animation in Looney Toons. Opening a can of anchovies would have fragranced the room like potpourri by comparison. Mom said it just needed to air out and be cleaned, so she sprayed some substance on the inside and we sat it out in the garage. A few days later, when she said I could decorate the outside with the stickers that had come with the purchase, the briefcase smelled like fish *and* chemicals.

Still, my mother swore it would be cute for me to carry, and I dutifully decorated the outside with stickers that wouldn't stay adhered to the grainy plastic exterior. What was worse was when I got it to school. Other kids hung their backpacks on hooks in the blue open cabinet that lined the wall. But I had to place that briefcase in the bottom, resting it on top of forgotten jackets. The first day that I had homework and had to pack textbooks inside of it, my hatred for that plastic, fishy piece of luggage grew tenfold. With just two textbooks in it, I swear it felt like I was hauling twenty-pound dumbbells in my tiny seven-year-old hands. I couldn't carry a single book in the thing and hold it with just one hand. I needed both. As I stood out front of the school, waiting for my Uncle Melvin to pick me up, the plastic handle pressed into my flesh, cutting and creasing and eventually causing my palms to sting and ache as I tried desperately to stand and hold that heavy ass thing up. Eventually, I developed blisters and calluses from the few minutes I had to carry it before and after school each day.

One afternoon, I attempted to move a little too swiftly with that briefcase, forgetting its weight of it and as I turned, it dragged me down in the opposite direction. I went skidding over the rocky paved front of the school and scraped up my hands badly as I let go, and it bounced over the ground, textbooks flying out as the plastic latches broke. All I cared about was my scraped-up hands that burned like hell. That was the last day I ever carried it.

Sans briefcase, I was still always styled from the crown of my head to the soles of my shoes for school each day. The more my teachers praised me for my appearance and how cute I was always dressed, the more my mother seemed to feel a sense of her own accomplishment. I know this because she came home to share with the family that a co-worker of hers at Zales had a friend who worked at my elementary school. Mom said something like, "She said the whole staff thinks you are just the cutest thing and are always dressed *so* nice." My mom's chest lifted with pride as her face lit up like an open sign in front of a convenience store: bright and welcoming. I suppose it did make me feel a bit more special at school knowing that the other teachers even discussed me beyond the classroom.

It wasn't just my dress that got me attention back then, either. I had long hair that hung down well below my shoulders. Mom had given my thick, natural hair a relaxer for the first time at the age of three. With regular maintenance and oiling, it had grown to hang low on my back, something that, at the time, I was taught was to be viewed as a source of beauty for a Black girl. A form of beauty, not of our culture, was attached to me like a red stamp of approval. I knew a handful of other Black girls at school; none had long hair like me. The same at church. My hair was a talking point, a source of status within my own people's community, and I didn't quite understand why it mattered so much. I didn't mind the flattery or attention I received over it.

"What relaxer do you use on her head?"

"Girl, what moisturizer are you using on all that hair of hers?" The ladies at church always questioned my mother as I stood beside her in the church parking lot after service, pretending not to be listening to the conversation going on about me. Mom would reach over and run her hair down the length of my ponytail or run her fingers through it if it were down.

"I water weigh it," she would say. It was a technique where my mom would use Johnson's Pink Lotion moisturizer and add a little water to the boar bristle hairbrush and go through my strands with it. She believed the combination of water and oil kept my chemically-straightened hair healthy, shining, and, most importantly to her, long.

Before school, my mom would slick my hair into a ponytail, bun, or pull it half up on occasion so the rest could hang. But it was always, always, smoothed and curled neatly.

Looking over the map, stories, and a few flashes of blurry images in an apartment with putrid green kitchen tile is all that I have from my earliest years. The first full memory is of daydreaming at my window at our home on Flannigan Street.

Flannigan Street was where Nathan molested me when I was five. Flannigan Street was where Dustin wanted to play house when I was six.

My eyes don't leave the paper. I didn't want to look at the faces following along with my story even though they had all gone before me. I had witnessed each of their emotional journeys, shed tears with them, hugged them. I was the last of the group to speak, and this felt more daunting than comforting.

"Dustin didn't know what Nathan was already doing to me," I begin.

While I was still in elementary school, Dustin had started middle school. He and I would hang out in front of his house, listening to Gloria Estefan and Steve Winwood music on his little brother's plastic boombox, talking about life at school and the movies we both liked. I told him about the boys I had crushes on and how I had hoped to get their attention. His little brother was just a toddler and wasn't allowed to join us outside yet.

Dustin's house wasn't directly in line with ours, so it left a blind spot out of our front bay window to the narrow part between his house and his neighbor's. We would sometimes sit with our backs against the brick wall, cross-legged on the grass in front of the fence in this little space, just talking.

It was in that little sliver of property, after months of hanging out together, that he asked if I wanted to play a game. I knew what he was getting at. It was the same type of game Nathan had been playing with me for about a year. Dustin called the game "Mommy and Daddy" and said we would pretend to be married and do things like mommies and daddies do.

177

If any words left my mouth for consent or otherwise, I can't remember. I knew that this game would involve touching me between my legs.

I made a big dramatic show playing the part of the mommy. I mimed washing dishes and made comments about the baby. That's when he asked if he could touch the baby. I paused, feigning misunderstanding. He stepped forward, and I stepped back, the threads of my cotton shirt snagging against the brick wall of his house, latched down like a rat tail in a trap.

He said the baby was "here" and put his hand between my legs. He began to rub and massage the spot. I looked at everything but his face as he made groaning noises to simulate sex. He took my hand and placed it over the crotch of his jeans, and that's when I said I had to go home.

I scampered away with a feeling that was commonplace at this point: shame. As I stepped through the front door of our home, I filed Dustin's new game under my growing list of secrets. That wouldn't be the first or the last time he'd seek me out for playtime.

Dustin was problematic, not just because of the abuse he inflicted on me and shrugged off as a game, but because of his behavior at home. He had run away more than once. I can remember his stepfather coming to our house one afternoon after school, asking if I had seen Dustin. I answered honestly that I hadn't. He asked if Dustin had said anything to me about leaving. I again responded no.

Mom told me later that evening that Dustin had run away, and his parents and the police were looking for him. I don't think that I even worried about him. The haze of that conversation and that day faded with me not caring if he was out in the darkness alone or if he had food or shelter. If he had run away, I told myself, it must have been for a good reason.

Eventually, he was found, no one seems to remember exactly how they tracked him down, but it was a brief reunion with his mother and stepfather. They shipped him off to Louisiana to live with his birth father, so I was left to ride my bike and roller-skate up and down Flannigan Street unmolested. I was free, and every breath I took outdoors on those days was a relief.

"Before Dustin wanted to *play*, there was a time in kindergarten when a boy in the class had wanted to play in the same way," I explain. "He had thrown a blanket over one of the large cubbies, pulling me inside with him. All the other kids seemed to have known why we went in there. I don't remember doing anything, but I knew what he was hinting at."

Someone had snitched to the teacher, and she had thrown the blanket back, revealing the faces of two scared kids who hadn't yet done anything out of line.

Playing with boys always seemed to come back to the same thing.

My cousins were the first true female friends I had, even though they were older. My cousin Serena was like a big sister, and I spent many weekends with her at my grandparents' house or her townhouse with her mom, my "Ainty."

My cousin Lena was the oldest of the grandkids. I'd spend the night with her on a Saturday, and we would all go to church on Sunday, where I'd meet up with my mom and JJ.

One weekend, I was invited to take a trip down to Houston with Lena, Aunt Kathy, and her new husband, my Uncle Junior. His sister, Francene, lived in Houston with her husband, Victor. Francene frequently visited Dallas and the church where both her mother, Mrs. Donaldson, and her brother were members. I liked her, too. She always had a gift for me or would slip me a few dollars to get myself a treat.

I was seven and excited about the road trip despite the circumstances. Victor was sick with some form of cancer, and they went down to visit as his condition worsened.

We made the four-hour road trip down I-45 to Houston's Third Ward, a historically Black neighborhood of prominence. I pretended to sleep most of the way, laying my head on Lena's lap as she played with my hair, treating me like an infant in her care. With my eyes closed, I listened to Tears for Fears and Cindy Lauper along with Billy Ocean and Chaka Khan.

When we made it to Francene's house, we were not the only visitors there for the weekend. Another relative of Junior's was there with a team of boys around my age or slightly older. I don't know how they were connected to Junior, but they were comfortably settled into the house.

I said hello to Francene as she hugged me, but I didn't go into the bedroom to see Victor. The house smelled different. It had the odor of old homes, the lingering scent of thousands of meals in the wallpaper, and the dank aroma of an old bookstore because of the frequent floods in Houston. I sniffed something else when we walked in—the faint odor of sickness and approaching death. Victor's bedroom was upstairs, and Lena and I had a guest room to sleep in down the hall to avoid disturbing him. I didn't venture up those stairs until it was close to bedtime.

As adults do, they left the boys and me to entertain ourselves so they could sit around and catch up on Victor's latest health reports and family gossip. A part of me resented Lena for being old enough to be a part of the conversation while I was banished outdoors for playtime with kids I didn't know. I could always find ways to adjust, though, so I stepped outside onto the wide front porch. The cement above the stairs had been painted a dark forest green at one point and was chipped in spots from years in the Texas weather.

The memory of that day doesn't carry forward in a sequence of events. It doesn't establish my conversation with them or even introductions or any of their names. Instead, the scene cuts to me on my back, lying still against that hard, weather-worn porch, chipped green paint underneath my head and limbs, and the boys circling around me like warlocks around a sacrifice.

I was told we were all going to play doctor. As the only girl, I was the patient. The four or five boys there either crowded closer for a better look at the lamb's body or to execute some part of the imaginary procedure I had to undergo.

I have no memory of consenting to another game in which my body would be touched, only that I ended up on my back with a familiar fear flowing through my veins.

One of the boys lifted my shirt and couldn't have seen anything impressive as I still wasn't even fifty pounds, underdeveloped, and without so much as a hint of breasts. The same boy told me to spread my legs a little wider. I hesitated, and he frowned, so I did it. Various hands rubbed at the juncture of my legs. I am unsure how I could have remained awake or even alive because, like so many times before, I held my breath. Maybe from all the times with Nathan, I had already developed the lungs of a scuba diver.

The leader of this medical examination told me to sit up. He then instructed me to kiss his little brother, a boy a little younger than me. I adamantly shook my head.

"Yes," he shot back. "Or we'll tell."

Now, how in the hell *them* telling on *me* for not wanting to kiss a kid I didn't know after they had rubbed their grubby little hands all over my body and frightened me to the point of compliance, I would love to explain. But I can't. I was a kid. Just like with Nathan, more than anything, I feared getting in trouble for "playing dirty."

What that gaggle of boys didn't know was that I was used to that threat—that it had been enough to silence me before and keep me in submission.

I expected my first kiss to be a whimsical, fantastical moment of pure love, a deep expression of burning passion. It was supposed to be just the way Humphrey Bogart wrapped his arm around Katherine Hepburn, clutching her shoulder while his hand pressed to her cheek, tilting her face upwards as his lips met hers after weeks of tension building between them on that rickety ship in one of my favorite films as a child *The African Queen*.

Instead, the gang of voyeurs leaned in for a closer look as I closed my eyes and felt sandpaper.

His lips were rough and cracked, and I wanted it to be over as quickly as possible. I tried to shut down every part of me that could feel. But that day, I couldn't find my mental safe haven. I was very present. Someone said for me to keep it going, that it had to be more than just a peck, so I kept my lips pressed against his crusty little mouth before finally pulling away. That, *that*, was my first kiss.

The memory cuts to me being on my back again and a hand under my shirt, against the flesh of my hip, when the front door swung open. The boys scrambled, talking quickly as one of them grabbed my arm and yanked me up to my feet so fast I almost fell over. They began pretending to act out some game of play, speaking faster than a speed reader. All I could do was stand there, petrified with fear that we, *I*, was going to get in trouble.

The scene dips to black, and the only other memory I have is a trip to the mall with some money Francene gave me. All the while, walking over linoleum buffed so hard I could see myself clearly in the faux marble, passing ammonia-wiped windows, and riding up the jerky escalator, my mind replaying what had happened with those boys. It stayed with me much longer than the episodes with Dustin and Nathan. The fear of getting in trouble didn't fade when we left the house either. It clung to my shoulders, fingers of an invisible skeleton, squeezing to remind me it was there. It was always there.

I returned home from Houston that weekend, and when I entered our house, I finally filed that weekend into the part of my brain that liked to forget.

It was not until a few months later, when Victor passed away, that the file cabinet was reopened. We drove down to his hometown of Hearne, a three-hour trip to an old white, wood-frame church on a clay lot. I wasn't expecting to see the perpetrators because the funeral was not in Houston. There was no anxiety about the trip itself, although flashes of what had happened that day popped into my mind with each mention of Francene's name.

Mourners were seated shoulder to shoulder, thigh to thigh in that small-town church, and my family was relegated to sitting in the choir stands so there would be room to accommodate the crowd saying goodbye to Victor. I couldn't have spotted them even if I had been looking.

After the funeral, my cousin Lena approached me with a smirk. Her eyes always turned up a bit at the corners like a cat, so stretched over her wiry braces, her smirk, intentional or not, came across as sinisterly feline. She stopped me in my tracks and began the sentence by naming one of the boys. I hadn't even remembered their names, so I squinted as she began to relay what he had said to her.

"He said you looked pretty today." Her eyebrow arched with intrigue and amusement.

I wanted to vomit. Lena felt the need to share this with my mom and aunts, who all fawned over the cuteness of it all. The name she spoke, I had no way of knowing if he had been one to actually touch me, but did it matter? In my eyes, even if he hadn't, he was an accomplice. There was no differentiation between the bystander and the executor. All shared guilt.

I said nothing as I marinated in disgust on the car ride back home.

I was too young to process how all these instances of sexual abuse were building a trauma profile for me the size of Mount Everest.

It was affecting me in ways I didn't quite understand. Yet, I was becoming more and more aware of what sex was and how your body could respond to it.

I began acting out in ways I didn't even know were acting out. I was still the doll my mother dressed me to be on the outside, but my playing, even at school, was becoming far more adult than for a child my age.

One day after recess in the first grade, I sat at my desk, sweaty from being out in the white-hot sun of late spring in Texas. I was trying to slow my breathing after running all the way from the back of the playground to line up at the school's backdoor to return to class. Grass stickers stuck to my cotton scrunch-top socks, and I wiped my forehead before bending down to pick off a few. When I sat back up, the other teacher from the class that shared the same large space as mine was striding towards me, her lips pressed together; wrinkles stretched out from them like cracks in pavement.

We had a reward system back then. If you had a good day, did all your work, and showed good behavior, you got a stamp on a piece of paper with a calendar on it that was taped to the top corner of each of our desks. I had already earned my stamp for the day from my reading that morning. As she approached, I sat up straight, almost ready to throw my arms in front of my face. I didn't ever expect a teacher to strike me, but she looked like she was two steps away from doing so. Then she raised the permanent red marker in her hand and put a bloody X over my stamp. "No." She sneered at me, staring me down.

I nodded my head shamefully as she spun on her heels and marched back across to her part of the classroom.

She didn't have to explain what led her to put the X on my stamp.

Our school's playground stretched on for nearly a full acre behind the school, all the way up to a fence that neighbored a creek. Near that fence was an old silver slide that would burn the hell out of your legs if you got on it in the summer or spring and a swing set. I don't know why it was so far away from all the other equipment, but when you were out that far, you could only just hear the whistle signaling for all the kids to come back in.

I had ventured back there with a girl whose hair was so thick and black it looked like a wig, and a platinum-haired boy. His hair was so blonde, in that sunlight it shined like a dime caught in the light. I think he was a student in that angry teacher's class. Maybe he was a favorite of hers, or maybe he was popular and well-loved by the other kids and teachers. I don't remember much about him other than that white *Village of the Damned* hair.

He pitched the idea to us of playing "Mommy and Daddy." This game was becoming more of a way of life than a novelty to me, and the other girl agreed. I agreed out of habit. I agreed because I knew what I'd feel when we played.

We had to be careful on that end of that slide that none of our skin touched it, unless we wanted a burn mark that would blister up later.

He deemed that I should be the mommy, and she was to be the baby. He told baby to go lay down, and she sat down under the shade of the slide, pretending to be asleep. With me, he sat me down on the very edge of that slide and lifted the hem of my dress, exposing my panties. He positioned himself between my thighs and began pumping in his jeans up and down against me, bumping and acting out sex.

I fixed my dress when I heard the faint blow of a whistle and ran with my classmates to line up.

This teacher must have seen it all from a distance.

There was no lecture, no pulling me aside, not even a phone call to my parents. I wonder now, if I *had* gotten in trouble the way I suppose I should have, what would have happened? Would I have sat in the principal's office or with the counselors and told them this kind of thing had been happening to me for more than a year? That I was sorry, and I didn't want it to keep happening, but it was like a record on repeat and I was the artist singing the same track over and over and over again?

I don't know if he got an X or if I was singled out in the discipline. Shame reached out for me at my little desk, clutching me and not letting go.

When my teacher finally came over to my desk to hand me a reward for having another great week as one of her best students, she stopped and stood up when she saw the red X.

"What is this for?" she questioned.

I played dumb and lied. "I don't know." I shrugged pitifully.

She glanced at the other teacher, who was busy with a student. Something in her eyes told me she was questioning why I had been a target. There was something about this other teacher that I could read from her face that she didn't trust. She never suspected I had been doing something *wrong*, so she ignored the stamp and handed me my two Jolly Ranchers and a pencil for a week of hard work.

By the time I entered second grade, the abuse at home had continued whenever Nathan came around, but there were no other violators.

***

"Multiple abusers and assaults." Tennie frowns.

"I wish I could say it stopped there," I say. I pause for a moment and study the life map, a compass pointing from one painful event to another.

"Middle school fucking sucked," I say to break the tension, and everyone laughs.

"Middle school is hell," Kim returns.

"When I was in the seventh grade, I started in theater." I finally look at the group as I talk, looking into each of the faces.

"There was this boy in class. I don't remember his name. I just remember he was considered one of the bad boys. He was already getting into trouble, and people said he was part of a gang. Even though he was in the seventh grade with us, he was a few years older."

"We were working on a production of *Charlotte's Web*. I was playing the Gander. It wasn't much of a production, seventh grade and all, but we were working on the stage in the cafeteria and creating the set. The curtain was closed, and there were just a few of us behind it with the stage lights on as we made parts for the barn. We had a little worktable."

"That boy, he'd made comments to me and seemed like he was flirting, but I didn't think much of it. I didn't think boys even liked me then cause I was so awkward. But all of a sudden, just out of the clear blue, he grabbed me by both my arms, lifted me up, and threw me on my back on the worktable. I was scared and in shock, so I wasn't fighting. I lay there, my back burning from hitting the tabletop so hard."

"He said something about 'getting at that pussy' and then jammed his hand down the front of my jeans. I was frozen."

"Someone said something. I don't remember if it was a girl or a boy, but somebody said something, and he stopped and let me up. I think it happened during sixth period. I spent the rest of the day walking around school, trying not to think about it and wondering if any classmates would say something, but no one did.

"I rode the school bus back then. There was a girl named Lauren who lived on the street below mine, and we'd gone to elementary school together. I sat at the back of the bus, angled in my seat, and told her what happened."

"Why don't I feel like I believe this happened?" she'd replied casually.

Words stopped flowing from my lips. It was the first time I'd tried to tell anyone about the violation of my body, and it was met with skepticism. The saddest part was that I was confiding in another teenage girl, and she was already programmed not to believe me.

"Later in the school year, that same boy got expelled for groping a teacher's ass when she was bent over," I explain. I see Julianne blow out a breath as Tennie shakes her head.

In middle school, I wasn't allowed to date. I could wear fingernail polish to parties when I was thirteen but immediately had to remove it the next day.

My first true longing to be with a boy, to feel his kiss and hold his hand, to be somebody's somebody in life, was Joseph Miller. Biracial, the son of a white mother and a Black father, Joseph was tall, athletic, and unlike any boy I had known before. I had never actually been in class with a student of multiple ethnicities.

His almond skin looked so warm and smooth. I imagined it felt like satin or warm cream to the touch as I would stare across math class at him timidly that first year at middle school. His hair wasn't textured but bone straight and gelled into a perfect arch on his head. His eyes turned down at the corners as if he were sad, but he was always cracking jokes and making his classmates, especially me, without specific intention, laugh.

I wouldn't refer to Joseph as my sexual awakening. Not yet. There was still an innocuous tingle that trickled up my spine and a quickening of my pulse whenever he looked my way or remotely acknowledged me.

Childlike infatuation that it was, my mind convinced my heart that melodramatic yearning was the only way he could possibly be my "true love." Summers spent at granny's and granddad's watching *All My Children* and *General Hospital* had taught me that there was no passion without sobbing, no caring without obsession, no tenderness without struggle.

Someone told someone who told someone else that I liked Joseph. I'm all but certain this started somewhere with my best friends in middle school, Erica and Thao.

Thao was the daughter of Vietnamese immigrants, and when I met her in the sixth grade, she had adopted the custom of taking on a more American nickname to be called at school. When roll was called on the first day of class, as the teacher tried to pronounce her name, Thao knew she was referring to her, interrupted and told her she went by "Jenny." In the eighth grade, she began wearing blue contacts. Even though her parents only spoke Vietnamese when I was around, she always only answered in English.

My goth, Mexican-American friend Erica was effortlessly pretty and even more effortlessly cool. She wore Converse with wide-leg jeans and flannel shirts, usually all in black or dark green. Her hair, black as a raven's wing, was always shiny even when she claimed she hadn't done a thing to it. She had a terrible habit of calling me and singing along to Mariah Carey badly and offkey at the top of her lungs. When I'd hang up on her, she'd just call back and keep calling. I was held hostage by the ringing phone until I allowed her to complete the song. Later, when she had her first car, we would speed out of the high school parking lot, voices raised along to Violent Femmes and rapping along with the Beastie Boys.

Memory serves me here to remind me that after my romantic inclinations were part of the sixth-grade gossip mill, I asked Thao to find out if Joseph did like me back.

Oh, woe to my anguished young heart when he told her he liked me as "just a friend." Banished to the cage-like cordial boundaries of *ugh*, friendship, my fixation deepened. The more it seemed I couldn't date him, the greater the longing. I'd listen to sad love songs, and the theatrics of my brain would produce entire scenes where my unrequited love was dismissed, I, the victim of cruel, malevolent love. I would come home from school and detail in my diary even the tiniest of interactions with him.

In eighth grade, my fixation began to border on obsession. As a student council member, I had a class period where I served only to assist the school's administration office. Two other students and I would make copies, put away files, send notes to teachers to retrieve students from class for appointments, and read the morning announcements. We also had access to student information cards and files. I purposefully searched for Joseph's. I knew where his locker was, and at the time, one hallmark of a middle school couple in love was sharing a locker. My fantasizing led me to open that card file and memorize his locker combination.

One day, in a deep pretending episode, I walked straight up to his locker and began turning the knob to the combination from the card. I wasn't a good five seconds into this process when a voice came from behind. "What are you doing?"

I cringed and snapped out of whatever realm I had been in and back into that moment to turn slowly and looked into the angry eyes of my crush.

"Uh," I stammered, mouth open. All cognitive abilities failed me.

He said something else angrily, but I didn't even hear it. I slowly began to ease away, head lowered and berating myself. I wrapped my arms tightly around my books and headed to class.

"What were you *doing*?" Erica asked me later at lunch.

I shrugged. "I don't really know."

"He's pissed," she added.

"Yeah ..." I said distantly.

I had no rational explanation for my actions other than I had wanted so badly for my fantasy to become real, to be sharing a locker with the boy of my dreams; I immersed myself into actions that took me completely out of reason and the present moment.

Had Joseph even considered me as girlfriend potential, I would never have been allowed to date him. I imagine that dating in middle school would have been an offense punishable with a chastity belt if my parent's lectures indicated the consequence for disobedience with the opposite sex.

Still, there was nothing sexual about my preteen love mania. In my head, the most we would have ever done was kiss and maybe a little heavy petting above the waist. Good touch/bad touch, there was no distinction for me. Any intimacy with boys landed me on the naughty list.

One summer, Thao became friends with a few high schoolers from a neighboring school district. They were freshmen, and we were just preparing to enter the eighth grade. Thao, Erica, and I spoke on the phone with them daily, a summer practice that saw us all reaching for our clear phones as soon as we woke up.

With Thao's new high school pals, I was on the receiving end of a coveted three-way call. Back then, this innovative breakthrough let you hold a call with two other people on a landline phone. You had to pay extra for the feature, something my parents would never have dreamed of doing, but Thao's parents didn't mind. It was on a three-way call that I was first introduced to Shawn. He was funny and made me laugh. The three of us would spend the entire day on the phone talking about music, movies, and our other friends until I had to bail out just before my parents got home. On a few occasions, Shawn called me without Thao on the line, having gotten my number from her.

I had explicitly told Shawn during a call that I was not allowed to talk to boys on the phone. Still, one evening, the house phone rang. Since it was evening, I thought it might be my grandmother or aunts for my mom, so I let it ring. A minute later, my bedroom door flung open with such force the knob hit the wall. Mom's face was contorted with contempt.

"Some boy is on the phone for you," she said and shoved the cordless phone at me.

Afraid, I slowly reached out and grabbed the phone. I gulped and took a moment to compose myself before my own anger rose. "Hello?"

"Hey!" I heard Shawn reply.

I glanced up at Mom, her hands on her hips by then. I was in trouble, and, in that moment, the blame shifted to him.

"I told you I can't talk on the phone to guys!" I hissed.

"*Okay*," he defended. "Sorry!"

I didn't say another word. I pressed a button and ended the call.

Mom's words hurled at me were a jumble but ended with me agreeing obediently to not talk to boys. My phone was taken away for three days. When I finally was able to get it back and call Thao, I immediately asked about Shawn.

"Yeah," she said. "He was sort of sad."

"I got in trouble, though!"

"I know," she said. "We won't do calls anymore."

And we didn't. I lost a fun friend that summer, even if we had never met face to face.

It was also during middle school that I became something like an aunt for the first time.

Nathan and his girlfriend had become pregnant, and during my seventh-grade year, she gave birth to a baby boy. They found a place to live together in East Texas. Even though the sexual abuse at his hands had stopped, I was still happy to know that he lived more than two hours away. He had begun his own family life and seemed to be out of mine.

At the time, I had no fears that his son may be in danger of being molested. It never entered my mind as even a possibility. As Nathan's victim, I assumed I was targeted because I was female.

I tried to play the role of a loving guardian. I tried to be excited about the birth of this child and taking on a new family title other than daughter, granddaughter, sister, and cousin. It was extremely hard for me to feel excited about the new member of our family. I found it even more difficult to connect with the infant emotionally, even the first time I cradled him awkwardly in my arms. I played the part when necessary, helping to give him a bath in the sink or feed him bottles and change his diapers when they dropped him off for a weekend visit. But the loving bond of family, the connection and protection I felt I should feel as his "aunt" was not there. A part of him was from a person who had hurt me for a very long time. I never blamed the child for that or resented his existence because of it. It wasn't his fault, just like the abuse had not been mine. Mentally, I disconnected from any responsibility or obligation expected of me to care for the baby.

He was born as I was entering a new stage of my life. My body was changing, and so was my temperament. The following summer, at age thirteen, I would begin my period. I was foolishly excited the day it arrived, so much so that I called my mother at work to tell her "Aunt Flo" had arrived in town.

"Already?" she exclaimed. I found that reaction puzzling since all my friends had already gotten their periods, and I was the late bloomer of the group.

I was also feeling down more days than I felt up. I was sad at my awkwardness, immaturity, and the archaic family beliefs I was raised by. As I was becoming a teen, depression was coming along for the hormonal ride.

The short amount of time when students gathered in the gym each morning at middle school could set the tone for the entire day. I would deboard the bus and make my way to the gym, the walls trembling with teen talk. We would wait about twenty minutes until the bell rang, signaling us to disperse to our first-period class.

One morning, I ascended the bleachers and dropped my backpack down beside me as I gathered with Thao, Erica, and a few other girls, including Melissa Beddingfield. Melissa and I had gone to elementary together and were sort of friends. She would invite me to her birthday parties, and she sometimes sat with us at lunch, but I wasn't as close to her as I was Erica and Thao. She, like us, drifted in and out of the uber-preppy and popular crowd to the alternative kids that seemed to have no rhyme or reason for their union. She was also one of the very first mean girls I ever knew.

Unsuspectingly, I sat down, not realizing I would be a target for her random ire. I was barely even adding input to the conversation, just trying to catch up after my late arrival to the chat, when she suddenly stomped her feet repeatedly, pumped her fist, and looked at me.

"I'm gonna jump you today," she declared and began to laugh as she stomped harder.

My forehead creased like a dress shirt out of the washing machine. "What?" I replied, bewildered. My mouth hung open.

"I said, I'm going to jump you today." She slowed her words as she repeated herself, glaring at me as if I was stupid for not understanding her the first time.

"Uh ... why?" I shook my head in disbelief.

"Cause I want to." She shrugged. "And you need to get your ass beat."

My head jerked, and I looked to my other friends for confirmation that I was hearing her correctly. None of them made eye contact with me. No one interjected. What the hell had I walked into that morning?

"I don't understand," I finally said through narrowed eyes.

She let out a cackle. "You just wait. During PE, I'm jumping you."

My body began to quake with a mixture of fear and anxiety; although it was a small movement, not visible to others, I could feel it. Something was making my blood pump faster. *I don't deserve this.*

Then the bell rang.

Melissa spent the rest of the day telling anyone who would listen, from homeroom to the lunch line, that she would make good on her promise and jump me. My friends were sympathetic, but no one was offering up any defense for me. I walked through the halls, feeling the eyes on me as the clock ticked closer to the seventh period when we had PE. I was quiet most of the day. I was nervous and sad. I had never been in a fight, and I was afraid of the pain that may come with each punch or kick, but also because no one for the life of me could explain why Melissa had decided I "needed my ass beat."

When seventh period arrived, I went to the girls' dressing room and into one of the stalls, pulling on my sweats for our run. Melissa was still flapping her gums, and I was muted in reflective and petrified silence.

Our teacher told us to line up at the door. When the door opened, I sprinted right out the door until a hand crossed my stomach and stopped me. It was another girl in my class, a Black girl with pigtails. We were acquaintances in class but didn't speak much outside of it. She had heard Melissa's talk that day and knew what was coming.

"Don't run," she said.

I locked eyes with her. My instinct had always been to run away from harm. My instinct that first afternoon when Nathan had put his hands on me had been to run. I understood her meaning. I needed to stand my ground. This was middle school, and I would never live it down if I ran off like a coward.

So, with her at my side, I began to walk slowly towards the tennis courts where we needed to run laps.

Melissa appeared in front of me with a group of onlookers ready to watch the beatdown. She had the same cackle from earlier that morning. I was walking forward as she took steps backward, but I kept my head up.

"You ready?" she said to me, an eyebrow steeply arched.

"Melissa." I sighed and lifted my hands in penance for whatever perceived wrong I had done. "I don't want to fight you."

"Shut up!" she snapped.

We both stopped walking, and the circle of girls around us drew closer.

Then she shoved me. With the force of her hands on my shoulders, she pushed hard, and I took one step back to balance myself. But I didn't fall over.

My back straightened.

"Don't put your hands on me," I said in a voice that seemed disembodied. It felt as if someone else was speaking, though I was certain I had said the words.

She laughed like the wicked witch of the west again, stepped forward, and shoved me with all her might.

Time stopped. The sun in the sky was eclipsed. The world went silent. I saw nothing but the front of her face and then total and complete darkness. A second later, I felt the cut on my knuckle.

The sun appeared in the sky again, and I could hear the "ow's" of the girls around me as Melissa yelped in pain. Confused, I looked down at my hand. There was a cut on my right hand, on the knuckle of my third finger where my fist had made contact with her tooth.

She began to cry, sobbing and holding her bloody mouth. I was stupefied. I had done that? I hit her? I didn't even know how to throw a punch, but somehow, I had and with enough force to knock her teeth loose and bust her lip open.

She cupped her hand under her mouth as blood rolled out, and she ran away from me, crying louder.

I looked around at all the wide eyes that were on me. I exhaled, looked at the cut on my knuckle again, and then was freed from my trance.

Melissa didn't run to tell the teacher. She couldn't. She had provoked it. If she had tried to retaliate, I felt like I could have grabbed a piece of her skin and pulled it all away, like lifting a sheet off the bed. Barely even a tug, and I would have dismantled her.

I assume she ran off to tend to her bloody mouth. I pushed through the group of girls and walked on, alone, beginning the jog with tears running down my cheeks. I wasn't crying out of remorse. I was crying out of fear.

What had burst from my body that day was the same fury I felt as a child in church, abandoned by her angel: rage.

I look at Kim. She grins and gives a fist pump that makes the entire group laugh, and despite my residual astonishment at my teenage actions, I smile too.

"The full weight of your vengeance was in that fist." Tennie tilts her head. "She paid the price for everyone who had hurt you."

It feels like I have learned an entirely new trade in that moment as her words enlighten me.

"Yes." I nod my head vigorously. "She did."

Part 3

Chapter Sixteen

Day 3 Continued

May 20, 2015

I learned I was still a virgin one drunken night in September 2004. I was twenty-four years old.

I'd met Trent when I moved to Tyler for my first on-air reporting job at one of the East Texas TV stations. He lived locally, and we'd met while I was on assignment. It was more than chemistry. He was a magnet, and I was an iron nail.

Trent was a former college football player who had grown up in the Metroplex just as I had. He'd taken a job in medical sales, Tyler being a hub for hospitals and young health professionals. At the time, we both found ourselves, two city kids, living in a town that was trying desperately to be more metropolitan than it was. Tyler was stuck somewhere between old traditions and even older money and an influx of entrepreneurs and young professionals from the big Texas cities.

Trent met up with my co-workers and me at a club one Saturday night. I'd had a few drinks, but I was already strongly attracted to him. The alcohol in my system only churned faster through my body, giving me that euphoric feeling of freedom by the way he made my heart race whenever he was near.

"Trent is the kind of guy who will have you on your back and get in your panties so fast you'll be trying to figure out how it happened," I'd told one of our photographers on a car ride to the scene of a story.

"He's a charming S.O.B.," he confirmed.

Trent had a female roommate who was like an annoying older sister to him rather than any possible love interest. She dated here and there and was a socialite within the young oil baron's crowd. She'd come with him to the club that night. After last call, we'd spilled out into the Texas night, summer still clinging to us like a black bat enwrapping us in its winged heat. Trent's roommate was adamant that she wanted him to drive her home.

"What happened to that guy you were talking to?" he asked as I lingered at his side and leaned in, interjecting myself into the conversation.

"I don't want him to take me," she whined with heavy eyelids and words that strung together without the usual polish of her articulation. "I don't want to do anything with him tonight, and if he drives me, I know I'll end up hooking up with him."

Trent's gaze firmly met my own, and the hair on my arms rose. We'd danced, bodies pressed together under a nicotine cloud amongst other writhing bodies. My ears were ringing from the volume of the music in the club, but I'd ignored it all and felt only him grinding against me as I moved in rhythm with the music and his hips.

"Just let him take you home. You don't have to do anything with him," I said. She looked at me, baffled. I could see she wondered why I would have anything to say in the matter. My eyes flicked back up at Trent and saw the same look of curiosity as he bent his body over mine. Then he flashed that panty-tearing smirk.

"No!" she protested and staggered. Trent reached out and grabbed her arm to steady his inebriated roommate. He looked back at me apologetically. He let go of her once he felt she was steady. He turned to me, and I leaned into the hug he gave me. My hand snaked around the back of his neck as he held me to him, and his large hands circled my waist. He felt warm. He felt safe. He smelled of cologne and cigarette smoke from the club.

"Goodnight," I whispered into his ear as I raised onto the tips of my toes, the hug lingering as my body slid down against his, and I rested back on my heels.

Silently, he let me go, but his hand dragged down my hip before his touch was gone. He grabbed his roommate and pretty much tossed her into his truck.

I shouldn't have driven, but I did. I drove the two blocks straight up the road to what was my very first apartment, all on my own. I'd taken the job at the TV station five months before. I met Trent almost immediately. We'd been friends, though we both knew we wanted more. He had a girlfriend back home—I was aware that he'd had several flings since arriving in town. We'd gone on beer runs across the lake to where the liquor stores were located right at the county line. Our little part of the woods was dry, and we had to cross the bridge like bandits to grab our stock of fire water.

One night we raced along the highway, windows cracked in his truck. I breathed in the lake air, aware of my heart beating almost as fast as Trent was driving. I was relaxed in my seat, content with being in the small cab with a foot of space between our bodies. I was becoming my own woman away from home. I had started a new job and was living in a new city. The life changes were staggering, but I was blinded and distracted by desire. I ignored all my red flags, the same way I ignored all of Trent's.

He'd turned up the radio and played a song for me by Babyface. The balladeer cooed about the next time he'd get to see his love again, completing him. Trent reached for the volume knob and turned it up as I looked at the full white moon reflecting on the nighttime waters.

"You like this song?" he asked.

"I love this song." I smiled.

Trent was happy with my response as his smirk appeared, and he drove with one hand, eyes looking towards me. It became our unofficial song.

That night after the club, I was back at my apartment undressing and peeling off my clothes, damp from the humidity and a full night of dancing, when I heard it. Trent's truck had a distinct sputter from the exhaust, and it roared when he accelerated. I knew to listen for it on the nights he picked me up to go to dinner or across the county line. I wasn't expecting to hear it that night.

My phone rang. I looked at the caller ID.

"I know you're outside," I answered.

"What?" He laughed. "How do you know that?"

"I know what your truck sounds like," I said, moving to my bedroom window and looking down into the parking lot. Sure enough, his black F-150 was parked right next to my Mustang.

"Look at you, Nancy Drew," he teased. Then he paused. "Should I not come up?"

I'd wanted him at the club. I'd wanted to go home with him or have him come back to my place; I didn't care which. I wanted to have sex with him that night. I'd abandoned that idea when we left the parking lot. Now, here he was without a direct invitation.

"No." I began to slide my jeans back on as I moved away from the window. "Come on up."

I fastened the button on my jeans and waited near the door. I heard footsteps outside, ascending the stairs. Then a knock.

When I opened the door, I was met with a set of confident brown eyes and a mischievously arrogant grin. "You know the sound of my truck?"

I ignored the jab at my acute awareness of all things *him*. "Come in." I motioned and stepped out of the way. Trent walked inside and looked around like it was his first time there. It wasn't, but we both knew this night was different. It smelled different. The scent of the club was still on our clothes, overpowering my potpourri on the coffee table. Even the air blowing through the vents felt different against my hot skin.

I bolted the door and then faced him. "What are you doing here?"

"It didn't seem like either of us was ready to say goodnight ..." There was a minuscule movement in his brow.

"No, it didn't," I admitted.

Trent's tongue moved over his lips. In defeat, resignation, and anticipation, I extended my hand to him, and he squeezed it tight as I led him to my bedroom. His mouth was on mine in a way I'd never kissed anyone. This kiss was filled with opportunity, not wonder of when I needed to stop things.

I was on my back, out of my clothes, and in my panties in minutes. He knelt on the bed between my legs and removed his boxers, watching me watching him.

When I saw him, *all* of him, I froze. Not just from the sight of his sizeable manhood but because I thought to tell him, *I'm a virgin*. The thing was, I wasn't sure if I was.

Trent hooked his thumbs into the sides of my panties and began to drag them down my legs as I looked up at him. My mind was screaming to say something. My voice once again was muted.

Condom. Ask him to put one on, at least. I said nothing. I was on birth control after years of battling endometriosis and polycystic ovarian syndrome, so I was protected in that regard. But I didn't know how many partners Trent had bedded without protection.

Say something. His mouth was between my thighs, soft kisses at first. Slippery, warm, and erotic, I tried to focus on the immense pleasure he was giving me, but I was stuck in my head. I thought I had time to say something. He came up, and I felt the weight of his muscular physique on top of my body as he lowered onto me. We kissed, and I tasted myself.

Then pain—a searing hot pain radiated through my core like a stabbing. I didn't cry out as he began to move. He didn't know to go slow, to take it easy with me; he just began to thrust. I knew the pain wouldn't last the whole time, so I stayed quiet and bore it. Then something warm and wet rolled down my body, dampening the sheets below me. I gripped his shoulders and gritted my teeth until something gave.

I began to moan, repeatedly crying, not mimicking what I had seen in porn and doing what I thought I should do. He coaxed genuine reactions from me as my metal headboard thumped against the wall. It was almost one in the morning, and I was sure my neighbors could hear my cries of "oh god" over and over again with that consistent thumping. I imagined they both hated and envied me.

He pulled out. Warm liquid splashed against my belly, and he rested his face on the pillow next to my head. Hot bursts of his breath tickled against my ear as he laughed lightly. "Damn. Wow. Are you okay?"

Was I?

"Yes," I murmured. I hadn't orgasmed, though it had felt good. I looked up at the ceiling as he rolled off me. When I stood, I felt my legs wobble, and in the soft lamplight of my room, I looked down and saw the crimson-soaked sheets, quilt, and comforter of my bed. I quickly grabbed the edge of the comforter and threw it over the blood stains to hide them as he rolled over onto his side.

I headed to the bathroom to clean myself up. I used wipe after wipe between my legs until they stopped appearing red. When I returned to my room, he was asleep. I grabbed an extra towel, lay it over the bloody sheets, and then climbed in beside him. Trent rolled over and draped an arm around my waist as I internally berated myself for not waiting for a committed, loving relationship.

The next morning, I pounced on his still sleeping form curled in my bed. I was sore from my navel down to my knees.

Startled, he jumped and looked at me as I grinned with childlike innocence at him, ignoring my discomfort.

"Hey! Wake up! I've got to go home today to Garland," I said as I straddled his waist, fully-clothed.

"Hmngh?" He yawned, half awake.

"I have to go," I repeated. He rubbed his eyes and groaned. Looking at me, he attempted a smile though sleepiness pulled his chin and lips down.

"So, um," I said. "There's something I need to tell you." I stayed on his lap, my butt resting on his thighs.

"What's up?" His hand stopped moving over one eye as the other brought me into focus.

"What we did … last night?" I gulped. "I never did that before."

"Seriously?" His hand flew away from his face, and he inched up closer to me, leaning on his elbows. The sheets rustled, and the bed creaked with the swiftness of his startled response. It forced me back and to move off him.

I gave a tiny shake of my head meekly in the affirmative. "You couldn't tell?"

"I thought it had been a long time for you or something." His voice shook without his usual pompousness.

"No. That was my first time."

"Oh." He nodded slowly. "Oh." He repeated louder and more strongly. "Well, now I feel bad." His brow creased so deeply that his eyebrows became one.

"Why?"

"Because that was your first time, and it should have been like ... special or whatever."

I reached out and gripped his shoulders. "It was what I wanted to happen."

"Should we have used something?"

"No, no." I tried to ease his concern, but he looked skeptical. "I've been on birth control for a while for a condition I have. We're okay." At least, I thought we were okay. I wasn't certain, but I wanted to calm the terrified young man in my bed. I didn't consider my own fear.

"Oh," he said in the same way as before.

I hugged my knees, feeling pain in my abdomen, as I scooted closer to him on the bed. Chewing the inside of my cheek, I looked at the television on my dresser. It was off, but I stared at it like it was on. "So, was I ... good?" My need for validation may have been more prominent than any time prior.

"How could you possibly have been bad?" He sat up shirtless with the covers over his waist.

"I don't know. I've heard girls can be bad in bed."

"If you just laid there, maybe. That wasn't you. Honestly, I'm surprised. You moved like you'd done those things before."

I wiggled my head and gave a cheeky grin. "I've watched a lot of training videos."

He smiled at me as he tilted his head back with laughter.

"We good?" he asked after a moment.

"Yeah, we're good. I'm sorry to have to wake you, but I'll text you this afternoon. Okay?"

"Sounds good." He rose from my bed while my eyes inventoried his naked body, and he began searching the floor for his clothes.

"'You didn't give me a choice.' That's what he told me a few weeks later," I explain as I look at the twenty-to-twenty-five-year mark near my right hip on my life map.

It's the last day of the individual intensive sessions. I am the very last in the group to have my turn. After sitting through four other sessions, I am worn out before I even begin to speak.

It reminds me of a time I got caught in the undercurrent at Galveston Island when I was seven. The tide was swelling, rolling out the sand beneath my feet, dragging my solid footing away and battering me as the waves crashed into my slender body and tossed me forward. An unseen hand seemed to wrap around my ankle and yank me back and underneath. I came back up, sputtering and gasping, as JJ held me.

I was standing still in front of a wall, but I felt like I was sputtering.

"We slept together a few more times. Then when I called him up and told him one night that I was going to cook dinner and he should come by, he got angry and said, 'Going to girls' places and having dinner with them is not something I do.'"

"But going to your place and having sex with you was something he could do?" Kim interjects.

"Yeah." My voice fades, the sound turning down as the images of Trent and our nights together fade from immediacy to another sad memory. "I'd saved myself just to give it up during a drunk booty call. I wasn't even sure I'd had anything to save."

"How did you feel after he said that to you?" Tennie asks.

I pull the cap off the marker and put it back on with a click for no reason. "I felt terrible. I felt like I'd taken away his choice, but I wasn't thinking about that then. I felt like I couldn't say anything. Then he threw it back in my face. I tried to understand it from his side. I went through this obsessive period of inability to let it go. Finally, almost a year later, we bumped into each other. He had a new girlfriend. He asked if he could call me. I went home for a few days while my parents were out of town, and he was back in Dallas, and we met up for dinner. I slept with him. Then I stopped responding to him and calling him. I guess I did to him what he first did to me."

"How'd that make you feel?" Tennie continues.

"I thought empowered. I thought I was the one in control again, but I never was. And Trent was only the first. After that, I habitually slept with guys who weren't available. I called up Christian from high school, and he came down for a weekend, and we hooked up. I found out he was starting to use drugs badly. I left him alone after that."

"I had a completely unhealthy relationship with a guy from work for three months. He had bipolar disorder. When he broke it off with me, I started comforting him even though I had every right to be hurt and angry. I put my energy into trying to help him. I flew to Miami for a weekend and hooked up with a guy I had been an intern with that lived down there. He was engaged and planning his wedding. His fiancé called him while we were having sex, and he answered, but we didn't stop. I kept telling myself I was just a sexually-free-minded woman. That this was my sexual revolution; none of them could or were willing to love me back, though. Not till Everett. Even then, when he and I first met, he had a girlfriend and got engaged. Nothing ever happened between us until she called the engagement off. There was a period when I was ready to dive into things, and he wanted some space. I kept pushing."

"I always joked that I thought about sex and treated sex like a dude because it wasn't okay to be a sexual woman where I had grown up." I blink as revelation strikes. "It wasn't the sex I wanted. I wanted them to love me, and the only way I knew how to get their attention was through sex. After feeling like a pariah in school and college, I finally liked men who liked me back. But they liked the sex part of me, not me-me."

I look at the entries for the most recent years. I had been miserable at work, and I finally could admit to being miserable at home too. My sex and love addiction peaked in the wake of my unhappiness, as I started to engage in daily sexual activity with strangers online, even while I was at work.

I catfished a few men. I hated myself for it even though that was part of the allure, I could be anyone else, and that appealed to me. I was even playing in sex chat rooms on nights when I was just about to put Charlie to sleep. Some of the worst parts of my addiction were going into chats and participating in roleplay that I found disgusting in real life but I went along with the requests for the sake of giving someone else the high, repeating what I learned as a child: I exist only for someone else's pleasure.

I recall the long list of confessions in my Step 1 Recovery Worksheet. I pictured myself reciting it all to a priest, leaving him stunned into a stammering mess, and no number of Hail Mary's could wipe those sins away.

"My marriage is suffering," I continue. "I feel like what I thought married life and motherhood would be like were just a fantasy, and because Everett isn't meeting that fantasy and Charlie was so hard to console as an infant, I feel this great resentment. Everything has to be a struggle. Everything has to be so hard when the first part of my life was hard enough. It doesn't ... it doesn't seem fair.

"I know it's not Everett's fault. I'm just one big paradox. I desire independence but also protection. I want solitude but nurturing. I crave tenderness but distance. There's always war in my spirit. I'm the good guy and the bad guy." Shaking my head, I look to Tennie, beseeching her to help end my battles. "I have no idea what I want."

"Maya, grab one of the pads," Tennie instructs as Kim rises to her feet. I grab a blue pad, the type you'd see in a self-defense class or training video, and slide the straps of it around my forearm, the way I'd seen Julianne do the day before.

Kim stands in front of me, feet parted in a defensive stance as she holds two pads over her chest. I shove my pad against her body blockers time and time again as Tennie throws questions at me.

"What would you say to Trent or Nathan right now?"

I push, shove, and beat at Kim's padded arms with my own, but I feel no sense of gratification. I do not feel a release. The rage that is there simmering won't boil over. At thirty-four, in this moment, I wish I could unleash the same fury I had at twelve against Melissa. The difference this time is that I am fully aware of my actions. It is hushed within like all my life secrets and pain, afraid to come out, not even when I tell myself it is safe.

I am too self-conscious, too fearful of judging eyes to let go. Part of me feels silly. What was I so worried about?

If people knew the real me, even others in recovery, they wouldn't like me. I was always the charmer, tap-dancing girl with a cocktail in her hand. I'd been hiding the real me for so long that I didn't even know how to be myself anymore. I believed in my soul that no one would want to befriend me or get to know me if they knew I was addicted to pornography and sex chat.

When the pushing and shoving result in no substantial change in me, Tennie asks me to grab the padded bat. There is a stack of thick vinyl mats in the corner.

"Hit them!" Tennie yells.

I bring the bat up over my head and slam it into the center of the mats, making them fold like an accordion. My strength and my weight are behind the blow but not my heart.

She encourages me to growl, to scream, to pull deep from my belly some primal howl and release it. It comes out soft, and I blush, feeling foolish. None of the emotions emerge naturally or freely. If something doesn't happen soon, will I ever heal? Maybe I should just act the part of the transformation, play the role of metamorphosis until I believe it happens.

Kim moves away from me. I put the pads and bats away and just stand there. Kim brings a chair into the space and motions me to sit. My palms are on my thighs, my feet on the floor, and my back is to the rest of the group. Facing away from them, I feel less like a freakshow.

"What would you say to your parents right now?"

It's a sobering question. I am angry at them for not protecting me the way I believed they should. But I had been so good at keeping secrets; how would they have ever known?

This is the first fissure that begins to form in Mount Maya's Trauma. As I reflect on Tennie's question, it rushes from the bottom toward the peak with the speed of a bullet train.

"I would tell them it's not their fault."

"Whose fault is it?"

"Nathan's. Dustin's. Those boys."

"You're right. It was their fault. It was never your fault, Maya."

I'd heard this before. I was quite self-aware in therapy to string the thought together that it had never, in fact, been my fault. I didn't remember a time before this moment that anyone else had ever said it to me. I'm sure someone did. But this singular moment brought the tsunami that the padded bats and body blockers didn't release.

My chin drops towards my chest. I am sobbing.

"If you could ask any of them one thing, any of your abusers, a question, what would you ask them, Maya?" Tennie's raspy voice is soft and gentle, motherly.

I shake my head no. I have no questions for them.

"Fuck all of them!" I shout, and then my face is in the palms of my hands.

"Who are you most angry with?"

I don't have to think. A name flashes in my mind's eye like a marquee.

"God," I spit out so forcefully that drops of my saliva hit my palms.

"God's listening. What is it you want to say?" Tennie prods.

"Where were you? Where were you?" I repeat through broken sobs. "I was a little girl! Where were *you!*" I shout and ball my hands into a fist and then flail my hands in the air. If I could have hit something, then I would have. I had nothing to grab hold of. Facing away from everyone else, I had only myself and my feelings. Uncontrolled, unfiltered waves of emotion break free.

"God can handle what you have to say," Tennie adds.

"I was just a little girl." I cry, eyes squeezed tight as drops of saltwater release from the corners, wetting my forearms and sleeves.

There are some whispers behind me and then the instinct that someone is coming close. I'm wrapped in a tight embrace. It's Julianne. I know it from her frail arms, but they feel like guardrails, tight and secure, as she holds me and lays her head against mine. I don't know what to do with the hug at first. I don't know how to accept the comfort. Not now with my wounds so open and fresh. Slowly,

I breathe through my mouth, my nose too clogged to inhale or exhale through, and I rest against her chest. We cling to one another from mother to mother, adult child to adult child, addict to addict.

After some time and Tennie's direction, Julianne lets me go and returns to her spot on the floor. I am aware now of the sounds of others crying. There are sniffles and the sloppy blowing of noses. Someone hands me a tissue. I accept it and wipe as my heartache recedes like the afternoon tide. It will be back again, but that's all for today.

"Maya." Tennie clears her throat, and I wonder if she was one of the tearful neighbors behind me. "I want you to think about that picture you drew of yourself as a child. The image of you happy," she encourages. "I want you to now think of that child, so tiny she fits in the palm of your hand. She's not shrinking; she's just so tiny she rests right there for you."

The pink, Snoopy T-shirt, bare legs, pigtails, and a missing tooth with my Christmas morning smile return like I'm holding the Polaroid again.

"I want you to open your palm and imagine she's in it."

My hand turns over in the air, and I picture a Tinkerbell-sized Maya hugging her knees and looking up at me with big, hopeful eyes.

"Now, take her and put her in your heart. Put your hand on your heart and place her there. Keep her there and tell her, she's safe now."

I cradle my palm carefully, truly seeing myself in my hand, gently moving me closer and closer to my chest. I place my hand over my heart and tilt my chin down.

"You're safe now, Maya," I whisper.

There she stays. At the epicenter of love, I placed the version of myself to which I had never given that very thing.

"She will reside there for the rest of your life," Tennie tells me.

I sit quietly for a moment and inhale. It's deep and clearing; my lungs expand, and I am reborn.

"Thank you, Maya," Tennie says.

I gather myself up from the chair, feeling the type of exhilarating exhaustion I felt after running a 5k. My body aches and is so tired. Yet, I have done it.

Six smiling faces look back at me, some with pink-rimmed eyes and splotchy red faces, as I take my seat on the floor next to Julianne. She doesn't care about rules and leans over and hugs me again. I pat her knee and hoarsely say, "Thanks."

"Maya," Jean calls. I can feel the puffiness under my eyes as I turn my head. Little residual sacks of tears wobble as I face her. "Oh my. There was a moment when your back and chin lifted, and you looked ... you looked absolutely regal."

For the first time since I was five, I feel the scope of my power.

Chapter Seventeen

Day 4

May 21, 2015

I released a torrent of emotions to the Heavens during my healing session, and God is responding tonight.

Hail pelts the window next to my bed, sounding at first like gentle sleet falling on a frigid February day before the tinkling becomes loud thwaps. I fear it will shatter the glass. I pull the vertical blinds to the side and watch the brilliant show, lightning stretching across the belly of black clouds like skeletal fingers reaching toward the house. Nickel and dime-sized pieces of ice bounce like hammers on piano strings against the cement. Water swirls in from each direction, carried by the wind, collecting leaves, ice, and more bloated raindrops before yanking them back into the yard that now mirrors a pool.

Thunder rattles our room, and I peer around me, squinting in the darkness, but no one else seems to be awake to hear nature's drum solo. I can't fathom how they are so deeply asleep.

I'd already been awake, so I was more inclined to hear it. The nightmare shook me, forehead damp, mouth dry, chest moving up and down like a pogo stick with my breath trapped inside. In movies, I'd always thought it silly dramatics when people would wake with such fright and sit up straight, gasping as they grappled with leaving the dream realm and returning to reality. Yet, that's exactly what I'd done. I jerked awake and sat up, only to hear the beginning of the thunderstorm's assault outside.

After my intensive session yesterday afternoon, I ate with a T-Rex's appetite, clearing my plate of what was possibly the best meal of my life. Despite my earlier animosity towards being trained how to eat, I ate slowly, chewing until the food was a watery pulp, mindful of what I was placing in my mouth. We had meatloaf, cabbage, zucchini, white rice, and a salad. There were notes of home in each bite. I disregarded the overall nutrition and reveled in the flavors of comfort baked into each dish. Though home wasn't always safe, I tasted my mother's sometimes manic devotion to her family and my grandmother's influence on the generations in that meal.

Then I showered and collapsed. I was too tired to journal. I had said everything I needed to before the group and God.

It appears God is reciprocating.

The storm lasts no longer than twenty minutes, but I remain awake until I hear it subside. When I'm certain the window won't send shards of glass into my body, I tuck the covers tightly around me as exhaustion pulls me into darkness.

Juana knocking at the door is the next thing I hear.

After washing up and getting dressed, I plop down on the sofa and write about my dream. I drop the log sheet in the bin in the kitchen.

Our group climbs into the SUV and returns to the dining hall. We roll carefully through what has become creek beds, not streets. Water is standing in yards and on the clay roads. We ease past some downed tree limbs and clumps of leaves torn at the stems from their homes.

After breakfast, we meet up with Tennie and Kim in the activity room. In the distance, there is the buzzing of some machinery.

"We lost one of the oldest trees on the property to last night's storm," Tennie laments as we take our seats on the floor. "An old oak tree, at least 150 years old, got struck by lightning. The burst was so powerful it didn't just split it; it made the trunk explode. Pieces of wood are everywhere. They are cutting what's left of it down. That's the chainsaws you hear."

My shoulders slump. I feel God had answered me by punishing Shades of Hope. I feel the war between us is at a truce. We've both had our say.

When Tennie pulls out the log I'd written hours before and begins to read it, my ears perk up. There's no embarrassment this time.

"I was inside of the mall near where I'd grown up. I was thirteen again, or in middle school at least. At the beginning of the dream, there was a giant ant, the size of one of the mall's stores, its abdomen knocking over clothing racks and perfume on counters. It chased me to the other side of the mall. I ran as fast as possible to where I finally felt safe, and the ant disappeared. As I made my way through the mall, I encountered a group of middle-school-aged girls that I didn't know. They taunted me, pointed at my clothes, and made jokes about my appearance. I stood there at first and took what they all said. But then I began to scream so loudly back at them and wave my arms so wildly that I scared them away. I wandered around the mall until I passed my favorite music store. When I looked through the glass windows, I saw Nathan picking up a CD and holding it. I quickly ran back in the opposite direction, wondering if the ant had returned. I ran so hard that by the time I made it to the other side of the mall, I tried to race down the escalators but lost my footing, and I woke up just before my face hit the gliding metal steps."

Tennie lowers the paper and lifts her eyes to mine pensively. "You dreamed it all, didn't you? It all came up. Every fear, every life obstacle was in that one dream."

"It was pretty scary, but I could go back to sleep."

"Have you been prone to nightmares before?"

"Sometimes. I dream, but I always remain pretty lucid during them, and I'm aware that I'm dreaming, if that makes sense? Last night was one of the few times that I was submerged in a dream. I didn't know I was dreaming. I felt fear, anger, and hurt. When I was a kid in elementary school, I had the same recurring nightmare. I was hanging out of a car or off the side of a plane's wing. The highway or a runway was rushing up too fast toward my face. I watched the yellow lines whizz by and get so close I could see the cracks in the pavement and the sparkle of granite in pebbles. I never hit the ground. Whatever it was just carried me along this way, in terror that I was about to lose my head."

I become very still as awareness pumps through my veins. That childhood nightmare had been a metaphor for my entire life.

"Do you remember the last time you had that dream?" Tennie inquires.

"No, ma'am." My voice is soft and reflective.

"You all may notice that you may have dreams related to your traumas or addiction while you're here or even when you go home. You've tapped into parts of your brain that have been closed off. When the door opens, a lot can come through it."

"I've had a few unsettling dreams," Julianne pipes up. "Revisiting some things I'd forgotten. Relationships I had that I didn't think about anymore and how they impacted me."

Tennie looks around to see if anyone else has more to add before taking a deep breath that seems to signal a segue into the next part of the morning. "You've been writing your First Step Preparation essays for the last few days. I want you to pull those out now."

Every green bag in the room rustles as we grab sheets of paper and notebooks.

"We are going to read those today. Who would like to go first?"

Star pupil that I'd always been, my hand shoots upward. "Me. I went last for the sessions. I'm not doing that again."

"I hear you, Maya," Kim replies. "You had to sit through everyone else's process and wait and wait. You're not doing that again. You're ready?"

"Yes." I grip thirteen pieces of ruled paper in my hands.

Kim and Tennie angle their heads in unison for me to begin. I focus on the pages, not the faces attending to my every move and rapid blinking of my eyes.

"I am powerless over my obsession for sex," I read. It's not until the words leave my mouth that I grasp the extent of what I am doing. This activity room is my confessional. Tennie and Kim are the pastors, and the congregation of four is hearing me repent.

I know what follows. I become uncomfortably aware of how deviant my behaviors sound even to me. I fear judgment, though I know this is the safest space I will ever be able to speak these words.

Every broken part of that old oak tree seems to wedge in my throat—cutting, restricting, and drying my air passage. I cough hard before I begin.

My unacceptable, hidden, and unhealthy sexual behavior includes a sexting relationship with a former co-worker. I am a married mother, and in my heart, I know what I am doing is cheating. We send pictures of our bodies and genitals, tell each other the sexual thoughts we have about each other and express our desire to have healthy communication, but we feel incapable of doing so. We text each other daily, calling each other at least once weekly. The texts are scattered throughout the day.

I also engage in sex chat online with strangers. I visit an adult chat room and often use a screen name that will reflect my desire to engage in taboo roleplay chat. I have even played parts to satisfy strangers' fantasies online that I know are sick and wrong. I usually engage in the chat about once a week.

I also created a fake profile of a college student as I began to chat frequently with one stranger. We began to email each other with a fake email address I created. From there, we even began to chat through Google Hangout while I was at work. This man believes I'm a twenty-year-old, single, college girl. I have not returned to this profile in a month, but we spoke on and off for almost a year this way.

If I am not chatting or sexting, then I am viewing pornography and masturbating. I have stayed home from work intending to rest but ended up viewing porn and masturbating for several hours. I masturbate almost daily, sometimes multiple times a day.

I realize I have led a double life. I have kept my addiction hidden from my husband, pretending to work or lying about needing to use the bathroom so that I can sext. I also realize the fake profile I created was secretly out of a desire to have a simplified, carefree life, such as the 'girl' I made up.

My thoughts move to sex almost constantly. If I'm in a meeting I'm not leading, I think of sex and fantasize about it with men I am attracted to. When I meet men, especially men in leadership positions, I often visualize a sexual encounter with them.

Usually, my thoughts are initially triggered by boredom, isolation, or loneliness. When I am alone, these are often the times I seek unhealthy sexual gratification, but at the same time, I also crave time alone. I welcome the rush of excitement I get from my fantasies, even when some of them are dark, or I imagine having physical pain or heartbreak from sex inflicted on me.

I often reflect on sex I had with previous partners and have thought of reaching out to them again.

I do not feel I control my thoughts about sex, but my mind often wanders to it when trying to focus. I feel a rush or a high when thinking or even talking about sex.

I often view men entirely as sexual objects, which bothers me. When I meet a man, through professional or personal relationships, I often wonder what type of lover he is and if I'd enjoy sex with him. In meetings led by younger men as well (men twenty to forty), I often fantasize about their bodies. While most of my fantasies revolve around men, I have at times viewed lesbian pornography for stimulation.

I believe, at one point, I thought my masturbation was healthy as well as my use of pornography because it wasn't 'hurting anyone else,' and I wasn't engaging in sexual behavior with others. But then it progressed to chatting, sexting, and photo swapping.

I realize the consequences of this could end my marriage or greatly damage my husband's trust. I have realized I need help for this addiction. I cannot control it alone. I have tried on my own and failed over and over again.

I have made plans to initiate sex outside of my marriage but have not gone through with them. I have supported my sex addiction by lying, manipulating and being dishonest.

I often isolate to masturbate or just have a mental escape during which I often think about sex.

I have had days where I planned to go shopping, work out, read or just clean the house and have leisure time, but I end up masturbating.

My behavior is getting worse, and I know in sex chat, I discuss or roleplay things I find immoral or against my beliefs, but I feel powerful and sexy and in control of the stranger's desire and arousal. I am turned on by turning others on, which feels so twisted.

The sex in my marriage is often routine, and I do not find it as satisfying as I do masturbation or chatting. I am more aroused through porn. It's less personal.

Masturbating is my line of release at times when I feel stressed, pressured or conflicted. The only other means of self-gratification is comfort food.

I have attempted to control my sexual behavior by reaching out to a friend, who, in turn, hit on me after I confided in him. I have also been working to control my behavior and thoughts through counseling, deleting emails and contact information, drinking alcohol, eating fast food or sugary food, and buying things compulsively online.

I have also recalled my first real dating experience. It was a man I met online and began messaging. We eventually moved to having phone conversations that ultimately led to us mutually masturbating while we were on the phone and having regular phone sex. Eventually, we met while on a work trip in San Francisco. On the first night of our meeting, we engaged in oral sex, and I stayed the night with him. He eventually ended the relationship, and I felt shame over what I had done with him.

II. My Life is Unmanageable.

I am unsure when my life took the path it did or when I fell into the rut I'm in. My days and nights are the same. I often feel depressed and sometimes anxious when I'm alone. My sexual behavior is often triggered by stress, anger, boredom or apathy. My behavior generates in me fears that what I am doing will get progressively worse, i.e. I will begin to engage in a physical affair, my husband will catch me, naked images or video of me may ultimately be seen by someone I know, or my marriage will end because of the behavior.

I often feel like my life happens by chance, not choice. I feel some resentment towards my husband, although it was my choice to leave TV, when I walked away from the career I wanted to be a wife and eventually a mother. I feel like having a toddler often dictates my mood as if when he has tantrums, cries or is sick, I feel my stress level rise. I feel a great deal of shame over my past sexual behavior and my current sexual behavior. Although I realize the situations in which I was a victim as a child were not my fault, I still feel shame because in some cases, I was a willing participant. I did what I knew felt good, which no child at those ages should know. Now, I feel guilt and shame as an unfaithful wife, and I feel like a bad mother because of my behavior. While most topics of sexual perversion would seem to turn me off, in other ways I am often aroused by what I see or hear and for this I feel shame.

My sexual behavior has affected my health by adding to my depression. The guilt and shame make me feel dirty and worthless, and the cycle of depression continues. I have trouble sleeping most nights unless I take a sleep or relaxation aid. I sometimes have strange and disturbing dreams. I typically wake up at least two to three times a night. Conversely, I feel tired during the day and will take two to three-hour naps.

My sexual behavior has hurt my mental creativeness, both professionally and personally. While I pride myself on coming up with new and exciting concepts for my job, I have fallen into a rut of simply doing what is familiar. Although I desire to start my own business, the energy I could devote to this effort is often spent on sex chat or masturbating. Even in my family life, I have not been interested in trying to experience new things as I would normally. We mostly spend our weekends inside and at home.

When I am at home, I tend to isolate. I do not want too much time out of the bed, and I will find reasons to close myself off in the bedroom, even when my son is up and playing. I often go to my work office when I know I can work alone and not be bothered. I have turned down invitations to events and functions in order to just sit at home and lounge, not desiring to go out for a meal or even public places.

I often feel shame for how I treat my husband. I am very independent and don't typically rely on others for help, so reaching out to my husband is rare. He stated once that I take him for granted. I realize that I do. He has his faults. He is only human, but he has been a good man to me, a good father to my son, and he's a good husband. I am dishonest with him regarding my online sex chat, emotional affair, pornography use and sometimes by not revealing my true thoughts and feelings to protect his.

As much as I don't want to admit it, I use sex to manipulate people through flirtatious charm or even in marriage like some type of prize or a reward for my husband. I admit that I am self-centered and insensitive and want only to do things my way. My sex addiction has affected my relationship with my husband because I keep secrets, have been dishonest, and have broken my marriage vow by engaging in sexual relationships with other men. With my son, I have shifted my focus from him or even been distracted during our time together while I text and chat. With my parents, I have kept secrets and lied. In other relationships, I have engaged in sex to keep unhealthy relationships going, and I used seduction to boost my ego.

I have spent more time engaging in my addiction than focusing on my faith. I have spent Sundays at home alone, chatting online with strangers, watching porn, and masturbating. I have spent more time indulging in what feels good and worshipping perverse means of sex rather than what is holy and pure. I always believed my masturbating and porn viewing was okay because it hurts no one but me.

My spiritual life was empty and void for so long. I did not have a strong belief system, and now I am moving forward in getting a closer relationship with God. I was very angry with God for a long time because I felt I was not protected as a child should be. My sex addiction has created a barrier between God and me and I know that while He blesses me, he does not bless my behavior, so I need to change. Adultery is a sin. I could devote the time I spent masturbating to meditation and calming my nerves.

My addiction has limited my patience and tolerance when working with others because I often feel, short-tempered, angry, and want to be left alone. I no longer feel the same rush of creativity I once felt. I usually feel too tired or irritated to put extra energy into projects, which is a big switch from my previous burnout as an overachiever.

While at work, I have engaged in sexting and sexual discussions. I know this is risky behavior and takes time away from my job, but the rush I feel from it breaks up the boredom and monotony of my day. I often leave work early at least once a week for therapy. There have also been many days where I lied to my co-workers and said I didn't feel well and wouldn't be in the office to stay home, sexting, chatting, or masturbating.

"Thank you for sharing, Maya." Tennie exhales.

"You're not alone in your behavior," Kim offers in comfort.

Rebecca, Julianne, Lucas, and Jean all read their essays, sharing their lowest lows, and I scoot back further and further away from them, resting my back against the wall.

Kim notices first that my arms are folded across my chest, my legs extended but bouncing rapidly, the backs of my knees hitting the carpet over and over.

"Maya? How do you feel?" she asks.

"I don't feel anything. I feel numb."

"Numb isn't a feeling," Tennie reminds me and points to the chart on the wall. I review the five primary emotions again: Anger, Fear, Sadness, Disgust, and Enjoyment.

"I guess I'm angry." The words leave my mouth with the speed of throwing a fast pitch. They want an answer; there it is.

"You look it," Tennie retorts.

"I'm madder at myself than anything."

"Why?" Kim urges me to keep talking.

"Because of the other stuff? The stuff that I talked about yesterday? That's stuff that happened *to* me. I didn't have control. This stuff? This is stuff I did *to me*." My words drip with self-loathing and contempt. "I did these things. I caused this!" I lower my head, and my forehead rests against my palm. It feels hot to the touch, feverish, though I'm not sick in the traditional sense.

"Maya?" Tennie responds, her tone patient. I know I'm being watched again, so I finally lift my head. "If you think you were ever in control of what you were doing, by choice or not, you have a lot more work to do."

We take a field trip later that day. Puddles still ripple from the velocity of passing cars on the shoulders of the highway and in the grassy medians. Reminders of last night's storm hang in the overcast sky as the van pulls into the parking lot of a church in Abilene. It seems abnormally full for ten minutes till noon on a Thursday afternoon.

Kim is in the driver's seat this time, Tennie the passenger, and our intensive party is scattered on the three rows of seats in the back. I'd retreated to my familiar spot in the corner, Julianne seated to my left.

Kim opens the back doors and takes out seven Styrofoam carriers. I'd heard them squeaking as they bumped into one another and bounced along with the ride, the faint smell of food wafting from the back. Their contents, like our destination, were a mystery.

As we climb out of the van, unenthusiastic clowns flowing out one after another, we all study the steepled exterior of the church. Kim calls us and then distributes the containers.

Tennie leads the way into the fellowship hall of the church. She strides in with confidence that comes from the familiar. Kim walks behind her with the same discipline, the rest of us hanging back, glancing furtively at one another. I silently look down at my feet, watching them propel me towards the church, using the backs of the other's shoes as my guide.

There are men and women seated shoulder to shoulder around the walls of the narrow chamber. Some have seen fewer years of life than I have, and others have seen decades more. That, or life, has worn them to such haggard appearances that they seem older than their actual years.

A long rectangular table like that of a high school cafeteria, complete with plastic chairs, is stretched in the middle of the room and vacant. As Kim motions to it, I realize it's been prepared and saved just for us.

We sit at the center table, the center of attention, though conversations carry on, and no one seems to pay us too much mind.

I open the squeaking, white Styrofoam container in front of me to reveal a similar lunch to the very first I'd had when I arrived at Shades of Hope. This meal, however, includes a bright, crisp red apple—its polished reflection glints in the fluorescent light bulbs overhead. My eyes are drawn to the vibrant red—red like the blood of life. Everything else around me appears to be black and white. Real life has become void of color. In response to my uncertainty, I realize I am dissociating. I grab a spork, dig into a scoop of chickpeas, and let the flavor of dill bring me fully into my surroundings.

An older man in overalls, a plaid shirt, and a faded trucker hat cattle whistles and calls the meeting for Alcoholics Anonymous to order. My chewing slows—not from mindfulness, but as I see the connection of the day's activities. We had prepped for the first step; now, we were entering step one of a twelve-step program.

An excerpt is read from a companion AA pamphlet about struggling with sobriety but the restoration of sanity that comes with moving through each step. I look around the room at the nodding heads and those who "hmphed" in agreement. If there was ever a group to understand me, it was made up of the people in this room. Our ethnicity, gender, and socio-economic status don't matter. Addiction doesn't discriminate and is a uniting catalyst.

Though I considered alcohol a secondary addiction compared to my sex addiction, one complements the other the way a chime complements a doorbell. They were reactions to one another. I drink when I need to numb and cannot act out sexually. I act out sexually when the numbness of alcohol isn't enough to release me from my personal hell.

We come to the last part of the meeting, where those who want to share can do so. My head whips up when I hear Tennie's voice.

"I'm Tennie McCarty, recovering alcoholic," she says. I didn't realize responding in unison was real, but everyone in the room smiles and says, "Hi, Tennie." I watch and try to learn how to behave. Again, I thought this was something only done in movies and TV.

Tennie talks about her continued sobriety and that she has brought with her a group of friends.

A young mother speaks about regaining custody of her children. A father who hadn't spoken to his daughter in three years mulls reaching out to her and if he can promise her this time would be different. The sponsor, I learn, who is leading the meeting, asks if anyone else would like to speak.

Lucas's voice lifts and sounds sure and determined across the table. "I'd like to. Hi, I'm Lucas, alcoholic."

He explains his story and how he came to treatment. He shares how life might be pivoting toward something good for the first time in months.

While Lucas and the others speak, the shiny red apple stays untouched in my container. I am afraid to eat it. I am marred by the fear that my loud crunching will distract from some despairing soul's step toward wholeness. Mostly, I'm afraid someone will truly see me. I keep my eyes on the red skin, wary of being noticed.

The time comes when the sponsor asks if anyone would like to take a chip. He explains there are chips for those committing to sobriety, for thirty days sober, and for months and years. Lucas is the first in our group to ask for a chip. He cheers as he accepts it.

I meekly raise my hand to the applause of the others in the room. "I want to commit to a life of sobriety." What felt like an insurmountable goal a week ago doesn't seem so grave at this moment.

I am handed a silver plastic coin from the box that looks like a fishing tackle. It is marked "24 hours recovery." My last drink had been the Saturday night before checking in at Shades of Hope, five days before, but today, when I had laid bare the most vulnerable aspects of my addiction to the group, today felt like the true start of sobriety. Around the '24 hours' is a triangle with the words UNITY, SERVICE, RECOVERY and "To Thine Own Self Be True." The opposite side of the coin contains the serenity prayer, which I can fully recite now.

I hold the sobriety chip in my hand and run the pad of my thumb over it, feeling the engraved letters. I close my hand around it tightly.

Step one.

Chapter Eighteen

Days 5 and 6

Day 5: May 22, 2015

S ix days wasn't enough to *fix* me. Tennie levels a concerned look at me. "We are recommending you stay for the full forty-two-day residential program."

A hot blast of air is forced through my nostrils as I "hmph."

Staying isn't that simple.

American medical insurance being what it is, most companies don't recognize some mental healthcare techniques that don't fall into neatly packed psychology, psychiatry, or counseling diagnosis. Weeks of equestrian therapy may help you overcome trauma, but it's unlikely insurance will cover the cost[1]. The body-based therapy techniques and trauma expulsion exercises at Shades of Hope didn't fall into one of those tidy, checkmark boxes. Simply, insurance isn't going to cover the price tag for me to stay, which was somewhere around $22,000.

We can't afford it, not on a teacher's salary and a consultant's income.

There is also the more important matter of my kid.

"Charlie turns two in three weeks," I reply, lamenting the upcoming milestone. "I can't miss that."

"Your son isn't going to remember his second birthday party or that his mama wasn't there for it. He *will* remember if his mama becomes more out of control or hurts herself." Tennie's terse reply seems unsympathetic as I initially take it in.

---

1. Insel, Thomas. *Healing: Our Path from Mental Illness to Mental Health*. (United States: Penguin, 2022).

I know she is right. I know mothers and fathers are capable of sharing their legacy of trauma, handing it down to sons and daughters like a cursed gift. I know that much from my own upbringing. I don't want Charlie to be more impacted by my mental illness than he already has been. This is not guilt or shame they are using to coax me into staying. We all know I need more help.

The work over the last few days has left me susceptible. It is how a hermit crab must feel in the frantic moments of leaving one shell for another. The tender parts of me are exposed. I am moving towards a better fit in life, but my previous guards sheltered me. Any moment it seems some terror could pluck me away and take me deeper into darkness.

I want to stay. I need more time. The healing is just beginning. Here, I am surrounded by care providers and others in recovery. Beyond the Shades of Hope property line is an uncompassionate world that only demands, doesn't listen. There isn't a broken copy machine, a phone call at the end of a work shift, road rage, snarky cashiers, or one of Charlie's tantrums to catapult my day from good to bad. I prefer to stay here in the shade rather than return to the spotlight as the star of Maya's presentable life.

For wanting to stay, I feel selfish. I am "should"ing all over myself. *I should want to go home. I should want to see Everett. I should want to hug Charlie tight.*

"Maybe we can see if my parents can help?" They'd offered to cover my treatment for the six-day intensive. I can't speak for them, but I imagined the offer came from some sense of responsibility to a child they felt had been left defenseless.

I am almost certain the offer didn't extend to this particular dollar amount.

"We will contact Everett, first," Tennie explains. "I'm not really allowed to handle the financial side because, if left up to me, everyone would have their expenses covered."

Later that afternoon, I walk with Lucas, Tennie, and Kim to the administration building. Their office manager had made a compulsory call to my insurance in the hope they may cover a portion of the expense given my years-long severe depression diagnosis.

There was no miracle today.

I sit in the waiting room while Lucas is on the phone with his family. The door to Cam's office is closed, and I try not to listen but find it impossible, given the small space. His family is willing to do whatever it will take to help their son. Somewhere on another part of the property, Tennie is on the phone with my family.

Lucas opens the door and steps out. There's a flash of eye contact before Cam summons me to a chair in her office. I take a seat as she plucks away at the keypad of the desk phone and hands me the receiver. I tug the coil as far as it can reach and press the phone, still warm from Cam's ear and Lucas's, to my own. It rings once before I hear Dad's, "Hello?"

I feel very much like a child in trouble. I am asking for too much.

"Hey, Dad."

"Hey, sweetheart," comes his usual reply. "How are you?"

"I'm okay," I lie. "They told you they want me to stay?"

"Yes, they did." Dad's calm reaches me, and I prepare for the "but." "... But without insurance, we just can't afford something like that. I'm sorry. I'll see you tomorrow ..."

My back bows and my shoulders feel too heavy for my body. I swallow the sour words.

"Okay, love you."

"Love you."

I hand the phone to Cam like I'm holding garbage I can't get rid of fast enough.

Financially, the decision has been made. No amount of reasoning lessens the anguish I feel over having to leave.

Back at the activity center, we are all seated on the floor.

"Your husband loves you," Tennie says.

I blink slowly. "I know."

"He was trying to stay calm and figure something out. He just wanted to do what's best for you. Also, I got to see what you meant about your mom," Tennie chuckles.

I grimace. "Oh, God. What did she do?"

"She was in the background shouting over and over as Everett was trying to talk, 'Tell her to come home! Tell her to come home now!'"

"That sounds about right," I say.

With the exception of Rebecca, it's recommended that all of us stay. We spend some time back at the house. They give our cell phones back to us. My stomach becomes as hard as a rock as I press the power button. Do I have a message from Tony?

I have one text. It's from Everett. He'd taken Charlie to a children's museum back home, and my curly-haired son is standing with big eyes in front of a display with species of butterflies. One bright blue variety near his puffy-from-smiling cheek, catches my eye.

I stare at the picture as I listen to Julianne on speaker phone seated next to Juana at the kitchen table.

I hear the exuberant cheer of a child as Julianne says, "Hey, baby!" Her voice rises octaves. I wonder if Charlie will be as excited about our reunion.

Julianne's husband comes to the phone after she speaks to all three of her girls. She explains to him that they are recommending she stay for the full forty-two days. She tells him she wants to be here.

"Babe, those people fixed you. You're good. Come on home. We need you here. I need you taking care of the girls. You're fine. They fixed you."

His words send my blood cells simmering. I imagine platelets vibrating with the anger that shoots through me. I lift my head and watch Julianne's shoulders slump as she whispers, "Yeah."

I'm angry for her. I'm angry for me. *Fixed.* No, we aren't. We are lug nuts being tightened during a repair. A wrench was around us, making the first turn. We are far from secure.

My rage rises to the point I stomp away from the couch out to the back patio, where Jean is on the phone with a friend asking for a loan so she can stay.

Immediately, I feel the intrusiveness of my barging in, so I keep moving. I step out into the grass, wandering, pacing. Right now, I have no place suitable for me to be.

We gather with Tennie and Kim in the activity room one last time. The van is ready to take us to Abilene for a night at a local deli. The goal is to teach us how to make healthy food choices even when we are away from home.

There will be no celebratory drinks for our party of five after our time together. Instead, we are emerging into society like ex-convicts and re-entering the world with salads and processed meat.

Since I will not be staying, I'm given an aftercare plan for my next three months of life. The recommendation for the forty-two days is listed, and I skip over it, an ingredient in a recipe that I can't afford.

I check the boxes next to what I am capable of doing for myself—what I need to do for myself.

- Attend 12-step Support Groups (90 meetings in 90 days) to include:

Al-Anon Family Group meeting per wk/mo
Sex and Love Addicts Anonymous (SLAA) meetings per week/mo

- I will have a sponsor upon completion of treatment.

- Other support/treatment/individual therapy: Continue sessions with Counselor

- I will have a daily program consisting of: prayers, meditation, reading, exercise, prop-

er/nutrition/meal plan, meetings, phone contacts and others

- Recommended long-term goal is Abstinence from:
sugar, flour, nicotine, caffeine, alcohol,
street or prescription drugs

I sign my name, and Tennie signs hers beside it. Lucas is the only group member who will stay for continued treatment.

Julianne, Jean, Rebecca, and I are given packets with phone meeting contacts and lists of in-person support meetings close to our homes. It becomes obvious there are many options available in Dallas and Houston but few in my East Texas community, especially for sex and love addiction.

"We have something for each of you," Tennie announces. "We give this to our clients before they go. For a while, it may have felt like you were going crazy."

Kim stands up, holding a small velvet pouch. She slides the drawstrings open and reaches inside. "Your time here was to ground you. You've done some very difficult work that you should be proud of. If those feelings of being out of control ever come up again, just hold these."

I look at Kim's grinning face, and I hold out my hand. She places four green marbles resembling cat eyes in my palm.

"This way, no matter what, you can remember you've still got all your marbles."

We laugh as we each take our parting gift. I slide mine into the inside pocket of my bag.

There is a period of fellowship. There are no teachings, journaling, or deep sharing, only laughter and smiles. I pull my phone from my pocket and show Tennie and Kim the photo Everett sent of Charlie.

"He is a doll!" Tennie coos.

My heart swells with a mother's pride; then, there is a crumbling within me. *What if I'm not returning to him better than when I left?*

I need more time.

Misty, the cook who had made every healthy meal delicious and, most of all, edible, steps into the activity room.

"Misty sings in the choir at our church," Tennie says. "She has a beautiful voice and I asked if she would send us off tonight with a song."

Misty gives the humble smile of a Baptist singer who knows she has the pipes to tear the sheetrock from the walls but won't flaunt it.

"May we join hands?" she asks.

I stand between Tennie and Kim, and my fingers link with theirs.

Misty opens her mouth, and though she is one, the strength of her voice sounds like a fifty-member choir as she begins to sing *Amazing Grace*.

I am crying by the second verse. Was I saved? Was I still just a wretch? The tears aren't hard and fast. They trickle over the apples of my cheeks and gather like a faucet leak on my chin.

I need more time.

My sight is narrow; I don't see a bigger picture, yet. As the tears fall, I lift my eyes to find Tennie studying me. Her hand squeezes mine tighter.

Day 6: May 23, 2015

I sign a piece of paper saying I'm not going to kill myself.

"Maya, in all honesty, we're concerned about you the most," Tennie says, sitting at the kitchen table in what had been home for six nights. Kim is beside her, and I am on the other side of the table, hands in my lap.

"You are very vulnerable right now. We told Everett as much. Your thinking may be skewed by that vulnerability."

I'd opened the crypt of the secrets in my life with a crowbar, and there was no way to seal it shut again. Trauma costumed as ghosts and demons were flying out, sure to haunt me in the coming weeks.

My focus tracks from one face to the other—their concern is visible. I detach from any sense of being alive then. The next seconds are void of the five feelings. I react and respond like an A.I. programmed to do so.

"We want you to commit to not hurting yourself," Kim adds.

"Write a letter to Kim and me saying you won't take your life."

In ho-hum fashion, I push my chair back from the table. I don't feel my feet on the carpet. I don't hear the conversation between Julianne and Rebecca even though I see them seated on the couch. I retrieve my notepad from the green bag on the bed and plop back down in the chair. I scribble these exact words:

`I, Maya, promise not to kill myself.`

With a flourish and large exaggerated signature, I drop the pen on the table and then push the paper at Tennie. I fold my arms over my chest and look from her to Kim.

"Thank you. We are going to hold you to this promise."

Sure.

Kim double checks her phone to confirm she has my cell number.

If there was a big goodbye, I don't remember. Lucas moved his things from the guest house to the residents' dorms. Jean's flight was leaving the next day, and she had to stay behind until she could check in at the hotel later that afternoon. Rebecca's Jeep and Airstream pull away as Juana backs the van carrying Julianne and me off the gravel and onto the road. The gate to the white picket fence is left open. It seems to tell me I am welcome if I need to return. I scroll on my phone, so I don't have to watch Shades of Hope, Buffalo Gap, and Abilene fading away.

Julianne and I are on the same flight to Dallas, hers connecting before she continues to Virginia. Not all of my ties with Shades of Hope are ending yet.

We sit next to each other on the plane, holding each other's hands, our green bags in our laps, as we wordlessly soar through the sky. It seems cruelly blue that morning. It's shining on one of my gloomiest days.

"Are you going to be okay?" I ask Julianne as we make our way to the gate.

"Are you?" she retorts.

We laugh sarcastically. It feels like a "no."

"I've got your number and email. Call me. Let me know you've made it safely. Keep in touch." She forces me to look in her eyes.

"You too," I croak. She throws both arms around my neck. We're two new best friends linked by unimaginable circumstances.

"Take care." I rub her back.

We let go before either of us starts to cry. I turn towards the escalator leading to the baggage claim and give one more look back. Julianne waves her hand high over her head before she turns to head back to her life and me to mine.

It's JJ who picks me up from the airport. He greets me with a hug and a "Hey, Sis."

During the car ride back to my parents' house, he doesn't ask me one question about treatment or my time away. I am grateful for the lack of interrogation. One, because I am physically, mentally, and emotionally spent and don't have the words to describe the last week. Two, because my brother's driving scares the hell out of me. It's the go-kart rides through the alley when we were kids all over again. This time in a two-ton vehicle.

I grip the door handle as we weave around cars. I'm departing the airport as chaotically as I'd arrived a week prior.

The numbness returns when the car stops in Mom and Dad's driveway, and my death grip on the door releases. I have to face them all. I am back at the epicenter of so much turmoil.

I had fear during the car ride to remind me that I didn't want to die. I think of the letter to Tennie and Kim.

My fear now is that I am returning to the circus, my tightrope act without a safety net. There is no Tennie, Kim, or Juana to link hands with if I slip. There is no Julianne to pull me up from a fall.

Charlie's face and hands are pressed against the storm door glass as I walk up, pulling my suitcase behind me.

"Hey, Mommy!"

The afro of little brown curls and his big dimpled cheeks brings me to my knees. I pull open the door, and he bounds into my arms as I kneel. I press my cheek to his and remember that I didn't come this far to lose hope and faith again. He hugs me, and I kiss his cheek, which he wipes away. He bounces on the balls of his feet and flings his hands and wrists rapidly, making a growling sound, which for Charlie, means happiness.

From my squat, I look up into Everett's uncertain eyes.

"Hey."

"Hey," he mimics as I stand. My husband embraces me for the longest amount of time that I can remember in our nine years together.

Mom and Dad are next. My hellos to them are intentionally brief to avoid questioning. For once, Mom leaves it be. JJ brings my luggage into the house. Charlie resumes playing with a jazz-inspired toy on the floor, a frog scatting as it sings.

I move to the guest bedroom after the salutations cease. I close the door and change out of my travel clothes and into my pajamas before climbing into bed.

When Everett walks in sometime later, I'm not asleep, just lying there.

"You alright?" He sits next to me on the bed, and I feel my body tilt to the side as the mattress bends. He places a hand on my knee.

"I'm just ... overwhelmed," I admit.

Everett gulps, a frown forming, the corners of his mouth turning down hard, like the thought was a puppet master yanking strings to pull his lips down. "Tennie told us you had more than one abuser."

"Yeah ..."

"Your mom has been trying to figure out who."

"I'll tell her someday. Right now, I need some time."

Everett leans over and kisses my forehead before leaving the room.

I look at the green Shades of Hope bag next to my suitcase on the floor. I remind myself that I still have all of my marbles.

Chapter Nineteen

90 Meetings in 90 Days

June 2015

The automated messaging system gives an enthusiastic welcome as it prompts me to dial in the access code. Like the serenity prayer, it hadn't taken long for it to become part of my repertoire.

My thumb moves in such rapid taps the key tones are a second behind them before I press pound. The feminine electronic voice tells me to wait for the meeting's host.

Scattered around me are adult coloring books, a linen sack of colored pencils, some pamphlets, and a pen and pad.

The door to our bedroom is closed as it has been at 5:59 p.m. every day for the last three weeks. Each evening, I wedge my EarPods snuggly in, connect them to my phone, and wait for the start of the women-only phone meeting for Sex and Love Addicts Anonymous. I'd gone through a meticulous screening process to gain access to the meeting code. The sponsors confirmed my condition as a sex and love addict through specific questions in order to protect the safety and integrity of the other members before I'd been given the phone number and the five numbers for access.

I'd started meetings three days after leaving Shades of Hope. We left my parents' house the day after my return from West Texas. As soon as I was home, I began to line up my recovery support. I'd have started sooner if I could, had the new member screening fallen earlier in the week.

Through the meetings, not only did my self-awareness grow, but so did my commitment to learning more about sex addiction and those who suffer from it. Counselor gave me a helpful chart and diagram that showed the cycle[1] addicts like myself are stuck in.

As children who suffered trauma during our developmental years, we formed a skewed core belief system. Our core beliefs are how we see ourselves, how we view other people, and our general outlook on life and our futures. Survivors of childhood trauma commonly hold four core beliefs that are fallacies, but they are the roots from which our mind's journey grew: I am a no-good person, unworthy; If anybody really knew me, they wouldn't love me; I cannot trust others to meet my needs; My most important needs are ... sex, drugs, food, my spouse, etc.

These core beliefs lead to irrational thoughts, which lead us to a thought or act that validates the irrational thought. I'd believed very early on in life that I only existed for other people's pleasure, and, because of that, I thought I was no good due to the "dirty" things that kept happening to me. So, if a guy wanted to use me for sex, whether in a relationship or online, I let them. It brought validation to that distorted core belief.

I'd long been terrified that if anybody really knew me, they wouldn't love me. I kept my addiction secret while putting up a virtuous front for decades. From the first time I pressed play on a porno to the first reply of "Hi There" in a sex chat as a married woman, I'd developed a CIA agent's ability for clandestine behaviors.

For addicts, after we've done the validating act (watched porn, photo swapped, had a sexual encounter with a stranger), we feel guilt and shame, again affirming that core belief system. As Dr. Brené Brown says, "If you put shame in a Petri dish and you want to make it grow, you give it three things: 1) silence, 2) secrecy and 3) judgment."[2]

---

1. Hal B. Schell's adaptation from Carnes, Patrick. *The Sexual Addiction*. (Minneapolis: Compcare Publications, 1983).

2. Brown, Brené. *Dare to Lead: Brave Work. Tough Conversations. Whole Hearts*. (United States: Random House, 2018)

The goal of recovery is to develop new core beliefs, renew thinking, and choose a different, healthier act that brings us to self-acceptance. Guilt and shame that have tortured us and been our captors in addiction can no longer thrive when we change how we see ourselves. We pull ourselves from the soil we emerged from by the roots and replant ourselves to bathe in warm sunlight, not wither in the shade.

I was learning more and more about the source of my mental ailment through SLAA meetings and Al-Anon. In the packet of printed information handed to me at Shades of Hope, I found a local church hosting Al-Anon meetings twice a week.

That first meeting, I'd pulled my car into the parking lot, the AC blasting on the highest setting in the June heat with the windows up. I was a few yards from the entrance and watched the door askance. With my hair in the fake ponytail, I rubbed at the back of my neck, which was wet with perspiration. I cut the engine and hopped out of the car before my nerves bested me, and with breaths quicker than my steps, I walked into what appeared to be a Sunday school classroom.

They immediately noticed the new face. I also wondered if any of them recognized me from the local television station. Cheeks burning a deep maroon and eyes cast to the floor, I pulled out a metal folding chair and sat down at the table, hugging my purse in my lap.

I introduced myself as a recovering alcoholic and an adult child of an alcoholic. I was given the Al-Anon book and several pamphlets, including an envelope to keep them in. On the outside of the envelope were the phone numbers for others in the group, should I need support on a day of struggle.

Despite being in-person, the meeting functioned in the same manner as my phone meetings. I tried not to make eye contact for too long with anyone while also appearing attentive.

I listened to a father talk about the grim heartache of setting boundaries with his alcoholic son whom he'd let return over and over again. He finally had to put him out of his house when he became violent during his last binge. I learned my own addiction had as much to do with my core beliefs as it did with boundaries, or my lack thereof. I'd been violated as a child and shamed into perfectionism. I'd never really known what healthy boundaries were.

When I got home that night after the meeting, I delayed my shower and sat down on my bedroom floor and pulled out some pages from the green and white tote that had become my bag-o-recovery. I located the list titled *Shades of Hope Signs of Unhealthy Boundaries*:

- Acting on the first sexual impulse

- Being sexual for your partner, not yourself

- Going against personal values or rights to please others

- Accepting food, gifts, touch or sex that you don't want

- Letting others direct your life

- Expecting others to fill your needs automatically

- Self-abuse

After my first Al-Anon meeting, I was tossed about like a cargo ship during a hurricane at sea with an increased understanding of self. I thought of all the times I'd expected Everett to be some type of mind reader and magically understand what I was thinking, feeling, and needing, and come to my aid.

Tucked away in a box on the floor of my closet, I had journals upon journals (most only half-used or a few pages written in) that detailed my struggles with perfectionism and my inability to say no to people. I'd been harming myself all these years by trying to be better, smarter, prettier, thinner, and never uttering the words "no" even when something was a stressor or huge inconvenience.

There was one bit of information that seemed elusive in my studies. What is sex addiction? How do you know you are an addict and not horny with a high sex drive?

A friend once told me, "Everyone looks at porn." While access to free porn is easier in the era of smartphones, it might seem like an accurate statement. In truth, not everyone does. Not everyone engages in sex chat, and not everyone searches online for a hookup.

Sex addiction itself can be hard to quantify because there are so many societal stigmas with sex, and stigmas harbor silence. These stigmas and taboos date back for many cultures through religion, slavery, colonialism, and even systemic programs like the American military's once-enforced sexual orientation program "Don't Ask, Don't Tell."

On the other end of the spectrum, we are experiencing another sexual revolution as women are encouraged to buy vibrators and satisfy themselves. Porn created by women for women is being championed online through ad campaigns.

During the early part of the 2020 COVID-19 pandemic and global quarantines, it became social media buzz and news headlines when PornHub made premium services free. If you were staying home, you could access porn all day at any time. There were tweets celebrating the announcement. Some vowed publicly to take advantage of the costless service.

Films like *365 Days* and *Fifty Shades of Grey* toe the line of consent, as do number-one hit songs like *Blurred Lines,* while racking up the streams and bringing in millions at the box office. It may seem like society is fixated with sex, but for millions of us, there is a silent struggle that is true obsession.

Sex addiction is defined as a neurological disorder. It is characterized by intense, sexually-arousing fantasies and urges or behaviors that persist for at least six months, causing distress and impairment in the professional, social, and personal life of the individual, despite repeated attempts to cut back or stop. Compulsive sexual behavior is recognized as a mental health disorder.[3]

---

3. Yasuhiro Kotera and Rhodes, Christine. "Pathways to sex addiction: relationships with adverse childhood experience, attachment, narcissism, self-compassion and motivation in a gender-based sample," *Sexual Addiction and Compulsivity*, no. 26 (1-2) (2019): 54-76.

There is both a comfort for me in having read that information while conducting research for this book and writing it now. There's a reason that I, like so many others, am battling sex addiction that moves beyond what many see as instant bodily gratification. The word "disorder" comes with mixed feelings that gnaw like a puppy with a chew toy. It says that something is wrong. However, part of recovery and self-acceptance says that this also proves how my brain works was reshaped by trauma.

Historically, sex addiction in female-identifying persons wasn't researched extensively until the 2000s. It was a professionally held misconception that this was a male affliction. However, with the number of women who experience sexual abuse in their lifetime, the statistics for female sex addicts are likely higher than we know. Most sex addicts aren't exactly lining up to share with the world the actions they consider the worst things they have ever done or experienced. Add the pressures of being a mother, daughter, an employee, or whatever other hat women are wearing, and the stigma is increased. It hampers research.

But the direct correlation between sex abuse and later forming sexual addiction is there. Among addicts, the rate of those who experience childhood trauma is extremely high.[4] In Patrick Carnes's pioneering work in the 1990s, ninety-seven percent of sex addicts reported childhood trauma. In a study by Tedesco and Bola (1997), of forty-five individuals who identified as sex addicts (twenty-four male, twenty-one female), ninety-six percent reported having experienced childhood sexual abuse. Adverse childhood experiences enhance long-term hyperarousal, which victims may attempt to neutralize by engaging in addiction behaviors[5], including exposing themselves to a situation reminiscent of the original trauma.[6]

---

4. Carnes, P.J. *Don't call it love: Recovery form sexual addiction.*(New York: Bantam Books, 1991). And Carnes, P.J., Green, B.A., Merlo, L.J., Polles, A., Carnes, S., & Gold, M.S, "A brief screening application for assessing sexual addiction," *Journal of Addiction Medicine*, no. 6(1) (2012): 29-34.

Many times, when I engaged in roleplay with narcissists and perverts online, it was an unconscious feeble attempt to reclaim the power I'd felt was taken away from me as a little girl. Nothing could ever satisfy this *need* to neutralize. So, I continued until I found someone who made me feel sexy and powerful.

A study about compulsive cybersex[7] found that seventy-six percent of women and fifty-eight percent of men were victims of abuse in childhood.

"Sex addiction often entails individuals neglecting their health, and they derive no pleasure from sexual experiences.[8] The forging of neural pathways and addictive responses explains the addict's relentless and self-destructive yearning."[9]

Neuroimaging tests among sex addicts found their sexual desire dissociated from their inherent liking.[10] I experienced dissociation during the first experience of molestation and would form dissociative disorders as a result. It was the same dissociation that placed me in a sex chat room typing away while also preparing dinner.

Kotera and Rhodes (2019) found that anxious adult attachment mediated the relationship between adverse childhood experience and sex addiction, in contrast to earlier studies. Sex addicts crave the intensity of intimate relationships while also avoiding it.

How do you treat sex addiction? It's still being studied. Methods beyond what we know as "talk" therapy are being examined. More extensive work, like the

---

7. Schwartz, M.F., & Southern, S., "Compulsive cybersex: The new tea room. Sexual Addiction & Compulsivity," *The Journal of Treatment & Prevention*, no. 7(1-2) (2007): 127-144.

8. Goodman, A., "What's in a name? Terminology for designating a syndrome of driven sexual behaviour," *Sexual Addiction & Compulsivity: The Journal of Treatment and Prevention*, no. 8(3-4) (2011): 191-213; Rosenberg, K.P., Carnes, P., & O'Connor, S., "Evaluation and treatment of addiction," *Journal of Sex and Marital Therapy*, no. 40(2), (2014): 77-91.

9. O'Brien, C., Volkow, N., & Li, T., "What's in a word? Addiction versus dependence in DSM-V." *American Journal of Psychiatry*, no. 163(5), (2006): 764-765.

10. Voon, V et al., "Neural correlates of sexual cue reactivity in individuals with and without compulsive sexual behaviors." *PLoS One*, no. 9(7) (2014): e102419.

intensive treatments I experienced at Shades of Hope, are being called upon to help sex addicts.

On the support calls, I listened to something much more than data and statistics could capture. I heard the human experience languishing for a few seconds of clarity and triumphing in the smallest of victories measured in fifteen-minute increments of sobriety.

In some ways, few things changed at home. I was still in bed every evening, with the door closed on my phone. Now, however, I wasn't sexting. I was chatting with other women all seeking a healthy relationship with sex.

Our ages, locations, occupations, and ethnicities varied, yet we shared the commonality of sexual dysfunction. There was a woman in her late twenties who had prided herself on being a self-proclaimed "trophy-girlfriend" and used sex to barter with her "sugar daddies." There was a midwestern sex worker who had a dungeon in her basement filled with every sex play contraption imaginable. She'd crossed what she deemed a professional line and fallen in love with and stalked one of her clients. A caller included a church lady on the East Coast who had a habit of seducing deacons at the many churches she'd attended.

Then, there was me. Every night, there were dozens of women just like me on the call: moms, wives, functioning addicts. I participated in my meetings, worked the steps, and eventually found a sponsor and continued with the path to recovery.

She was younger, lived in California, and had been in recovery for five years. My sponsor had me text or call a daily check-in for accountability. She required that I include three things I was grateful for that day; Charlie's laugh, time to nap, and another day of sobriety made the lists many days.

Number eight of the 12 Steps is "Make a list of all the persons we had harmed and became willing to make amends to them all." As I moved deeper into recovery with the help of those calls and my sponsor, I started my amends with Everett.

Things at home were melancholy. We were too emotionally thin to put effort into the chore of growing together. We were moving, just not at the same rate. I was a steam engine pushing myself only to accept what brought me peace and calm, and Everett was stationary. We looked after Charlie and made sure he was happy and had both of us as playmates.

Everett and I became zombie soulmates. I talked little about Shades of Hope, even less about the abusers and my own misconduct. My birthday was just a few days before Charlie's, and it was lumped like a pebble in a runner's shoe. I was jogging along through recovery, and there was the nuisance of that single day to hinder my hopeful journey.

I would have preferred my jaw to be wired shut than to blow out candles this year. I'd thought about Nathan every day since leaving West Texas, one of the lingering effects of revisiting the trauma. My birthday was the constant shackle linked to him.

"You don't want to do anything today?" Everett's perplexed face and open mouth are five feet away from me in the kitchen.

"No."

"But it's your birthday!" He throws up his hands in irritation. "You're just going to mope around all day?"

"You don't understand."

"No. I don't." His voice wavers. "I don't understand because I don't know what happened to you out there! Ever since you've been back, all you do is go to work, measure your food, and you only talk to Charlie and the people on those calls!"

I knew I had to enlighten Everett. I'd been seeing Counselor once a week since I was home. We'd talked about bringing Everett with me to an appointment. I knew then it was time.

❦

Late one evening after work, we parked our cars beside each other's and then walked into Counselor's office.

"That's some picture," Everett says of the canvas image of Jesus.

I stay quiet, fidgeting instead with the papers in my hand.

Counselor welcomes us into her office. Seated beside Everett, I share it all: the emotional affair, the abuse, the sex chat, and the porn. I turn each page of my First Step Preparation, reading it out loud the same way I had at Shades of Hope. I didn't change a word of what I'd written to soften the blow. If I was getting clean, I had to come clean.

This time, I waited for my judgment like a defendant warily seated before a jury of her peers.

Everett sits very still. Then comes the outburst.

"I know exactly who it is! If I see that motherfucker, I swear it, I'm going to beat his ass!"

I calmly ask him who he thinks it is. He gives the name of an ex, and I shake my head. When I tell him it's Tony, Everett is incredulous.

"Really? Him?"

Wincing, I nod. "I wasn't even attracted to him, really."

Everett and I look to Counselor to mediate.

"Everett, if there's anything you want to say or ask, now is the time. Doesn't mean you won't have more to ask later. Right here and right now this is the time for you to talk."

Everett pulls at the bristles of gray hair in his goatee, a repetitive crunching sound between his fingers that usually makes me livid. I can only see the movement now. I know the sound is there in the quiet room. I don't hear it. My entire body waits for him to speak.

"I don't have the words." Everett's head moves from side to side, eyes filled with shock and awe. "First of all, to know you've been sexting with somebody for *months*," with each word he speaks, his voice becomes louder, growling with untethered anger, "then you're talking to some random dude, fucking catfishing people? What am I supposed to say to *that*?"

"You can say whatever you want." My voice comes out so small, a mouse peeking out from under the cupboard at night, testing to see if it's safe.

Everett huffs, pinching the bridge of his nose. He is silent for so long I look at Counselor, afraid. Is he a boiling pot about to spill over?

"I don't see how you had time to even do all that. Now, I see why you were always on your damn phone."

Everett is quiet again as he figures out what to say and do.

"I heard everything else you said, though," he continues. Then he looks at me. He looks at me with a stranger's eyes as if he had never seen the woman sitting beside him. He looks at me, his wife, and for the first time since we met eleven years before, Everett sees Maya.

"You really felt out of control, huh?"

"Yes." My voice carries the soft hush of a punished child.

Everett looks at Counselor, who sits tall in her leather rocker. "Is this common?"

"For people who have experienced childhood abuse to develop addictions?" she clarifies.

"Yeah. Like, what she wrote and said. She can't be the only one."

"It is not uncommon at all for people who suffered abuse in any form, but especially as children, to develop what can be called unhealthy coping mechanisms."

Everett lets her words settle in the room and then looks back at the strange woman he exchanged marital vows with.

"In some ways, do you feel bad still about what you went through as a kid, not just because it was so horrible but ... because maybe at times, you liked it? That you felt pleasure during it? Not intentionally! Just ..." Everett wrestles with the delicate wording. I understand every part of his fragmented question.

As gently as he makes his inquiry, it feels as if that one question knocks me flat on the area rug in the office, and a hundred-pound kettlebell settles against my chest.

I work my jaw from side to side, then raise my knuckles to my lips like a barricade as my eyelids lower. With watery eyes, I whisper, "Yes. Yes, and I hate that I did. I always felt so guilty, so disgusted with myself because I shouldn't have known at that age what any of that was supposed to feel like."

Everett reaches out and curls his fingers around mine, prying my knuckles away one by one from my mouth.

"Wasn't your fault," he says. It's there again. The same words that are meant by everyone with the best of intentions to set me free from the cell of blame I had locked myself in. He squeezes my hand. and this time the tears don't crest over the brims of my eyelids.

Everett runs his thumb against the back of my hand. "In a way, I thought when we got here tonight you were going to say you wanted to separate or divorce."

"What?" I balk. "No! Of course not!" I am petrified. "Is that what you want?" I would have understood if he had said yes. Given everything I'd unloaded on him in one sitting, I brace for it. I could barely stand to be with me; how could I expect him to stay?

"Maya." Everett sighs. "Not at all. I mean, am I mad? Yeah. Am I hurt? Yeah. Do I still love you? Hell yeah. I know you are trying to get better. I know it's not easy. I see you trying every day with your meetings and going to therapy. I'm just feeling so much right now; it's hard to explain it all."

"And your feelings are perfectly valid," Counselor says.

Everett squeezes my hand again. "I don't think she did any of this to be vindictive or spiteful or to punish me in any way. I don't believe she really intended to do this to harm our marriage or me."

"I didn't. I really didn't."

"I've had a lot of couples come in and sit on that sofa for many different reasons," Counselor says. "I've watched some and known they weren't going to be okay. You two? You're going to be okay."

Everett and I thank her in unison.

We leave the office that night and relieve my in-laws who had been looking after Charlie. I am turning down the covers at bedtime when Everett makes a request.

"Will you do me one thing?"

I would have said yes to standing on hot coals for him that night. "Sure. What's up?"

"Will you give me Tony's number?"

Every liter of blood in my body drops to my feet, and I gulp. "Honestly? I don't have his number anymore. I blocked and deleted him on social media too. All I have is an email."

"That'll do." Everett's stare commands a response.

I grab my phone, search my email and find a year old exchange with Tony. I copy the address and text it to Everett. When his phone buzzes on the nightstand, he nods at me. "Thank you."

Saying "you're welcome" didn't seem appropriate, so I don't reply and climb under the sheets. Everett rolls over and drapes his arm around my waist. I'm wide awake as I think of the endless possible outcomes of Everett emailing Tony.

In the dark of night, with at least five DJs blasting beats from each checkpoint along the route, my running shoes pound the uneven asphalt, my lungs straining for air as my arms pump. Everett is by my side.

A week after we'd seen Counselor, we'd decided to make a weekend getaway around a 5K Glow Run that I had registered for weeks ago. Mom agreed to watch Charlie to give Everett and I some time to reconnect. We booked a suite at a new hotel in Fort Worth, in an equally new outdoor mall that had a number of cafes and coffee shops and a movie theater. I used my new healthy eating skills from Shades of Hope to make menu choices at the restaurants, and we enjoyed an action movie with prehistoric creatures raised from the dead for a theme park.

We were a new couple. We had the same familiar quirks and idiosyncrasies that we had learned to accept from one another, but I wasn't hiding from Everett any longer. He didn't love me less for it; I could feel that he loved the authentic me more. It was in the way he looked at me, the way he sat extra close when we watched TV, the way he made full eye contact now when we spoke.

Running had always been my way to feel like a conqueror and I'd signed up for this race as my victory lap post-Shades of Hope. Everett decided to join me and registered the day before the race.

They'd given us white T-shirts with our race numbers. There are blasters that shoot thick foam in arcs into the air that gather like a wading pool on the pavement. Everett and I slow to a light jog as we navigate through the suds that make the bottom of our shoes slick. We wobble and slide and catch each other laughing. Once through one foamy obstacle, we headed toward the next. The foam creates neon pink, green, and orange glowing patches on the runners.

Everett and I pause to take a picture. He turns on the flash as we stand cheek to cheek. When we review the nighttime snapshot, we laugh at how bright the colors are against his pale skin and how you could hardly detect it against my brown skin.

"Hashtag interracial couple problems," I joke. Everett chuckles and puts his phone back in his pocket before we continue. We can see the finish line about a quarter of a mile away.

"Run for it?" he challenges, shouting over the music. "Everything we got left in the tank?"

"Yeah!"

He takes my hand. My legs burn with the power I demand from them to propel me faster and faster, Everett keeping pace.

We cross the finish line together, hand in hand.

Chapter Twenty

The Courage to Change the Things I Can

September 20, 2016

I am in full strut. My four-inch heels click like a rhythmic 808 beat as I hustle across the buffed Saltillo tile floors of the country club. Every detail about today has been reviewed and examined at least a hundred times in the last six months as I checked off one "To Do" item after another.

All preparation led to today.

My extensions are curled, my lips are glossed, my black, poplin dress shirt is pressed, and my heart rate is up.

Local radio stations and my former television employer have been running PSAs for the 1 in 3 Affects Me Kickoff Luncheon for the last six weeks. The announcement extended an invite to East Texans to join the newly formed 1 in 3 Foundation with special guest speaker Tennie McCarty of television counseling fame, for the organization's first public event.

The voice I'd heard while meditating at Shades of Hope, real or not, had been a call to action I couldn't avoid. It was the same as the sign in front of the old BBQ joint. Divine intervention or dissociation, my life was saved by both instances.

In my recovery, I realized I had the capability to help other survivors of sexual trauma find hope and healing. I knew, despite the financial barrier that ultimately kept me from staying in treatment, I'd been fortunate enough to afford the type of reformation that I experienced during the six-day intensive. It was the gilded key that opened my life to a new world of authenticity and calm.

I wanted to give that feeling to others. I did not want there to be any reason why women in need of help encountered any type of obstacle to recovery.

"Big checks are on the easels, table numbers are out, programs at each table," I say to Tara, the 1 in 3 Foundation's new Vice President of Finance and Governance. "Everyone who registered has a name badge, and if there are additional guests, these are blanks and here's a sharpie." I move around the table draped in a blue cloth that has been set before the entrance to the ballroom as our check-in area.

She smiles. "People are starting to show up."

"I see!" My eyes widen before I take a deep breath, count for four seconds, hold it, then exhale for another four counts.

I'd chosen the name 1 in 3 Foundation from the World Health Organization's statistic that 1 in 3 women will experience physical or sexual violence in their lifetime. That statistic was astounding and sobering. If you stopped to think about every third woman you encountered throughout your day, more than likely they were a survivor. These women are our mothers, sisters, daughters, friends, co-workers, and partners. For most of my life, I thought I was the only one who had experienced the horror of molestation. Shades of Hope, SLAA, Al-Anon, and the statistics told me my survivorship wasn't an island of one.

No one talked about it. Sure, we'd sat through assemblies about good touch and bad touch, stranger danger and the like. No one stood up and said out loud in those assemblies, "It's happening to me." I never heard growing up, "I know someone this happened to." I wanted to bring people together to begin the conversations I wished I'd had.

In July 2015, I used my knowledge from consulting nonprofits (a skill I didn't realize was preparing me for this) to file the paperwork with the Texas Secretary of State's Office to file the Certificate of Formation for the 1 in 3 Foundation. The website said a filing could take up to three to four weeks for a response. My filing was approved within five days.

The job I hated that was part of my PTSD triggering and search for escapism? As fate would have it, I'd reported to my boss, the organization's president, that

I'd be gone for a week for medical treatment a month prior to leaving. He'd chosen not to share this with the board of directors, who were preparing for an event that would take place just a few days after my return. When the event went off the rails, the finger-pointing came in my direction. I'd done my due diligence by telling my immediate supervisor that I had to go away. I chose not to share it with others at the time because I didn't want to answer questions that, legally, they couldn't ask me. He hadn't seen the point of sharing my absence with the board.

So, as I sat in a meeting with wagging fingers, berating, and the board forcing me to accept the position of scapegoat, I stood it until I couldn't any longer.

The thing about learning healthy boundaries is once you know what they are for you, you won't tolerate any violations against them. The knowledge that I would not be a people pleaser and concede to their lack of preparation and dropping the ball, led me to do something I'd never done before: I quit.

I quit the job without a plan. I wasn't going to ride it out until I secured something else. I took a tremendous leap of faith, and, with Everett's full support, I gave my two weeks' notice. Financially, it would put us under strain. I was no longer willing to sacrifice my mental health for the appeasement of others. My employers weren't safe and didn't have my best interest in mind. I quit.

Like many acts of blind faith, strengthened by a new dignity, I was rewarded.

The filing for the 1 in 3 Foundation as a nonprofit corporation in Texas was swift, and I received immediate funding from a donor I'd built a strong relationship with in my previous job. The grant they provided covered the startup costs for the foundation and helped to underwrite the kickoff luncheon expenses.

I'd also sat down and asked myself, "What makes you happy?"

I'd loved sports reporting. The burnout I experienced with the daily news grind was partly the nature of the business, but mostly my overwhelming, hyper-driven pursuit of being the best. I still had a good professional standing in East Texas with the schools and coaches from my days on local sports TV.

While serving as the station's sports director, we'd partnered with a regional cable network, to provide Friday night highlights from marquee games in the area. Through that partnership, I'd come to know one of the network's producers. I'd held on to my rolodex and his card had been one I saved. We connected through LinkedIn and one July afternoon, while I was still completing my two weeks at my soon to be ex-job, I shot him an email.

Hey Michael,

I hope you are doing well! I know it's been some time since we worked together, but I wanted to reach out and let you know that I am beginning some freelance work in East Texas and if I can ever do anything to assist us with highlights or Friday night football, please don't hesitate to contact me.

Regards,

Maya

The reply came back before that evening.

Maya! How are you? Our team met the other day and we were just discussing the need for a videographer in your area! I'm going to connect you with the head of our high school spotlight show and the Friday night football coordinator.

The first week of August, I filed my first freelance report for the network as a new weekly contributor. It led me to connect with a production company from the Houston area that offered me a contract for in-game sideline reports for college football.

During the weekdays, I would take Charlie to pre-K, come home and work on the computer to file more documents for the start of the 1 in 3 Foundation and begin building a steering committee to form the board of directors. On weekend nights, I was in stadiums across the state for high school and college football games, microphone in hand.

After years of banging my head on walls and pounding my fist against doors that weren't meant to be opened, after battling my biggest enemy—me—after a lifetime of being everything to everyone else, my courage to change was being rewarded by the universe. But this wasn't a time to rest.

I was putting my full energy into launching the organization I intended to build to help other survivors and back to doing the job I loved. I was also a healthier and better mother because I was being true to self and making sure I practiced self-care.

Guest by guest arrives for the luncheon. I smile and shake hands with several community leaders, hug a few colleagues, and greet family and friends from across the registration table as I watch more than one hundred people file inside for the event.

After a welcome by our board president, I step to the microphone, adjust it to my height and look at a room of expectant faces. Photographers from the newspaper and some of the TV stations are positioned at the back of the room, and I see red camera buttons power on and a white flash.

"I was in the car with my husband on the way over, and I was feeling a bit anxious," I admit. I can hear myself loudly from the speakers. "I was trying to think of my opening to these remarks for all of you who have joined us for today." I open the printed papers of the bulleted points I wanted to make and press my hand flat against the crease to open them and ground myself.

"As I do when I'm finding myself wrestling with my emotions, I listened to Prince." This draws a few light laughs from the crowd. "If you don't know me very well, I'm a huge Prince fan. We share a birthday, and my favorite color is purple; you do the math there." I shrug, and more laughs come. "Prince actually reminded me of something very important about today. You see, everyone I love is in this room. From my husband, to my parents, my in-laws, my friends and colleagues, people who have changed my life," I look at Counselor and then Tennie seated next to Kim at the front table, "you are all in this room." I quote Prince's famous lyrics from "Let's Go Crazy" to cheers and applause.

I continue, "Life hasn't always been so grand. I've experienced some amazing highs and the lowest of lows. That life's journey is why we are here. I don't just want to get through life; I want to live it. I want others to *live*."

My eyes drop to the paper on the podium before I look up and directly at Counselor. "Someone once asked me, 'Does the caterpillar hurt when she becomes a butterfly?'" Counselor had posed the question to me during a session not long after I'd returned home from the intensive. "It made me wonder if total transformation, from something that crawls and slithers on the ground to something beautiful that can fly and soar is possible without pain?"

"I want to tell you the answer to that question is *yes*. It does hurt. It hurts like hell. That metamorphosis, though? The moment you realize you are emerging from a cocoon and about to spread your wings? *That* is a feeling made only possible by allowing yourself grace to change. That is why the logo for the 1 in 3 Foundation is the blue butterfly. Transformation takes strength, and you can encourage other women to seek help, heal, and fly."

I detail the initial programs we would provide as services of the 1 in 3 Foundation: scholarships to fund therapy sessions for survivors with little to no income; lunch and learn programs to educate care providers and the community on topics relevant to sexual violence and trauma and to facilitate healthy conversations around those topics; and links between other care providers and service agencies in the area to connect survivors with the appropriate type of care and treatment for them. As an individual, I was launching our own local chapter of SLAA, with weekly meetings. I'd secured a space to host the in-person 12 Step recovery program.

I thank our donors and event sponsors and then introduce the woman who made me promise I wouldn't take my life almost a year before, Tennie. I hug her as she steps to the podium to give the keynote address as I sit down beside Everett.

Tennie's powerful endorsement of the need for support programs for survivors and more advocacy work in the community, as well as her personal story, brought the audience and the guest speaker herself to tears.

"Survivors tend to follow two extremes when we work with them. Either they have given up on life and are barely functioning, or they are profoundly driven achievers like Maya," she says.

Everett reaches over and rubs my knee. I don't bother to eat the catered lunch set out in front of us. My heart and soul are full.

After the luncheon, our board of directors help gather up all of our items. I am folding an easel when I look over to see Everett and my parents talking to Tennie.

I thank our president and directors as we load my car with the leftover programs, name badges and butterfly decorations.

When I return to the country club's main entrance, I hug Tennie and Kim farewell and thank them for making the trip to East Texas. I wish them a safe trip home as they make their way to their car.

Everett walks with me back to my SUV and takes the keys from my hand.

"Thank you," I sigh. After buckling up, I pull my feet from my heels and flex my toes.

"You know Tennie pulled me aside to talk to me after the luncheon." Everett gives me a knowing smirk.

"I saw. What'd she say?"

"She said, 'Did you ever think Maya would make it here?'" Everett leans forward and his green eyes dilate with the same look of love and pride I last saw from him as I walked up the aisle on our wedding day.

"And what did you say?"

He places a hand on my shoulder. "I told her, 'Yeah, I did. Because I know Maya. I know her, and I know when she's determined she's going to do exactly what she says she will do.'"

Epilogue

February 2, 2006

My pinky and big toe throbbed as I pulled my feet from the high-heeled boots I'd been wearing for thirteen hours on what was scheduled to be a nine-hour workday. I flexed and curled my toes into fists as I pulled off my grey wool peacoat and threw it over the chair in the one-inch-larger-than-a-storage-shed living room of my single-bedroom apartment. There was a sharp pain radiating from each toe, signaling both their new freedom and relief.

I stripped out of my clothes, dropping a sweater and a skirt on the carpet as I moved to the bedroom and unhooked my bra. I turned the switch on the lamp and, with liberated breasts, I arched my back like an ostrich and spread my arms, waving them and trying to shake off the tension from the newsroom. I opened my dresser and pulled out an old T-shirt. The cotton slipped over my skin, warming me and reminding me I'd left the heater off on that winter's day. I was so tense when I'd walked in the door from a day of cranking out news reports, I hadn't noticed the cool temperature.

My laptop lay on the top of my bed sheets where I'd left it that morning before leaving for work. Sipping tea, I always checked my work email and skimmed the news headlines in the morning, monitoring what had happened overnight around the world while I slumbered. Any decent reporter begins their day by checking out the news and their inbox for story ideas or tips.

On most days, the laptop was the second appliance I turned on after the lamp. That evening, I stepped over the skirt and the sweater on the floor and made my way to the thermostat and turned the heater on. At some point, I'd make a snack or microwave one of those low-calorie, low-fat meals for dinner, but my laptop awaited like my playful child in the evenings. I was still using AIM to talk to friends back home in Dallas, College Station, or wherever they had ended up after high school and college. All but one of the internet friends I had made as a freshman at A&M had faded away over the years.

I stepped over the sweater and skirt and climbed into my bed with a groan of comfort as the coils gave and the foam contoured to my body. I fluffed the pillows behind my back, pulled the covers up around my waist and pulled the laptop onto its appropriately-named position. I opened it, a mundane habit repeated on innumerous nights after work.

Something was different today. A surprise was lurking in my inbox like a thief in an alleyway.

The hot jet of air blowing from the vent above my bed helped to stave off the chill in the room I was still feeling despite being under the covers.

I opened my inbox skimmed over the product ads and store sales for my real mail and what I found there made me shiver. My body shook as if the cold from winter, and the shock of what was in my inbox, had passed through my dermis, bypassed my veins, slithered past my muscle tissue and gripped my bones.

The email was sent at 4:31 p.m.

I shuddered when I read the name under Sender.

Subject: Family Issues

Nathan had emailed. I hadn't spoken a word to him or seen his face in six years. And there he was, haunting my inbox.

Looking back now, I can't recall if I stopped breathing, but I must have. It was what I did when I experienced something unpleasant. I held my breath until the moments passed or until my lungs demanded air. It'd seemed like I'd been holding my breath since Nathan opened the bathroom door almost twenty-one years before.

At first, I thought to ignore it. *Delete it*. My brain instructed me to let the email disappear from my inbox. Out of sight, out of mind.

But, that wouldn't make him disappear. All these years, he'd only been out of view. The ramifications of what Nathan, the boy across the street, the boy on the playground, and the boys in Houston had done were leeches attached to my brain. The experiences had transformed the way even my Amygdala performed. When I wasn't thinking about the abuse or assaults, I was still reacting to it. I reacted to it when I received criticism from Mom, when a viewer wrote to tell me my blouse was too tight, when I couldn't let go of a man at the end of a dating relationship. They *were* my mind.

A tiny voice inside me that had more courage than the adult me currently held asked me to open it. She wanted to know what he had to say.

Maya,

How are you? I hope you are doing well. Your dad shot me an e-mail stating that there might be some unresolved problems that the family may be dealing with and need to be reconciled. We are now both mature adults and should not allow childhood mistakes to deter us from our lives.

I'm not a perfect person by far and when I was younger I did have some problems. For those mistakes I apologize and I hope that you find a way to forgive me. It is not my intention to be a trouble maker in any shape, form, or fashion. After taking a long look in the mirror and looking back over the past I am well aware of some of the problems I may have caused long ago.

Honestly, my focus is to please your father and bring him peace. I truly know what it is like to have a disturbing element in the atmosphere that is not being properly brought to the table. Maya I am an adult and so are you. I am confident that we can resolve this issue and restore peace in our homes.

He wrote his full name as if somehow, he'd become unknown to me. He left his phone number.

It was, no exaggeration, the biggest piece of bullshit I'd ever read in my life. *Childhood mistakes.* He wrote the email as if *I* was the one being unreasonable by breaking off contact.

I hit the X in the corner of the email box, and the message disappeared. My fingers hovered over the mousepad. I questioned if I should delete or save it. I dragged it to the Saved folder.

I didn't bring the email up to my parents then. Startled as I was and grappling with fury at his words, that night, disassociation helped me. I had filed the email away and I filed my emotional and physical response away too.

I talked about it with the psychologist I still saw from time to time back home, Dr. Goode. I printed Nathan's email and read it as if I was reading an ad for plumbing service. I was detached. She helped to ground me and let the emotions release.

"What do you want to say?" she asked.

I scoffed. "Go fuck yourself, to start with."

She grinned, one of the reasons I liked her. "You could write that. You could definitely say whatever flows from your heart and your mind. You have a chance to respond."

I scratched at my scalp and shook my head. "Even that's too good for him. Is it weird I still want to take the high road? Tell him off but in a way that feels ... calm? Not so ... violent?"

She shook her head. "It's not weird at all. Though make sure you are doing it because that's what you want and not what you think someone expects of you."

"I don't really care what anyone else thinks about what I have to say to him. It's my words, my chance. He started the conversation; I plan to end it."

"Good."

Over several weeks we discussed my reply but didn't harp on it. I would write it when I was ready.

One day, almost three months later, I was. I cc'd my parents in my reply. Mom would later write back that she was proud of me.

Nathan,

I was extremely disappointed by your email. Not only to receive it, but to read it and find that you take little responsibility for your actions.

Your "childhood mistakes" have resulted in years of therapy for me. I also believe, very much as Dad said, you were old enough to know better. I was just a little girl. You were a teenager who understood the right and wrong of what you were doing and you chose to do wrong. It has caused irreparable harm to me and to our family. I will never be the same because of you. Do not attempt to guilt me into some type of reconciliation so that you can feel better on your end and so that Dad will speak to you. This was your doing, not mine.

The isolation you are living is because of the crime you committed. You asked for my forgiveness, you do not have it. You cannot give me back what you took from me as a child. You cannot return the peace of mind you stole from me. For that, I won't forgive you.

I have only one hope for you.

I pray to God you get some help. Not just for yourself, but so that you never hurt anyone else in that way ever again.

Do not contact me anymore.

END

Acknowledgements

With love and gratitude for my son who shows me every day what empathy, honesty, vulnerability, and staying true to yourself looks like. For tickles, belly blowing, big hugs, shooting hoops, smooches and the best laugh in the world.

Immeasurable thanks to my husband for giving me time and space to write, to destress, vent, hold my hand after nightmares, rub my back after query rejections, and for sticking with me through the "for worst" parts. You make the "for better" even more than I could have hoped for. "I love me some you."

I want to thank my parents, my mother and father-in-law, my big brother and Ainty for their encouragement and support through this process.

Special thanks to the team at Rising Action Publishing Collective, Alexandria Brown and Tina Beier for taking a chance on this memoir and championing stories for survivors.

Thank you to Cassie Mannes Murray and Pine State Publicity.

"Dr. Goode" for helping me on my healing journey and for being the best possible introduction to mental health CARE. Counselor, for being a mentor, positive force and healer. Thank you for watching this journey unfold with love and patience.

The board of directors and volunteers for the 1 in 3 Foundation, and the souls who have allowed us to be a part of your healing and recovery. This is for you.

My marble jar friend, Brenda McBride, LCSW. Thank you for caring, for the lives you have mended, for your commitment to trauma informed care...and for being a fellow emotional gangster.

Anissa Centers, Brian Brandt, Nicole Brown and Lara Eastburn for your help with feedback, pitch and query input.

My La Madeleine Mademoiselle, Erin Irvin: Thank you for being the first person to tell me I was not an aspiring writer, but a writer. Thank you for your friendship and helping me to hog tables at our favorite coffee spot.

My friends since those awkward tween years: Thao, Traci, Monique and my Homebug, Erica. Someday, I want to be like each of you when I finally grow up.

Taylor Byas, Ashley Elizabeth and Mag Gabbert for assistance with early development and copy edits.

Bianca Marais for your phenomenal guidance and elevating my writing. I hear your voice in my head saying, "Show don't tell!"

Writing Workshops staff and instructors: Blake Kimzey, Alex Temblador, Sarah Hosseini, Jessica Hindman, Gordy Sauer, Katie Reilly and Lynne Golodner. When I didn't know where to start, it was Writing Workshops that showed me the steps to take.

Much love to the 2022 Mackinac Island Retreat crew!

Read Cook, KC Carmichael, Marthese Fenech for being so incredibly supportive. I look forward to your upcoming projects and am grateful to have connected with you.

2023 Debuts! Class of '23 changing the publishing game.

Ericka Freeman, LCSW for providing insight as a care provider to how this story could help others and what we needed to ask of readers.

Writer's League of Texas for being an infinite resource.

Garland Darling Bev Chukwu: Looking forward to the chapter after the epilogue.

To the people who saved my life: Tennie and Kim McCarty, Cam Balcomb, Misty (your beautiful singing that made my days), and the Shades of Hope staff, I am a better person because of you. Thank you for giving me room to grow and a safe space to speak the words of healing. It was with you that I learned vulnerability and took the first step in owning my story.

Thank you, Tennie, for writing the beautiful foreword to this book and for all of the lives you have touched with your wisdom. Sending love and light.

About the Author

Maya Golden (Bethany) is an Associated Press winning and Emmy nominated multimedia journalist. Maya is the winner of the Excellence in My Market Award (EMMA) from the National Academy of Television Arts and Sciences. She is the founder of the 1 in 3 Foundation, a non-profit organization that provides recovery and counseling resources to survivors of sexual trauma with little to no income in East Texas. Maya has been featured on Bally Sports, Fox Sports College, ESPN 2 and 3 and other broadcast mediums including Blackgirlnerds.com. She speaks as a survivor for organizations such as the Children's Advocacy Center, CASA (Court Appointed Special Advocates) and Kids Aspiring to Dream. The Texas A&M alum's career includes experience as a sports anchor/reporter and television production editor, newscast writer, field producer and print writer. She is a member of the Writer's League of Texas. Her first novel, a political thriller, The Senator, is releasing April 15, 2025 with Rising Action.

Book Club and Care Provider Questions

Created with Ericka Freeman, LCSW, Associate Professor of Practice/BSW Field Director, University of Texas at Tyler

1. Memories are made in layers of our senses. The more senses involved, the stronger the memory. The author describes distinct memories before, during and after the initial abuse event at age 5. What are some of the senses she described? How did these senses later serve as triggers? Do you have memories that are cemented because of senses, such as smell, taste, sounds?

2. Often, in survivors of sexual trauma, the abuser's gender is overgeneralized to the population at large. That gender (e.g., male) is seen as an enemy; however, the author does not do that. She is able to exercise discernment. Describe the dichotomous identity males have in the author's perception (her focus and her fear).

3. What was your first encounter with pornography? How did generational aspects influence the means by which you first encountered it (i.e. the internet, magazines, video tapes)?

4. "Disappointment" is a central theme in the author's journey. Where did it start? How did it start? How internalized was this theme?

5. Describe and unpackage, using your own perspective-taking, the author's relationship with her mother?

6. Discuss "shame" and "guilt" as extrinsic motivators for the author. When did these motivators stop being effective?

7. What are some of the protective factors and risk factors of being a southern, Black American girl in the 1980s? In subsequent decades of the author's life, as a southern, Black American woman?

8. The book takes the reader on a journey that includes the author's experience of complex trauma from a micro view, as an individual, to a macro view, as a non-profit organizer for other survivors. How did the journey help the reader understand the author's resiliency?

9. The concept of forgiveness is a large part of Christianity and American culture. The author rejects the idea of forgiveness for her primary predator. What are your thoughts on forgiveness for those who inflict harm and trauma?

10. The author's story takes place mostly in a pre #metoo era when most victims remained silent. Do you think the current climate for survivors, family reactions, or religious reactions would be different now?

(The following would be primarily for care providers and students)

1. Using a Family Systems Theory lens (Dr Murray Bowen, https://www .thebowencenter.org/), what were the roles, relationships and expectations in the author's family of origin (birth or "childhood" family) that may have contributed to both the abuse AND the response?

2. What was different for the author, from normative experience, in each stage of the author's life course because of the trauma?

3. What was similar to a normative experience in each stage?

4. Draw and label an Eco Map of the author as a child and, later, as an adult. Be sure to include all social environmental participants. What are the main sources of energy for the author? Where does the author give most of her energy?

5. Draw and label a Genogram of the author. Be sure to include all extended family of origin and family of procreation as identified in the book. What connections did you find?

6. What developmental needs were met and which were not for the author as a child?